'To be effective, project managers must learn the
Peter and this book will help you to do that.'

***Neville Bain**, Chairman, The Institute of Directors; Author of 'The Effective Director', 'The People Advantage', 'Winning Ways Through Corporate Governance', and 'Successful Management'*

'If all books placed as much importance on soft skills as this one then perhaps we might start to see a sea change in the way projects are managed. All too often the fact it's people that deliver projects is forgotten, something not lost on this book which should be applauded.'

***Chris Field**, PMP MBCS CITP, President, PMI UK Chapter*

'I recommend every Project Manager reads this book (in addition to PRINCE2!)'

***Andy Murray** CDir, lead author, PRINCE2 2009 refresh; Director, Outperform*

'Important contextualised contribution to the development of competence in the so-called soft skills, hard to master, but an indispensable component of effective practice in a profession whose time has come.'

***Andrew Bragg**, Chief Executive, Association for Project Management*

'I first spoke with Peter during 2007 about the need to develop self awareness and soft skills in project managers in order for them to become better leaders, and I was impressed with Peter's application of NLP at the time. It appears that this conversation seeded a book, and an excellent one too. Well done!'

***Sean O'Neill**, Vice President, UK Head of Programme Leadership, Capgemini*

'I have no hesitation in recommending this book to project professionals whether starting out on their career, or those with more experience seeking to constantly improve their performance.'

***Alistair Godbold**, Deputy Chairman, APM*

'Read it, apply it and not only will it make you a more effective project manager, it will also ensure the projects you are engaged in are more successful.'

***Steve Jenner** FAPM, Chairman, Portfolio Management Specific Interest Group; (Formerly Director of IT for Criminal Justice)*

'Peter's book brings analysis, insight and valuable pointers to improving those very important soft skills such as building rapport with stakeholders, handling difficult situations and being assertive. I recommend Peter's book, read it and help improve both your personal performance and your team's performance.'

***Paul Hirst**, Head of PPM capability, HMRC*

'For anyone who believes that people skills are important in the delivery of projects then this book is for you.'

***Paul Goodge**, Vice President, Bid and Programme Management, Thales*

'NLP is a perfect technique to help all project players to improve in this area – enabling misunderstandings to be avoided or spotted and difficult issues confronted which will lead to better project outcomes. I recommend that all project players spend time to learn from the topic and improve their own capability and performance.'

Martin Samphire, *Vice President, Hitachi Consulting*

'With NLP our people can learn to be even more effective in their dealings with their teams, clients and key stakeholders. The release of Peter's book is perfectly timed and fills a large void in the market.'

Peter Chana *MAPM, MCIOB, Programme Director, Bovis Lend Lease Consulting*

'The effectiveness of project leaders is defined by their level of emotional intelligence in conjunction with real experience in end to end delivery. Peter demonstrates both and we are pleased to work with him. His new book gives away some of his trade secrets and all project professionals would benefit from buying a copy.'

Matt Rawson, *MBA (Project Management) CPM; Director, Programme, Project and Change Management, Practicus – the outcome delivery partner*

'Peter's inspirational approach uses NLP to enhance project and project manager success. Common sense, mature, and professional.'

Sam Brown, *Director of Projects, Enable East (an NHS Trust)*

'One of the main reasons for projects of all sizes failing to deliver is the project manager's lack of soft skills for managing people. In this book Peter helps you to develop the skills in dealing with team members and stakeholders that are essential to be a successful project manager.'

David Lillicrap, *Head of Programme Management, London Borough of Ealing*

'Peter has demonstrated underpinning skills in leading, motivating and influencing in his work over many years. We are glad that he has now captured the essence of these and many other skills in his book on application of NLP for professional project managers.'

Chris Dunn, *Director, Hays Transformational Leadership*

'Soft skills are the difference that makes the difference in leadership of change. Getting change to work well is really all about people. Peter tirelessly promotes this in project management, both through Alchemy, and more specifically in this book, which is a major contribution to the discipline.'

Paul Matthews, *Certified Trainer in NLP; MD, Alchemy for Managers*

(Full and additional quotes can be found on the supporting website www.nlp4pm.com)

NLP FOR PROJECT MANAGERS

Make things happen with neuro-linguistic programming

BCS, The Chartered Institute for IT
Our mission as BCS, The Chartered Institute for IT, is to enable the information society. We promote wider social and economic progress through the advancement of information technology science and practice. We bring together industry, academics, practitioners and government to share knowledge, promote new thinking, inform the design of new curricula, shape public policy and inform the public.

Our vision is to be a world-class organisation for IT. Our 70,000 strong membership includes practitioners, businesses, academics and students in the UK and internationally. We deliver a range of professional development tools for practitioners and employees. A leading IT qualification body, we offer a range of widely recognised qualifications.

Further Information
BCS, The Chartered Institute for IT,
First Floor, Block D,
North Star House, North Star Avenue,
Swindon, SN2 1FA,
United Kingdom.
T +44 (0) 1793 417 424
F +44 (0) 1793 417 444
www.bcs.org/contactus

NLP FOR PROJECT MANAGERS
Make things happen with neuro-linguistic programming

Dr Peter Parkes

Claire

Practice, Practice, Practice

Peter.

Published by British Informatics Society Limited (BISL), a wholly owned subsidiary of BCS, The Chartered Institute for IT, First Floor, Block D, North Star House, North Star Avenue, Swindon, SN2 1FA, UK.
www.bcs.org

ISBN 978-1-906124-68-7

British Cataloguing in Publication Data.
A CIP catalogue record for this book is available at the British Library.

Typeset by Lapiz Digital Services, Chennai, India.
Printed at CPI Antony Rowe, Chippenham and Eastbourne, UK.

To Mum and Dad, who taught me everything they knew.

CONTENTS

FIGURES

AUTHOR

Peter Parkes joined the nuclear industry (UKAEA) in the mid-80s following a PhD and post-Doctoral research in solid state chemistry. He rose up to become head of capability for BNFL and actively involved in expansion into global markets and different cultures. Following an executive MBA in the mid-90s and a Master's dissertation on best practice for project management of technology, Peter's career took a right turn into delivery of complex platforms and technology enabled change. Since then, Peter has held Program Director roles in the private sector, public sector, public private partnerships (PPPs), and 'Big 4' consultancy practices.

Being dedicated to ongoing personal and professional development, Peter is a Fellow of several professional bodies including the Association for Project Management (APM), BCS and Chartered Management Institute, and is certificated with them to the highest level. With the APM he is Trustee and Board Champion for best practice groups. He sits on APM's steering group for the project management body of knowledge and is a contributor on topics of portfolio management, governance, sponsorship, and assurance. He is a regular speaker on aspects of project management to various management schools, professional bodies and industry conferences.

Since adopting NLP in a professional environment in the early '90s, he went on to become an NLP Master Practitioner and is a professional member of the Association for NLP. Today he is a Director with Peak Performance, offering consultancy, coaching, and NLP-based project management training.

FOREWORD BY MIKE NICHOLS

We can now buy almost any car and expect it to work perfectly from the start – very different from a few decades ago. So why not aspire for a world in which every project succeeds? That involves organisational change and improved processes and systems, but primarily it is about people – their attitudes, behaviours and relationships. Project management professionals are already driving this cultural shift. This book, by an eminent practitioner of both neuro-linguistic programming and Project Management, makes a valuable contribution by marrying the two fields to reinforce our understanding of how people can maximise their effectiveness in managing and responding to change. It provides interesting and useful insights for those at all stages in their career development. I am pleased to recommend it.

Mike Nichols
Chairman, Association for Project Management
Board Member, Major Projects Association
Chairman of BSI Standards Policy and Strategy Committee
Chairman, The Nichols Group

FOREWORD BY BOB ASSIRATI

Method and process are important in project management, but knowing how to use them is even more so. Most project managers can increase their effectiveness most by developing their soft skills, recognising that finesse can be more effective than brute force. Once developed, they will find that their skills are much more transferable across not only project types, but whole industry sectors. This book showing the application of tools like NLP to develop competences will help you on that journey and will certainly whet your appetite for more. Peter's lively style is compelling and benefits from his imaginative use of appropriate quotations and personal anecdotes. For me the book throws light on a major component of our journey towards greater professionalism in project management.

Bob Assirati
Deputy President, BCS The Chartered Institute for IT
Honorary Fellow, Association for Project Management
Major Projects Director, Office of Government Commerce

ACKNOWLEDGEMENTS

I would like to thank the following:

For assisting with content, editorial and proof reading (alphabetic by surname): Richard Allen, David Broughton, Brendan D'Cruz, Alistair Godbold, Paul Goodge, Jo Orchard, Sandra Parkes and John Zachar.

My numerous NLP classmates and assistants, particularly Jo Orchard, who has helped to ensure that all of this is teachable.

Paul Matthews from Alchemy who has been a guide to further learning around the broader subject. Arielle Essex and many other trainers. Anthony Robbins for showing how it can be done.

Geoff Lowe, a fellow board member of the Association for Project Management and former colleague from BNFL who introduced me to world class performance in project management.

Paul Goodge and Richard Allen, two lights in project management, for discussions on the application of NLP.

Liz Wilson and John Zachar for discussions on competence frameworks for project management.

BCS for commissioning this book and helping me to achieve another target. Matthew Flynn from publications for his patience when we had to re-plan due to an accident in Australia that scuppered the original estimates.

Finally my wife Sandra, a fellow NLP practitioner, for instilling some of the discipline from her Master's in Education for Leadership Development – the best trainer that I have seen. And also for putting up with some of my defective meta-programs for so long.

PREFACE

WHO THIS BOOK IS AIMED AT AND WHAT YOU WILL GET OUT OF IT

This book will help program and project leaders, and other project professionals, to be even more effective in managing three key resources for projects: themselves, their team, and the various stakeholders that they interact with. If you want to be even more effective in project management then this book is for you.

Dedication and hard work alone will not be the decisive factor in project success. In order to advance your career you will need to develop excellent 'soft skills'. In my journey through project management I have been on hundreds of days of training courses and read dozens of books, and from these have found the approach and toolset of NLP to be the most effective for developing soft skills.

As a project manager, this book will map out a journey for you, from the elements of method to competence in the key skills for effective delivery; from your first role as a project manager to the highest professional levels of chartered status and above.

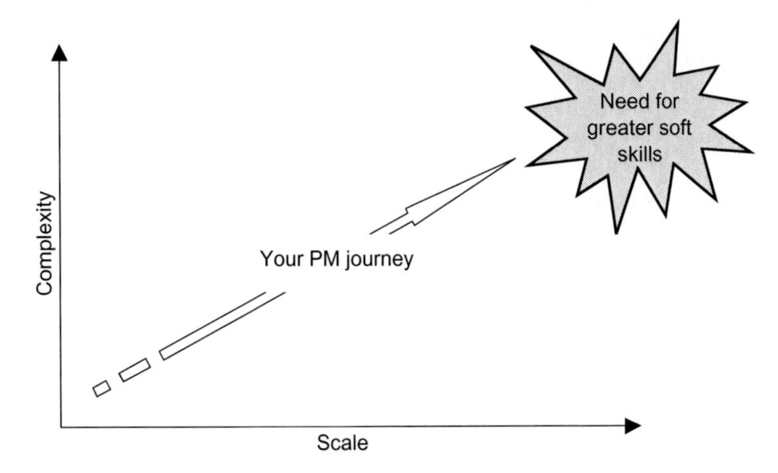

If you are working on relatively small projects that are well defined and with an in-house delivery model, then elements of this book will help you to develop your team motivation techniques. It will also show you how to present yourself and manage your state in potentially stressful situations.

For more experienced project and program managers, this book will help you to manage the increasingly complex stakeholder arrangements that you will face. It will also show you how to choose behaviours and language appropriate to the context and task.

For those responsible for portfolios of projects, this book will help you to manage 'the big picture' and the process of negotiation and accommodation. It will also introduce you to high performance coaching and modelling of excellent behaviours in others.

Effective leadership of projects and programs is a transferable skill, and this book applies across sectors and disciplines. Going further, it is my opinion that if you are not confident in managing projects in other sectors outside of your domain of expertise then you probably have not yet developed key skills to a sufficient level. After all, the exams and assessments for all levels of project management by all accrediting bodies are sector independent. This book will help you to make those skills transferrable.

Learning and applying the techniques of NLP has made my life in project management one with a bit more finesse and a lot less brute force. I am sure that it will help you in the same way should you choose to follow this route.

WHAT NLP CAN DO FOR YOU AS A PROJECT MANAGER

Once you adopt the approach of NLP and start to learn some of the tools that it offers, it will help your development enormously. For a project manager it will:

- give you an understanding of why you do what you do, and what other choices are available;
- help you to control the way you think, feel and act;
- manage stress;
- strengthen your ability to connect with others and develop rapport;
- help you to pick up and decode what is being communicated outside of the obvious – words will give you an edge in everything from negotiation to leadership;
- enable you to communicate more effectively and persuasively;
- motivate and lead;
- show you how to develop flexibility in behaviour to match the context and requirements;
- help you to develop new skills;
- enable you to model excellent behaviours from role models that you meet.

MY PERSONAL JOURNEY INTO NLP

As a student of formal project management in the early 1990s, I gobbled up all of those helpful tools and techniques to help me in my transition to manager of major projects in the nuclear sector. I became qualified by the APM, adept in the PMI Body of Knowledge, overly familiar with British and ISO standards, and took my PRINCE exams. They made a huge improvement compared to 'management by instinct', which seemed to be the default method at the time. My Master's dissertation, as part of an executive MBA at Lancaster University Management School, was on project management of research and development. (R&D was an area that until then had been seen as chaotic, and left to the scientists in case innovation was stifled.) Involvement with best practice groups followed, alongside papers and presentations to conferences.

As my career progressed, projects became even less well defined than in R&D. They became more about eliciting tacit requirements, encouraging cooperation, resolving conflict, accommodating divergence, managing expectations and realising benefits. At the same time, projects moved from being insular and in-house to international collaborations. We had to deal with a widening group of stakeholders, from regulators to politicians. These changes, and the complexity of human interactions involved in them, were not easily accommodated by the formal tools focussed on management of time, cost and quality.

While involved with graduate recruitment in the mid 1990s, a forward thinking professional from human resources (HR) recognised that the PhD graduates we were bringing into the company to become nuclear scientists and engineers did not have the most highly developed soft skills. It did not matter so much for technical specialists, but candidates for management and delivery roles were also drawn from this pool via promotion. Two five-day NLP modules were introduced into the graduate training program. I was invited to participate in these courses as a 'model' for some of the skills. At that time, the course proved unpopular with most of the male recruits, while many of the female recruits found it insightful. A couple pursued personal development to become certified NLP practitioners themselves, as well as excellent scientists, engineers and project managers. Of that small first group of scientists and engineers, one went on to be head of communications and another became HR manager. I observed first-hand the power and the results of some of these techniques.

As I followed my own personal development and ran out of technical courses, I started to do more and more training in advanced communication and behavioural skills. As well as traditional courses on mentoring and counselling, this included NLP practitioner, master practitioner, NLP modelling, hypnosis etc. Short courses with most of the NLP gurus, including Anthony Robbins and 'The Fire Walk', were also undertaken. The more of these I did, the easier delivery became, until I was convinced that, if things were difficult then it was because I was not using the most appropriate behaviour. Since then, I have used my NLP training as a project manager to communicate across cultures, reframe problems, align goals, manage stakeholder groups, resolve conflicts, find accommodations, motivate teams, mentor and coach managers, and generally be a better leader. So, if you too want an easier life, then get with the program!

WHY ME?

In writing this book I do not attempt to set myself up as the world's most proficient in soft skills. There are naturals who appear to effortlessly engage with other people and glide through the world. In contrast, in my early career I found that gaps in my own soft skills limited my effectiveness. Those naturals, however, being unconsciously competent, would find it difficult to tell you how they did things that were implicit in their nature. (Other project management competences may not be natural to them anyway). I have had to move through the cycle of conscious incompetence to at least a level of conscious competence. I do not yet consider myself to have fully reached the stage of those naturals, i.e. unconscious competence; my wife will tell you that I sometimes have lapses where my mouth is engaged before my brain. But hopefully, less frequently. I believe that the fact that I have had to study this subject, hard and in a structured way, puts me in a good position to help you on your journey.

In no small part due to personal and professional development, I have achieved the highest levels in project management, academically, with the professional bodies and in several sectors of industry. I have been able to progress from relatively small R&D projects, through delivery of infrastructure and business change, to policy-led projects. I have led programs in the private sector, public sector, public private partnerships (PPPs), and 'big four' consultancy houses. Of these, PPPs proved the most challenging, having to bring together two worlds, and two sets of values, behaviours and capabilities to deliver tangible outcomes for citizens and shareholders. As I write this book, I am managing the portfolio for a high-technology company in the automotive sector and dealing with government policies and politicians on a regular basis. A world away from the research laboratories where I started out on my career.

Like my life, this is a work in progress. I am keen to get feedback, either directly or via the supporting website (www.nlp4pm.com).

A BRIEF NOTE ON USE OF LANGUAGE

In a topic like NLP, language is important. The first thing to notice is that I have used a consistent spelling for the word **'program'** – Americans use this spelling and it is universal in NLP for terms such as 'meta-program'. Hence I have not reverted to the English spelling for references to projects and 'programmes'.

Project management means different things to different people. Some refer to themselves as 'program' managers, or to managing a portfolio of projects. As you will read in section 1.1.3, this is all subjective. Hence I have used the abbreviation **'PM'** throughout. Don't worry which flavour this refers to – it means you.

Similarly, I will use **'project management'** as referring to the whole domain, encompassing programs and portfolios.

NLP – some combine the words 'neurolinguistic', while others use two words. I use a hyphen to maintain the three letter abbreviation, but I will mostly use the three letter abbreviation, as it is a mouthful.

INTRODUCTION

STRUCTURE OF THIS BOOK

Other books attempt to teach you about NLP, or at least support training in it. The domain of NLP is very broad, and since it originated from modelling of successful therapists, guides and courses will generally focus on aspects such as life coaching, wellbeing, relationships, etc. This book is unique in that I will show you how NLP can be directly applied to project management in a competence based approach.

The structure of the book follows an NLP approach itself. At the core of NLP is the presupposition that we all have unique world-views, and we only communicate effectively when we find a way of causing overlap of these distinct worlds. Hence, I will first introduce the world of projects and the world of NLP, before going on to bring the two worlds together and describe the many applications of NLP for soft skills in project management.

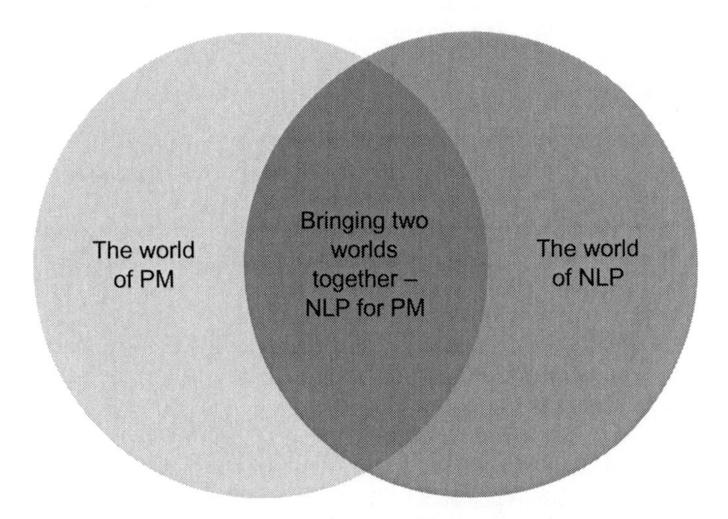

The first part of the book gives an overview of where so-called soft skills are relevant to the different aspects of project and program management, classic stages of the project life cycle, and the various bodies of knowledge (BoKs). Key skills and behaviours from the various competence frameworks are compared, and requirements for becoming an effective project professional are discussed, including those being assessed for a register of project professionals by the Association for Project Management. Now that project management has been recognised as a discipline in its own right, these competences will form the core of any new chartered profession.

The second part lays the foundations for understanding the world of NLP, leaving most of the application for the final part.

The final part of the book brings together the worlds of projects and NLP, and provides a large number of exercises specifically aimed at developing competence against skills and behaviours identified as key requirements for effective leadership and management of projects and programs.

THE WORLD OF PROJECT MANAGEMENT

Formal project management had its fiftieth anniversary around 2010. Methods, mainly for managing time, cost and quality, have been codified and form the backbone of the new profession. In the new millennium, however, Dr Martin Barnes CBE, former Executive Director of the Major Projects Association,[1] re-defined project management as 'Getting things done by people'. This innocent remark is striking because it was Barnes who set in stone the basic tenet of the 'iron triangle' for project management by the three dimensions of time, cost and quality.[2]

Our world is changing with increasing frequency, and much of this change is now being delivered through the discipline of project management. Projects themselves are becoming increasingly complex, as we move on from focussing on delivery of assets and technology to management of stakeholders, benefits, and emerging opportunities and risks. Hence requirements for project and program professionals must continue to evolve to meet these increasing expectations.

Without doubt, the structured methods of PRINCE2 and PMI codify good practice and have helped to guide entrants to the profession. They have become *de facto* standards along the way. Hundreds of thousands of people have now been taught, examined and certificated in these methods around the world. As yet, however, we have not seen a resultant increase in project success, especially in IT projects. Maybe this is because for complex projects:

Method + Soft Skills + Leadership = Success

I think so. In other words, as Louis Armstrong sang:

> 'Tain't what you do, it's the way that cha do it, that's what gets results'

Hence, I see what is introduced in this book as quite complementary to the structured methods. For professional bodies under the International Project Management Association (IPMA), there is certainly a requirement to demonstrate competence in delivery as well as knowledge and experience of method in order to advance beyond the basic levels of qualification. Chartered status for project managers, as proposed by the Association for Project Management, will certainly require demonstration of competence against a wide range of skills, which are covered in Part 3 of this book.

THE WORLD OF NLP

Neuro-linguistic programming (NLP) is defined in the Oxford English Dictionary as 'A model of inter-personal communication chiefly concerned with the relationship between successful patterns of behaviour and the subjective experiences (especially patterns of thought) underlying them.' I prefer to call it the modelling of success.

It originates from early work on cybernetics and systems, and the metaphor of the human mind being like a biological computer, running long established core programs as behaviours. Modelling of world-class therapists led to even greater understanding of the workings of the mind, and tools and techniques for understanding, eliciting and modifying behaviours.

NLP is well established in top level sports and is widespread in the pursuit of personal development, especially for removing limiting beliefs and modelling peak performance. It is increasingly gaining acceptance in training and human resource management. It has been popularised to eliminate phobias, change compulsive behaviours and manage stress. It can be used to deal with inner conflict and manage health issues. In this book I will be constraining myself to a fairly formal approach, but having had personal experience of all of the other areas, I will give pointers in a final part on 'taking things further'.

WORLD-VIEWS – THE COMPLETE PROJECT MANAGER

> 'The biggest room in the world is the room for self improvement'
>
> Japanese proverb

I believe that to be a complete project manager you need both hard and soft skills. When BNFL (British Nuclear Fuels) went through an initiative for 'world class performance' for project management in the mid-1990s, it largely abandoned trying to train poorly performing managers and instead set up selection centres based on behaviours of successful project managers. It then invested heavily in the development of those managers. Improvements in hard and soft measures of project delivery were significant, especially in forecast vs out-turn for time and cost.

But if you entered the profession via competence in processes and tools then take hope. It has been established that soft skills can be developed and improved. In Goleman's original book in 1997 *Emotional Intelligence: Why it can matter more than IQ*, he convinced a proportion of the five million readers that EI was important. But the book fell short in not showing how to improve it. This book *will* provide you with an approach and some useful tools to help to improve your emotional intelligence, even where it might already be considerable.

By the fact that you have picked up this book, I know that you will approach the exercises with an open mind, and trust that you will get good use from the knowledge in your own journey of personal and professional development.

All books are poor substitutes for personal coaching, hence the price difference. Neither can they remain practical and be comprehensive. (The encyclopaedia of NLP is 10 times the length of this book.)[3] This introduction to the topic and its application will stimulate those who are ready to take the next step and do some hands-on training. For the rest, I expect to at least broaden your map of the world.

'No man can reveal to you aught but that which already lies half asleep in the dawning of your knowledge'

Kahlil Gibran

PART 1 THE WORLD OF PROJECT MANAGEMENT

1.1 INTRODUCTION

This book does not pretend to be comprehensive across the body of knowledge for project management (PM BoK), but rather to bring out the soft skills elements in the management of projects, as these can be overlooked or taken for granted when the tools and techniques are taught. In Part 3 of the book, we will show how to develop these soft skills. I believe that the tools and techniques are also important, but these 'hard skills' are easier to learn, and fairly well understood and trained. As a first point of reference to tools and techniques, I personally use:

- *Project Management Pathways*;[4]
- *The Handbook of Project-Based Management*;[5]
- the PMI Body of Knowledge;[6]
- the suite of OGC publications, including those around PRINCE2[7] and Managing Successful Programs (MSP).[8]

Projects are carried out in all sectors, there are lots of types of projects and project management itself has a broad scope. I am conscious of the fact that many people with the title of project manager, sometimes down in the supply chain, have accountability for a limited subset of overall activities. Similarly, some holding the title act as client, and may have limited experience of execution itself, being more concerned with governance and assurance of work carried out by suppliers. Some are responsible for the front end of the life cycle, including assessment of options and business case, while others may be accountable for implementation and benefits realisation. Some focus on technical aspects and others on stakeholder management, etc. Hence, this chapter paints a picture of the breadth and depth of the profession, across all components through the life cycle, especially for those starting out their careers with limited experience to date.

Having scoped all aspects of project management, I then provide a review of the skills and characteristics for effective project management provided by relevant authorities, before finally looking at assessment models, qualification frameworks and requirements for career progression. Tools and techniques to improve competences and provide flexibility for behaviours will be provided in detail in Part 3, after laying out some of the fundamentals of NLP in Part 2.

If you feel that you already know all there is to know about project management, then skip to Part 2.

1.2 WHAT IS PROJECT MANAGEMENT?

1.2.1 Models for project management

In order to understand what project management is, and what skills are necessary to successfully carry it out, we need to agree on what projects are. That may sound a trivial question, but I remember a debate lasting half a day with the supervisor of my Master's dissertation on that very topic. His view was that it was adequately defined by the 'Iron triangle' made famous by Martin Barnes, now President of the Association for Project Management.[9] (Note that I have added 'performance'to the dimension of scope, as Martin always maintained that this is what he meant.)

Figure 1.1 The project management 'iron triangle' of scope, time and cost

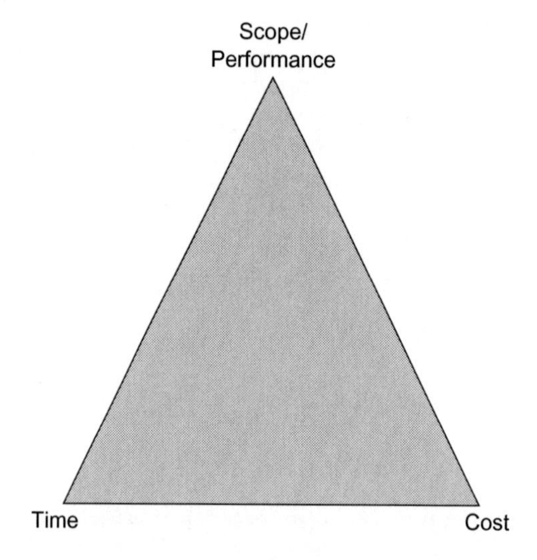

Various texts on project management, however, show this to be only one, rather restricted, model.[10] Personally, I prefer a definition promoted by Martin Barnes decades later:[11]

> 'Project management is getting things done through others'

With this model in mind, if you don't relate well to others then you are off to a poor start.

For projects, as against operations or 'business as usual' (BAU), we must introduce the fact that we are managing some change, whether that is creation of an asset such as a structure, an organisational change or other outcome. There are indeed some who say that project management is change management, and any

Figure 1.2 The classical view of management

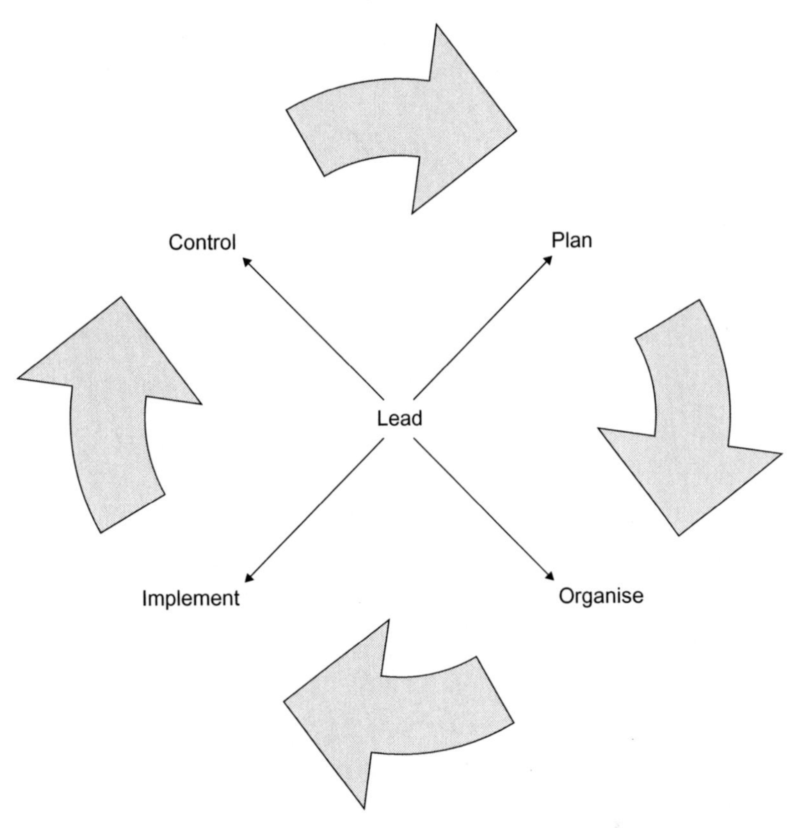

assets that are created are there only to support the change. *Project Management Pathways*[12] includes the definition:

> 'The controlled implementation of defined change'

A government grant-backed initiative called 'Rethinking project management'[13] attempted to redress the fact that project management had evolved into a tool-based system and was glossing over general management competences. I over simplify the outcome of this, but there was a move to create an alternative triangle, which was less 'iron'and more soft. This has found favour, particularly amongst consultancy based organisations.

One model/definition of project management that I would like to mention is that of a decision-making process. When I first came across this I thought that it had little substance, but having had the stress of working with stakeholders who couldn't make a decision to save their lives, or at least that of the project, and people who had no idea what information was needed in reports to support decision-making (none, too much, not relevant, etc.). I increasingly favour this model. Perhaps this is what led me to help develop frameworks for governance, sponsorship and assurance.

Figure 1.3 Managing the benefits

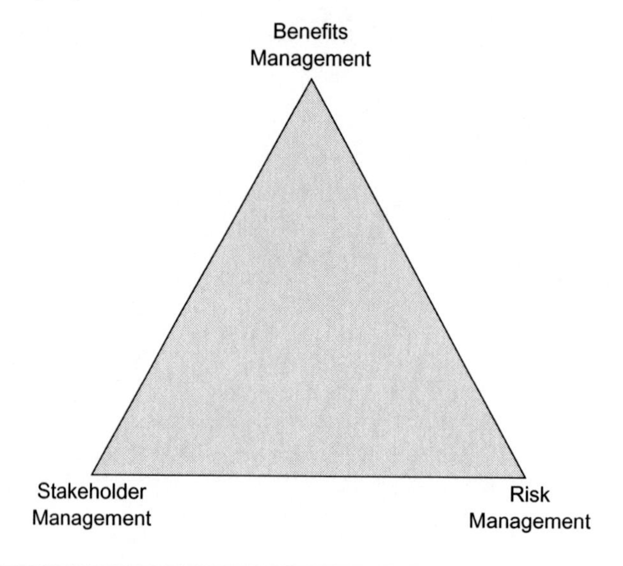

Figure 1.4 The decision-making model for project management

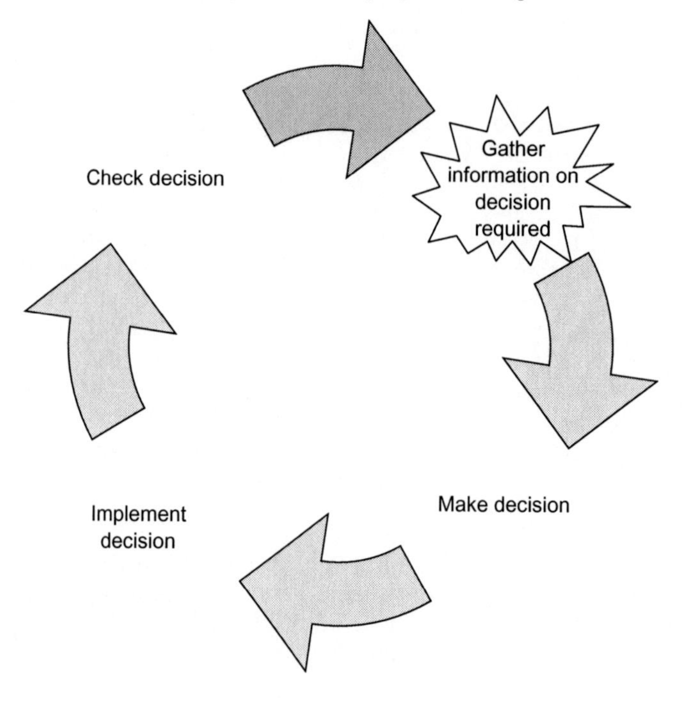

My favourite model, however, I save to last. In studies of attitudes to project management in different cultures, Rodney Turner discovered that adoption of even the best tools and processes by competent people was not sufficient, and concluded that:

> 'Project management is an attitude of mind'

We will discuss other aspects of project management under considerations of life-cycle aspects, components of bodies of knowledge and competence frameworks.

1.2.2 Management of projects versus business as usual

In the last section I blurred the relationship between definition of projects and 'business as usual' (BAU). This was intentional, as the availability of graduate and postgraduate level qualifications in project management is relatively recent, and in the past many people, including myself, entered the profession sideways after already achieving some success and competence in operational roles. Hence, the early definitive guide by one of the godfathers of project management, Rodney Turner, was entitled *The Handbook of Project-based Management.*[14] (In my view, this remains the most complete and practical guide to the nuts and bolts of the profession.)

Nowadays, on the face of it, people can directly enter the profession via education and training without necessarily having exposure to people management. This is a particularly worrying trend when some organisations offer online or five-day courses culminating in multiple choice exams to become 'accredited' PMs with no requirements for prior experience. The buyers, that is the people taking these courses, recruitment agencies, and the people employing them, often do not know how these very short knowledge-based courses fit in to overall qualifications and competence. After some attempts to introduce BAU competences into the PM BoKs, these are now reflecting only a subset of the differences of management competences in application to projects.[15]

So, apart from the specific tools and techniques of project management, what are the main differences in relation to BAU?

- Each project is unique, i.e. a PM must keep relearning context, fast.
- Short deadlines can impose severe time pressure.
- Changing sponsors and senior stakeholders rather than fairly static line management means that relationships have to be developed fast.
- Limited direct authority of PMs – must use influence/leadership.
- Constantly changing teams, as resources are usually drafted in and change through life cycle.

- Projects purposefully disrupting the status quo through change, rather than seeking incremental improvements, which causes resistance from some peers.
- Often a fresh team for every project, with little chance to develop resources.
- Don't have luxury of time to develop relationships with key stakeholders.
- Partnership projects put PMs in separate lines of command.
- Virtual teams are often used.
- Change of company and even sector from project to project.
- Increasing proportion of partnership projects where PMs manage resources outside their own organisation.

All in all, these elements constitute the key difference to me, which I refer to as:

'Management at the sharp end'

1.2.3 What's in a name? Portfolios, programs and projects

Projects have become very popular. Even things that I would judge as being BAU are now being called projects, perhaps so that the person managing them can call themselves a (project) manager and get a pay rise, even though they may not actually be managing staff. I came across a nice lady from a very small marketing firm recently who described herself on her business card as 'Project Director', even though she had no staff and no budget and managed nothing bigger than small customer engagements, usually consisting of herself. She seemed to have had no exposure to projects apart from having to meet client deadlines, and no knowledge of any body of knowledge. But enough of that gripe, and whether people call themselves directors or supervisors, what about the fundamentals?

Good practice says that we should use work breakdown structure (WBS) to make complicated things less so. Once we have a work breakdown structure then it assumes fractal geometry to those in it, and you may not be able to tell where you are in the structure, especially when things are contracted out, unless you are at the top or the bottom. Initially, everyone started to call themselves project managers down the chain. But some noticed that they had people calling themselves project managers reporting up to them, maybe from supplier organisations, and started to call themselves program managers. As the contagion spread, program managers found that they had program managers reporting to them, so they must be managing a portfolio…

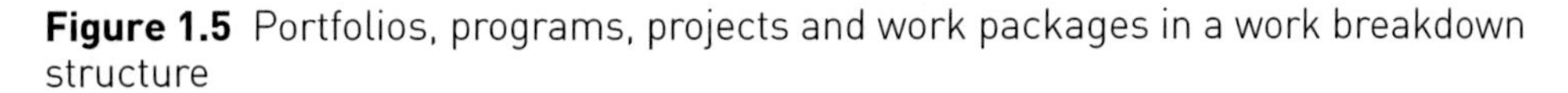

Figure 1.5 Portfolios, programs, projects and work packages in a work breakdown structure

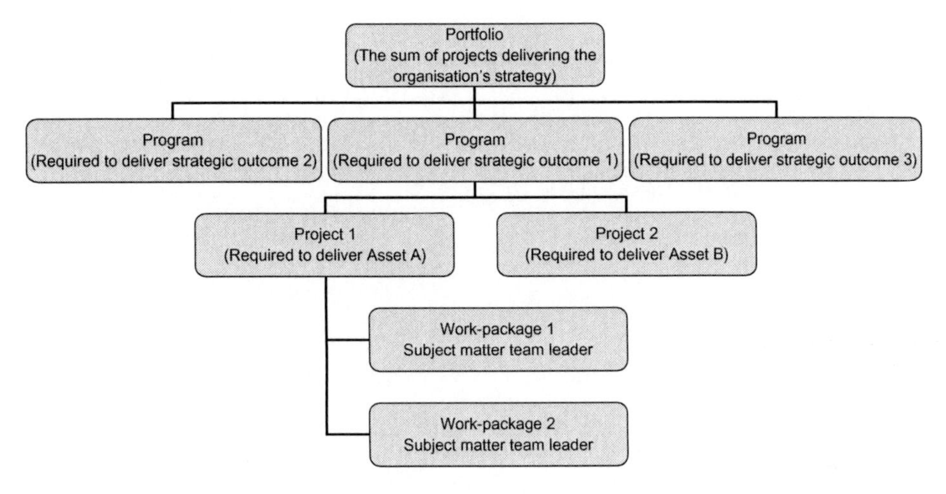

It is all relative, and you can find jobs advertised for PMs that vary in salary by an order of magnitude. To me, what matters are the main duties that you carry out. The table below is my own simplification, but illustrates the spectrum of activities from technical assurance to strategic alignment. But carry on reading, as the book is written to cover this spectrum, from beginners to grand 'meisters'. (And I will refer to all of them, for simplicity, as 'PMs'.)

Note that when I started out in project management, I thought I had to do ALL of these activities. Now, the role of sponsors[16] and governance[17] has been developed

Figure 1.6 Key responsibilities for managers of portfolio, programs and projects

	Key responsibilities	**Key activities**
Portfolio	Strategic alignment Resource pool Governance framework Assurance framework	Understand corporate strategy Management of context Management of senior stakeholders Development of PM capability – people and processes
Program	Delivery of benefits	Business readiness and implementation Management of risks Benefits realisation (leadership)

(Continued)

Figure 1.6 *(Continued)*

	Key responsibilities	Key activities
Project	Delivery of asset/ platform	Requirements and scope Planning of time and cost Managing issues Quality assurance Coordination (management)
Work-package	Delivery of components	Management of activities Technical assurance (supervisory)

so that duties are properly separated, and not only do we do the projects right, but we also do the right projects in the first place. Or so the theory goes.

1.2.4 Types of projects – complexity and uncertainty

I have found the matrix below, adapted from one first popularised by project management guru Eddie Obeng,[18] to be a useful framework to put projects on:

Figure 1.7 Do we know what we want and how to do it or not?

Not sure what we are trying to achieve	'Challenge'	'Quest'
Know what we are trying to achieve	'Factory'	'Capability'
	Know what processes and technology to use	Not sure how to do it

Perhaps most projects are mostly in the bottom left box for most of the time. For organisations with this type of delivery, e.g. construction companies and consultancies, they are likely to have well developed processes, capable PMs and supportive culture. Projects could be considered as their BAU.

At the opposite extreme, we have what appears at first sight to be complete nonsense. How can we be trying to deliver what we don't know, especially when we don't know how to deliver it? Unfortunately, these are some of our most prominent projects, as they are often the ones driven by politics and policy: someone thinks that something should be different, e.g. immigration or the health service, but the implementation is not thought through before deadlines and budgets are set, and often remains disconnected. Is it such a surprise that projects such as these are perceived to 'fail' so often?

The bottom right box contains the most interesting type of projects for me – knowing roughly what you want but having to work out how to do it. The most prominent example of these was President Kennedy's moon challenge, 'We will put a man on the moon…'. That project (program?) is credited with generating all kinds of intellectual property, but the biggest asset was probably to create organisational capability, the benefits of which are still accruing.[19] Strangely, it is in this context that the most formalised tools of project management were developed, including the use of PERT (program evaluation and review technique).[20] Undoubtedly, this was to help to manage the ensuing size of the resulting program, as traditionally innovation type projects shunned structure.[21]

Challenge type projects are the ones that most of us spend most of our time doing. The technical skills are probably within our organisation and we are trying to apply them to meet a new specification or extend functionality. Within such organisations the focus can be on the technical, and the less tangible side of projects can sometimes be omitted, for example by getting so caught up in the elegance of a technical solution that we lose sight of the functionality that is most important to the end user, or the price they were willing to pay. Gold-plated Rolls Royce anyone?

Of course, determining where your project fits on this grid helps to determine what your principle measures of success are. The figure below contains my suggestions:

Figure 1.8 Measuring what you want to achieve

Type of project	**Principle measures?**
'Factory'	Time, cost, quality
'Capability'	Benefits Functionality
'Challenge'	Innovation Capability
'Quest'	Outcome Stakeholder satisfaction Risks to organisation

1.2.5 Mega-projects

The term 'mega-projects' has recently come into vogue. Having myself come from the nuclear industry, these tended to be the norm, but can be quite threatening if you have only managed small teams before. In my view, these are quite manageable using the discipline of project management, and particularly work breakdown structure (WBS), governance and assurance. I had the pleasure of reviewing the UK's lifetime nuclear decommissioning program, which was £60 billion over 100 years, but this was perfectly well structured into manageable projects through effective use of WBS. If you are in an organisation that has not reached a level of maturity to consistently manage standard project management processes, then do not attempt to deliver these by the seat of your pants or you will fail. Where such 'mega-projects' have failed, subsequent reviews have found the maturity of the delivering organisations to be at fault, particularly on governance, and wide-scale capability programs have resulted.[22] This has not prevented individual PMs being named and shamed, effectively ending their careers. (See Section 1.5 on organisational maturity.)

1.2.6 Complex projects

There is increasing dialogue around 'complex projects'. From a purist point of view, I think of complex systems as those with 'emergent properties' such as swarms of starlings or shoals of fish, which behave like a single entity where the whole has behaviours that are almost impossible to predict from the components. I hope that people do not mean that they cannot forecast these huge projects, but are instead referring to size and the fact that they are complicated. Neither of these two factors on their own give cause for concern, as both can be dealt with through work breakdown structure and governance under a competent PM. (We will look at skills for 'chunking' from the big picture to the detail in Section 3.14.)

The only real issue is whether the organisation is sufficiently mature and the project manager is sufficiently knowledgeable and competent to do the job. In some cases this has not been the case. In terms of project management competence, although the International Project Management Association (IPMA) provides a standard grading of PM maturity on a scale of 1 to 4, with 4 being suitable for 'complex projects', most courses and qualifications only address level 1. I have seen disasters where 'level 1' PMs, or rather PMs with only level 1 training and experience, have been put in charge of large complicated projects without the safety net of close mentoring and support, with dire consequences.

We will leave competence of PMs to Section 1.8, but how do we determine how complicated a project is? A tool that I have found particularly useful is the risk potential assessment (RPA).[23] This was developed by the UK's Office of Government Commerce (OGC) and is used to determine the level of scrutiny that a project is subjected to. At the top end of the risk profile are 'high risk projects'; for these, external highly experienced reviewers are called in to assure the project at each phase. It is a pity that the RPA is not used to determine the level of PM that should lead the project, but maybe this is in the pipeline, with the OGC pushing for greater professionalism.[24]

Figure 1.9 Example risk factors for government projects

Factor	**High risk**
Political	Driven by legislation.
Public	Public facing, e.g. new system for taxation.
Financial	Budgetary size means that the project has to be approved and reported above government department, e.g. to the Treasury.
Impact on BAU	Operations may be significantly affected by the project, e.g. to take old system down to replace.
Dependencies	The project is dependent on other projects, managed separately to deliver components of the solution or other projects are dependent on it.
Security of information	Personal information that must be kept secure is being transported and could be accessible.
Stakeholders	Stakeholder map is complex and includes senior figures who have capability to de-rail the project, e.g. government ministers.
Supply chain	Significant components are delivered through partnership organisations and suppliers.
Senior support	Does the project have sufficient senior support to keep it on course?
Supporting capability	Is there sufficient capacity and capability in the organisation and applied to the project to deliver it?

Note how few of these factors are addressed by process-based management and how much they can be affected by soft skills. Basically, the higher risk the project then the more capable the PM needs to be in terms of soft skills, though even 'small' projects benefit from them.

Figure 1.10 Riskier projects require better developed soft skills

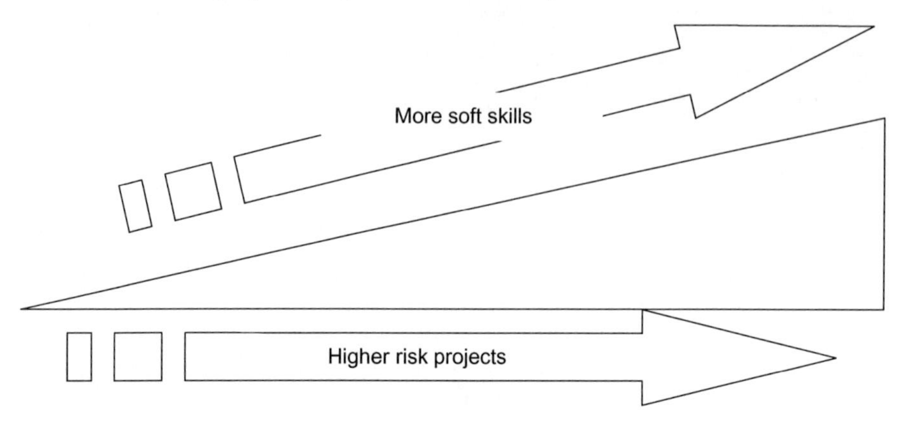

1.2.7 Small projects

Although there is a lot of focus nowadays on large and complicated projects, most organisations deal with what might be termed small or simple projects. These projects have challenges of their own, in that:

- Being small, the PM assigned may be relatively junior and struggle without the support of a mentor or proactive program management office (PgMO).
- There may not be organisational support to them, e.g. no project support office (PSO).
- The project may be viewed as less important and struggle to secure resources, including the time of the sponsor (assuming that there is one).

Despite being small in terms of budget, the project may be large in terms of consequence, e.g. impact on reputation or in providing avenues for future revenue of the company. In my mind, the best way to judge a project is using the risk potential assessment already introduced, as this includes other factors to budget, including criticality, complexity, and impact. This method of assessment should judge where your best PMs are assigned, not simply on size of budget. Of course, the project may only be small in current phase, but grow considerably as it passes through successive phases and gates, as for R&D projects. One of the big challenges for PMs of small projects is influencing senior stakeholders when the project may not appear very important. (Influencing skills are covered in Section 3.15.)

1.2.8 Partnership projects

Organisations enter partnership projects for various reasons, including sharing of risk and to fill capability gaps.[25] From a project management perspective, aside from aspects of virtuality and perhaps cultural differences, which are dealt with separately, the biggest challenge is that ownership of the project is less clear and there is no single chain of command. Best practice for governance recommends that there is a single sponsor for the project,[26] but stakeholder management undoubtedly becomes more complex. Rather than have success criteria for the project, these can degenerate into win-lose arrangements, with the PM stuck in the middle. Those projects found most successful have been ones where a superordinate goal can be identified that all organisations can align too. (In NLP this is referred to as 'chunking up' to a common goal.) It is also in the PM's interest to create a very strong project identity, i.e. separate from those of the parent organisations. (Creating project identity and motivation of project teams is dealt with in Section 3.)

1.2.9 Virtual projects

More companies are virtualising as they dispose of non-core assets, but the rate is exceeded by the number of virtual projects, where the overall capability is created by combining elements from different organisations, often in different countries, in different times zones, etc.

The element that I want to address here in relation to this book is the fact that much of the communication in these projects is via teleconferencing at best, and often by email. Both of these innovations are very welcome to the project manager, who like me used to have to spend half their lives in transit between different teams. The downside, however, is that the opportunities for miscommunication are multiplied, and multiplied again when we add in differences of culture, and again when people do not share a common first language. If we struggle to be effective in face to face situations, then the prospect of doing so without the face to face bit is daunting. In Section 3 we will read that most of our communication is non-verbal, and what to do about it.

I worked with one Head of IT, who in NLP terms had an aural preference, and he would choose to hold teleconferences with people who were on the floor above, let alone in the next building. Things did not run smoothly and each day was consumed by conflict and fire fighting due to avoidable misunderstandings.

Hence, if you are ever involved in leading such projects then remember the adage:

> 'It is difficult to see eye to eye until you have met face to face'

For those struggling to hear my tonality or to see my body language on this printed page, that means get on the plane for at least the first meeting.

1.2.10 Multicultural projects

Most projects are now multicultural in that people are more mobile, and so even a moderately sized project office in London is likely to have people from several races and cultures in the team. Turner pointed out,[27] however, that there are considerable problems in using the suite of Western-oriented techniques for project management in non-Westernised countries, as aside from the processes, project management is an attitude of mind and is strongly influenced by world-view – a concept at the heart of NLP. Cultural differences were studied in terms of the factors of: individualism, masculinity, uncertainty avoidance (fear of change), and power-distance (acceptance of authority and social inequalities). In NLP terms, we can view these as relevant meta-programs or unquestioned behaviours to be considered for effective project management. Turner's research also revealed that different combinations of these factors are better for the different phases of the project life cycle, and notes that, while Western cultures are better at delivery, they are relatively poor at initiation and close-out. Does this ring true with you?

From an NLP perspective we need to appreciate that even people from our own culture and background have different world-views to ourselves, and for different cultures this can be more different than same. There are some elements in our favour, however. Firstly, the well-known experiment giving the 'Maharabian statistics' showed that people picked up much more from tone than words, and much more from body language than both combined.[28] On the face of it, this means that you will convey more accurate information in person to someone from a different culture who doesn't speak your language than to someone in the next office via email! If they are aurally biased rather than visual, then even more so. This doesn't quite stack up when considering the need to relay technical content, but the point is that you will probably fail to get even this over unless you at least attempt to understand the world-view of your audience.

In a seminar on cross-cultural projects some years ago, one of the participants relayed a story from a joint project between a telecoms company in Scandinavia and an American company. The request to invite 'significant others' led to Americans leaving the plane in Hawaii shirts with their *wives*, to be met by a brass band and members of the *royal family*. Being visual, I have held that picture to my heart as I despatch each email overseas.

From an NLP perspective, it is worth noting that rapport is no more difficult to achieve across cultural boundaries, and this is the foundation for all effective communication.

1.2.11 Change management projects

As we have seen in models for project management, one definition (used in Project Management Pathways) is:

'The controlled implementation of defined change'

Some people, mainly coming from HR rather than project management backgrounds, think of change management as something different to project management, and regard the latter as too formalised. Personally, I prefer to regard all projects in terms of change management, and put the focus on outcomes and change of behaviours. I have certainly found this to work with IT, where the fashionable term is now 'IT enabled transformation'.[29] In frameworks like MSP (Managing Successful Programs), however, responsibility for the transformation part is separated out from the role of the PM, who is only there to deliver the physical asset.[30] A separate resource, usually from 'the business', is nominated to lead on change of behaviours.

I have worked with this framework and am not a fan of this aspect since benefits realisation planning, to me, is best left with the PM to make sure that it happens. The language in common usage for change management, with end states of target operating models via business blueprints, also lends itself perfectly to the project management discipline. Some change projects are referred to as process-enabled change, and again the PM is well positioned to address these aspects, especially since the business analysts carrying out this type of work usually report in to the PM during the requirements gathering phase. I suspect that the division arose because the PMs available were largely experts in the technical domain and were not deemed competent to address some of the softer work-packages such as stakeholder management, requirements management, communications, benefits management, etc. In Part 3 of this book we will be addressing the breadth of skills for change management.

I was challenged as to how construction can be regarded as change management. Working with colleagues in regeneration, or what was town planning, the vocabulary is entirely consistent, with a focus on building communities rather than building houses, and taking a macro-view of the urban plan, including transport, health, education, leisure, etc. Hence the overall program is definitely about creating change.

With regards to physical buildings themselves, even here the focus is on 'liveability', with many new schemes including associated leisure, shopping, etc. In many new homes you will now see the kitchen and bathroom being designed, and even built, first, as construction is being dictated to by the values and requirements of the end user, rather than the construction process.

For the UK's huge national program for schools, the focus moved away from providing buildings to provision of an educational environment, with ICT support, maintenance, operations, etc. packaged up and outsourced via contract with a focus on lifetime costs. What was contracted was not a physical asset but a changed learning environment.

With regard to what are referred to as cultural change programs, I think these exist mainly in the conversations of the boardroom. In one transformation program in a local authority where the sponsor asked me how I was going to do cultural change, I replied, 'I cannot do cultural change, as it is established that it takes five or more years to change culture, and I intend to be out of here within 12 months. What you will get is technology and process-enabled change that will give you effectiveness and efficiency.' He replied, 'That will do.' While implementing organisational design (OD) and business process re-engineering (BPR[31]) certainly help, I think that cultural change only occurs with change of leadership.

1.2.12 R&D projects

I include R&D projects here as that is where my career started out and has recently returned. While doing an executive MBA I was asked to carry out a study on how to manage small R&D projects. It was considered that we knew how to do big projects, but were not so good at small ones. Many of the small projects referred to were over £1 million annual spend (and big ones over £100 million). I wrote a dissertation on best practice for management of R&D,[32]

but the key features were not about size. The most important aspect was a focus on managing the overall portfolio rather than individual projects. It is well established that most R&D projects do not come to fruition. Some succeed technically but fail to go into production or fail to achieve market share. The real focus had to be on terminating projects early that were less likely to be commercially successful in order to concentrate resources on to new projects to take their place and give those that were likely to succeed priority for resources.[33] Cooper's Stage–Gate process became widely used across a number of sectors to crystallise these thoughts,[34] and independent 'end of phase' reviews became the norm. (A very similar funnel process is used in sales to convert leads.)

Figure 1.11 Innovation funnel/portfolio management for R&D projects

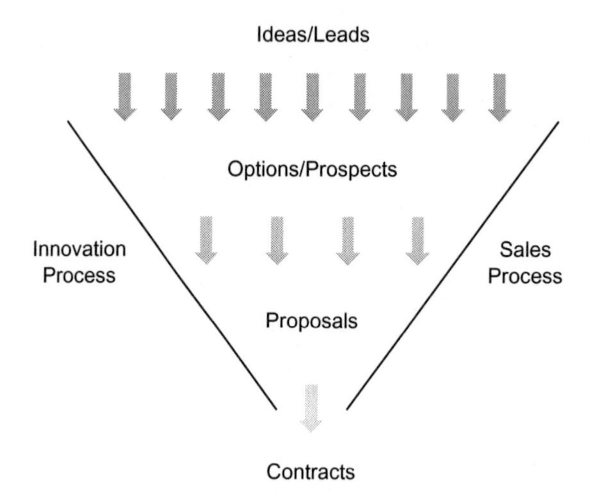

The Stage–Gate process morphed into the OGC's Gateway Review Process,[35] and independent reviews became project boards under the PRINCE method.[36] With Gateway, however, the process starts much later in the life cycle, effectively when decisions need to be taken on outsourcing of the project. The other key difference between the original 'stage and gate' and the Gateway process is that the former is designed to kill projects early, whereas Gateway is designed to improve the chances of project success, and it is not possible to recommend closure. Maybe it should, particularly at the early gates before too much resource has been consumed. It has been recognised, however, that the biggest influence on project success is early in the process, and there is a move to introduce earlier gates. Gate 0 has already been added as a review of the over-arching program.

Phasing of projects, and use of Stage–Gate processes, is now endemic across most industries, from oil and gas exploration to manufacturing, with some organisations introducing up to 10 review gates.

Scenario analysis was introduced from the oil and gas industry. To manage strategic risk one had to bear in mind that the context for the organisation, let alone the project, could change dramatically, especially as more than a decade can

Figure 1.12 The ability to influence a project diminishes rapidly with time

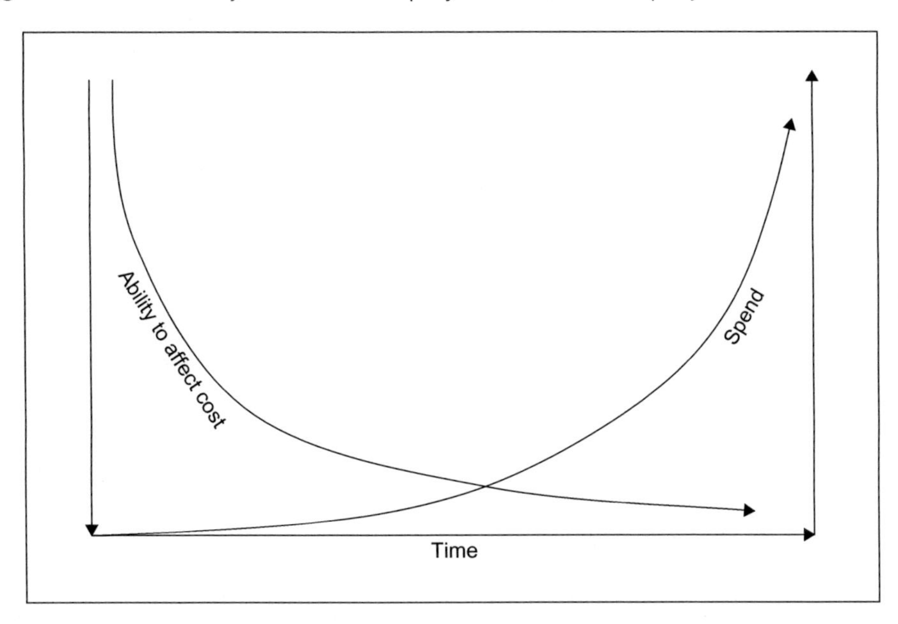

elapse from seed to germination. Given the increasing rate of change in the world, and the macro-changes to all aspects of life over recent years, scenario analysis will be increasingly used to test different sets of (project) assumptions. NLP offers great techniques to recognise and bring together different world-views.

So, other than a greater focus on scenario planning and portfolio management, much of which may happen over the head of the PM at project director level, what is different about project management of R&D? My answer to that is 'not much', though there should be a greater emphasis on resource management (across the portfolio), and capability management (across the portfolio). Risk management needs to explicitly include 'opportunity management', though it is in the best organisations anyway. (In Part 3 we look at those motivated by meta-program for risk and opportunity.)

I was cheered in support of these views by an article appearing in *Project* magazine in 2010 where a PM from the construction sector moved to the pharmaceutical industry, where the focus is on managing multiple R&D projects for the next generation of drugs, after completing an MSc in project management. On being asked what the key differences were between construction projects and research projects he replied, 'There aren't any.'

One aspect of R&D that did turn out to be quite different was the need to encourage a culture of innovation.[37] Up to that point, there had been a drive to push R&D into the operational business units to 'keep it real'. The result was that long term R&D gave way to short term operational support, and the organisation developed a shortfall in its new product development pipeline. Fortunately, good leadership established a strong identity and culture and the numbers of patents produced rapidly multiplied.[38]

Earlier this year, more than 15 years later, I was asked to participate in a study group for 'portfolio management of R&D', and a new 'best practice group' for portfolio management was formed in 2010.[39] Similarly, last year I saw my first presentation on scenario planning at a project management conference – something that we were doing for R&D portfolios decades ago. As with many things, life cycles are not just for projects.

1.2.13 Trends in projects

On the face of it, project management doesn't seem to be getting any better in that reports into rates of failure do not show an improving trend. Balancing this, however, we should recognise that projects themselves are becoming more complicated, as what was cutting edge becomes the expected. For IT projects, users have much higher expectations of functionality and availability based on what they can experience in top end leisure applications. Linking masses of data with web availability and still expecting total security clearly poses challenges.

Not so long ago, all functions of a project may have been conducted in-house, but today there are complex supply chains giving the integrator the job of not only making sure that all the pieces of the jigsaw arrive on time, but that they also work together as intended. Methods of contracting out the supply chain are slowly moving towards contracting for benefits, which forces the focus on understanding end user benefits and benefits realisation planning.[40]

Looking higher up the organisation, the boardroom is now seeking to get a grip on the overall portfolio of projects, and the link to delivering the organisational strategy. Above it all sits governance.[41] Not simply the rules that should be applied, but the complex human interactions that mean that they are followed, or not.[42]

The role of the PM is being forced further from the work-face towards the boardroom, and this demands a higher calibre of professional with a wider range of business skills. Those business skills include the competences described and developed in this book. I expect these to be tested more thoroughly in the next generation of qualifications for PMs.

1.2.14 Putting it all together

The element that I want to emphasise here, in relation to the objectives of this book, is that we first need to understand the challenges of the project objectives, context and organisation, before we even start to think about delivery of the project itself. Such factors will determine the seniority, skill-set and capability of the PM most likely to successfully deliver the project. These aspects are unlikely to be met solely by the formal processes of project management, although there are tools that can help, but it has everything to do with the competences being developed in Part 3.

1.3 WHAT IS PROJECT SUCCESS AND WHY DO PROJECTS FAIL?

> 'A thing which cannot be accomplished should never be undertaken'
>
> African Proverb

I remember being at the World Congress for Project Management in 2000 in London and the keynote speaker picked two high profile Millennium Projects: The Millennium Dome and the London Eye. The speaker asked the audience which one was a success. The audience almost unanimously voted for the London Eye, which still stands and does good business attracting lots of visitors. The Millennium Dome was subject to front page newspaper reviews on what a failure it had been. But in fact the Millennium Dome ran to time, cost and original scope, whereas the London Eye did not meet any of these. So why was the Millennium Dome considered a failure? The business case was fatally over-optimistic and the project, on tight time scales, had deliberately excluded the press, a key stakeholder for such a venture, during the construction phase. By comparison, the BA London Eye was intended to be a PR exercise and had enthusiastically courted stakeholders and particularly the mass media. The moral of the story? The physical assets of a project are less important than knowing who your stakeholders are and what they want, and keeping them involved. NLP provides a very strong set of tools for stakeholder management, and this topic will be covered at length in Section 3.15.

> 'The quality is remembered long after the price is forgotten'
>
> Versace

There are reviews every year of why projects fail, the most widely quoted of which are the CHAOS reports for IT projects,[43] but the National Audit Office covers the breadth of public sector projects in the UK.[44] What is most striking to me is the fact that those reasons don't seem to change over time. Are we not learning the lessons? One possible reason for the lack of apparent progress is the trend for projects to become more complicated. With IT projects for example, issues around interfaces, data security, web-enablement, volume of data, client expectations around functionality, etc. make it difficult to be sure of success. As one IT project director said to me when I was carrying out a review, 'When you put a million lines of bespoke code onto £10 million of hardware for the first time and ask it to search terabytes of data, it is difficult to predict where problems are going to arise and how long it will take to solve them.' Maybe these really are complex projects in the true sense.

Addressing the APM annual conference in London in 2010, Sir Peter Gershon stated:

> 'Projects do not generally fail for novel reasons, but for the same boringly repetitive ones'

The most frequently cited reasons for project failure are those on the NAO/OGC website.[45] These are:

- lack of clear links between the project and the organisation's key strategic priorities, including agreed measures of success;
- lack of clear senior management and ministerial ownership and leadership;
- lack of effective engagement with stakeholders;
- lack of skills and proven approach to project management and risk management;
- too little attention to breaking development and implementation into manageable steps;
- evaluation of proposals driven by initial price rather than long-term value for money (especially securing delivery of business benefits);
- lack of understanding of, and contact with, the supply industry at senior levels in the organisation;
- lack of effective project team integration between clients, the supplier team and the supply chain.

At APM's annual conference in London 2010 Sir Peter Gershon summed up the state of project failures by using the quote:

> 'We know why projects fail.
> We know how to prevent failure.
> So why do they still fail?'
>
> Cobb's Paradox[46]

You can view these reasons for failure through a number of prisms, and with a 'governance' hat on I could identify this aspect in most of them. For the purposes of this book, however, we can see themes of:

- lack of leadership;
- lack of engagement (with senior sponsors, stakeholders, supply chain);
- lack of team integration;
- lack of skills.

All of these are addressed through NLP tools in Part 3.

1.4 ORGANISATIONAL CULTURE AND THE MATURITY OF THE PROJECT ORGANISATION

To my view, one aspect of project management that does not get enough attention is the project context in terms of organisational capability and capacity.

Some organisations seem to have the view that you can send a candidate off for one week's training in project management and everything will be OK. Even if the PM comes back with their underpants on the outside like Superman, they are going to find it difficult to deliver when the organisation does not have structures, processes and capability to support them. Some organisations have taken to adopting versions of the PRINCE2 manual, but lack of support often means that these get the label 'PINO' – PRINCE In Name Only. A large-scale study by the University of Queensland into project failure in organisations where PMs were trained in PRINCE2 concluded that failure could be attributed to lack of project management maturity in the parent organisation.[47] (Subsequently, the state government of Queensland mandated use of maturity assessment for government departments.)

Where investigations have shown systemic failure in projects, these can create the 'burning deck' scenario cited by change management professionals as necessary to successfully carry out organisational change. Organisations such as British Aerospace and NATS (National Air Traffic Services) have successfully recovered from such systemic failures to substantially improve the maturity of their delivery capability.[48]

Figure 1.13 Project management maturity in an organisation[49]

Ad-hoc	⟶	**Mature**
Line management dominant	Matrix management	Management by projects
Stand alone projects	Some programs	Projects organised under portfolio to deliver strategic plan
Line managers do projects. No formal training or qualifications	Some professional project managers. Training in processes	Organisation is managed by projects. All managers are project managers
Simple processes, tools, and techniques	Standard method	Benchmarked processes, tools and techniques
Intuitive project managers	Process dominated project management	Project managers with appropriate traits and behaviours
Task oriented	Product oriented	Outcome oriented
Activity driven	Deliverable driven	Benefit driven

> I was asked to go into a failed local government council as interim Project Director to organise and execute an organisational turnaround. On the first day I was presented with a thick report on all the instances of failure and asked to put together a program to address them all. I pointed out that the first paragraph of the report said, 'This organisation has no capability for delivery or change management...'. I proposed that this would be my first change project, as if it was not then all the rest would be paper exercises doomed to failure.

Without waiting for catastrophic project failure, you may wish to look at the project management maturity of your organisation. There are a number of maturity models out there,[50] but I have found the P3M3 model the most pragmatic to use, as it tells you not only what your level is but also what to do to improve.[51] Note that this model addresses all three aspects from portfolio through program to project, as is necessary to address organisational capability.

Figure 1.14 P3M3 – Maturity of the organisation's portfolio management

	Level 1 Awareness of process	**Level 2** Repeatable process	**Level 3** Defined process	**Level 4** Managed process	**Level 5** Optimised process
Organisational governance Resource management Management control Stakeholder management Risk management Financial management Benefits management	Does the organisation's executive board recognise programs and projects and keep a list of its investment in them?	Does the organisation run projects to a method to a minimum acceptable standard?	Does the organisation have its own centrally controlled processes? Does it have a process for portfolio management?	Does the organisation obtain and retain metrics on its whole portfolio as a means of predicting future performance? Does the organisation assess its capacity to manage projects?	Does the organisation run continuous process improvement for the portfolio in order to improve its ability to depict its performance over time?

This leaves us with maturity of PMs. Who says you are a PM? Do you have a piece of paper? How long did it take you to get? A week, a year, five years? This aspect is covered in detail in Section 1.8.

1.5 PEOPLE SKILLS THROUGH THE PROJECT MANAGEMENT LIFE CYCLE

> 'A hen is only an egg's way of making another egg'
> Samuel Baker (English satirist 1612–1680)

Many advertisements for jobs state a requirement for experience of 'full project life cycle'. But is it reasonable to expect one person to have an aptitude for project concept, ideas generation and divergent thinking as well as having completer finisher behaviour for closure? In R&D portfolios we found that some people were very good at working with new concepts and project start-ups but were relatively poor at the discipline of managing delivery to time. Some were good at handling concepts, others at process, and some with people and relationships. (These are all described in NLP through various preferred behaviours or 'meta-programs' and are relatively easy to illicit.) Hence it is good to think of not only the type of project, but also the phase of project in order to define the most appropriate skills and most suitable resource. Of course, the ability to develop flexibility of behaviour, as discussed in Section 3.11, vastly extends the operating range of the project manager.

Figure 1.15 Extending the operating range of project managers

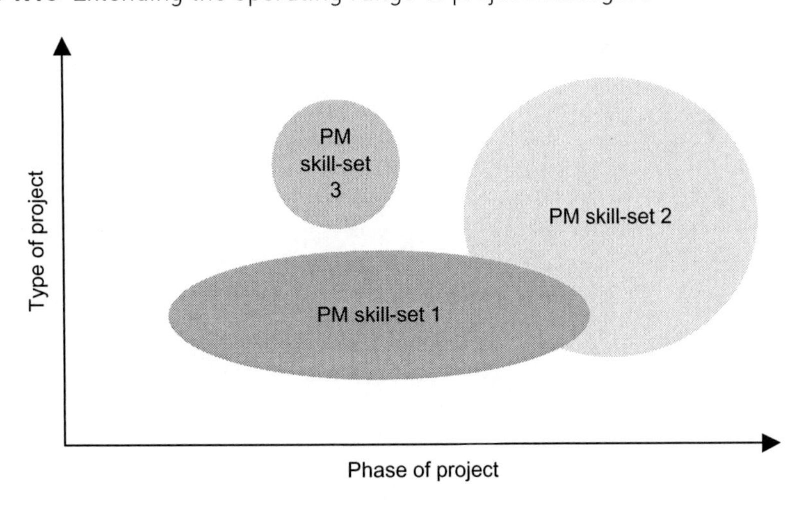

The table below looks at different phases of a project life cycle and considers what might be the key skills of a project manager working in each phase. Note that this is intended to be an encompassing terminology for the different life cycle models in use in different methods.[52] Many of the key skills identified are addressed in

Section 3, which is intended to develop your flexibility to handle different project demands.

Figure 1.16 Changing skills across a project life cycle

Phase	Key activities	Key skills
Research	Nurturing of idea	Listening Options thinking Reframing
Concept/Proposal	Formalising of idea Marketing of idea Initial Business Case	Presenting yourself Gaining support and approval
Initiation	Planning Resourcing Planning Benefits	Seeing the big picture while managing the detail Orientation to procedure
Start-up	Mobilisation	Teambuilding Communications
Definition	Requirements	Listening Finding accommodation
Options appraisal	Evaluation	Options thinking
Design	Design	Detail orientation Process orientation
Build/execute	Execution Reporting Issue Management Stakeholder management Management changes	Resilience Resolving conflict Problem solving Motivating Coaching and mentoring
Test	Identifying problems Fixing problems Managing configuration	Listening Problem solving Delivering bad news well Reframing
Implementation	Training Handover Operational support	Leadership Communication styles Team-working
Closure	Lessons learned review Staff feedback	Giving and receiving feedback
Benefits realisation	Post-implementation review	Listening Resilience

Some people consider **agile type methods**, which are iterative cycles of requirements-to-build inside a constrained resource box, as being an alternative to long development cycles. They are usually, however, constrained requirements-to-build cycles for only one work-package of the project, and the remainder of the project usually proceeds via a water-fall type approach such as that above. For example, a software application may use an agile method to time-box development, but the other work-streams of the overall project, such as hardware platform, manufacture, marketing and sales rarely adopt an agile approach. For the team leader of the agile work-packages, the scope is quite limited, as aspects such as business case, project sponsorship, communications, value management etc. as outlined in the next section are not their consideration.

As a final thought in this section, Rodney Turner reviewed data on the abilities of different cultures to perform projects, and noted that the Western philosophy of project management did not fit with some cultures.[53] Using some standard parameters for measuring cultural differences, he established that different cultural outlooks were more suited to different phases of the project life cycle, and noted that Eastern cultural attitudes were much more suited to project initiation and close-out, while Western cultural attitudes were more suited to delivery phases. So, think like a French woman for the initiation stage, turn Germanic for planning and execution, then Arabic for termination. In other words, the most flexible PM is going to be more successful. (Flexibility using NLP is discussed in Part 3.11.)

Figure 1.17 Preferred cultural approach at different stages of the project life cycle (Turner)

Trait	Feasibility	Design	Execution	Close-out
Power distance	High	Low	Low	High
Individualism	High	Medium	Low	Low
Masculinity	Medium	Medium	Medium	Medium
Uncertainty Avoidance	Low	Medium	Medium	High

1.6 PEOPLE ASPECTS IN PROJECT MANAGEMENT PROCESSES

As introduced above, some people considering themselves as project managers may be carrying out the duties of a technical line manager. Few have exposure to all components of project management across the life cycle without purposely seeking to do so. For accreditation at higher levels of project management, however, it is necessary to seek out such development opportunities.

The various competence frameworks consider both the knowledge and experience aspects of these components, with the latter dominant for higher levels of certification.

The list below is a compilation of common components of project management from various bodies of knowledge (BoKs). As this book is about using NLP, rather than a treatise on project management, I will only touch on those aspects of these 'hard' competences that require specific soft skills. These soft skills will be developed in Part 3.

Sponsorship[54] is sometimes carried out by people who have got to this level through project management, but often by people from the business who have no background in project management but may be accountable for the business benefits. Either way, amongst other duties, they have the difficult task of managing senior stakeholders and finding compromise between suppliers and users within the constraints of budget. They must also maintain the relationship with the project manager. As we all know, relationships are a two-way affair.

I run a series of talks on 'what is **assurance**?', as I came to the realisation that it depends on who you are assuring, and what they feel unsure about. If your sponsor feels unsure about where the project is, when it will finish, and what it will actually deliver, then you are likely to be in for a lot of health checks, visits from Internal Audit, reviews, etc. Maintain a continuous dialogue. Be the first point of assurance to your sponsor and other senior stakeholders, and don't assume that they are happy with the way things are going just because they are quiet. (Stakeholder management techniques are covered in Part 3.15.)

Legal awareness. Ignorance is no excuse in the eyes of the law, and this also goes for contract law. Legal action can often be avoided through dialogue and ensuring that boils do not fester in the absence of less adversarial channels of communication. Handling difficult situations and negotiation are explicitly dealt with in Part 3.

I am old enough to remember when **health and safety** was considered to be something of a joke. As a PM, however, it is your primary duty of care to ensure that your staff and those affected by your project return home to their families at the end of each day safe and in good health. This also encompasses mental health, and you are culpable if you unduly stress your workforce through your own deficiencies in planning, communication and management. Even if you don't suffer from stress, you may be a carrier for your team. (Stress management is specifically dealt with in Part 3.8.)

Until relatively recently, **environment and sustainability** were terms thrown into bids to help to jump 'the green hurdle'. Now they are being introduced into core responsibilities of project management. The onus is on you to consider how the project can be a force for good and minimise our impact on the environment. In the wider sense, it is your job to ensure that the project environment is supportive, rather than like running in wellington boots, and that the project team is managed in a way that sustains performance, rather than imposing crazy deadlines and excessive hours that quickly lead to poor performance.

Information security may not seem very important to us sometimes, but I have been inside organisations that have sustained massive reputational damage as a result of relatively minor leaks of personal information. I have also seen details of people's pay displayed to them and an audience of their colleagues during straightforward implementations of software systems. We wouldn't like it to happen to ourselves, so we have to set the standard and expectations for the team, and what are acceptable process and unacceptable shortcuts. (Setting team values and behaviours is covered in Part 3.19.)

Quality management used to be something to be avoided, but no one likes wasting time on rework, and the customer definitely doesn't deserve shoddy work. And as they say in the field, 'quality is free' (the avoidance of rework pays for any systems very quickly). Again, it is up to us to ensure processes are in place and set expectations that these are to be followed and not short cut. It seems strange to bring leadership up with quality, but leadership is about setting standards and behaviours as much as anything.

I have reviewed many projects at late stages, and even on final stage, where the **business case** was not yet complete or signed off. (I will not mention those organisations or projects where there was not even a business case to be found.) Many project managers don't like to do them (or any paperwork), but it is your job to ensure that they are done and signed off. (Actually, it is the sponsor's job, but I have not yet seen an instance where the PM has not ended up getting it done.) If you are running a project without a business case and plan then you are firing your arrows with a blindfold on, hoping that when it is removed some of them will have fallen near the target. It is a fantastic tool to help to get close to the business and understand what they want out of the project (and it is unlikely to be another room full of IT servers). Be professional. In preparing the business case it is good to understand the culture of 'optimism bias'[55] to avoid giving yourself unachievable targets, as for the Millennium Dome project in London. Did the project fail because it did not deliver, or because it was unachievable?

Finance and budgeting is another area that some PMs are reluctant to understand, preferring to leave it to an accountant to tell them how much they think they might have spent. The customer is relying on you to protect them from financial exposure. It is not difficult, though it does take a bit of study.[56] It also requires you to go over to the dark side and talk to some accountants. Try to see the world from their perspective and help to meet their needs too, and I promise your life will become easier.

The project management plan, also called a project initiation document (PID), sometimes gets left behind. For large projects, and especially ones with a complex stakeholder map, this is not only your 'contract' for the project, but also an essential communication tool. It should be a live document, maintained as changes to the way you plan to do things change, so that all parties can stay on the same page. Be sure not only to maintain and update it, but also to communicate those changes. That does not mean posting a new version in the document management system, but rather telling those that the changes may affect in person. Sounds obvious, but does it happen in your organisation?

Requirements management, in my view, continues to be badly done for even the basics. Either the solution provider ends up assuming what the client might want, or listening to an array of people too far down the organisation to understand where the organisation wants to be, rather than where it finds itself. Requirements management demands assertiveness to get the right people at the right level to agree on what opportunity or problem they are trying to solve, and also to push back on what is not practical and of value. This is a real trial of a range of people skills, including seeking information, facilitating change, chairing and challenging. It is also a true test of influencing skills.

Documentation and information management may appear too boring for some PMs, but for larger assignments it will keep the project on track and prevent a real muddle near the finish line, especially for long projects where there are likely to be many changes in personnel along the way. The real test is understanding the nature of information as against data, and of purpose/value of documentation as against volume.

Configuration management is essential in many industries but seems to be poorly done in IT, where the nature of the beast is that we expect to have to fix and change things through the project life cycle, let alone the full product life cycle of the application in service. Many good software systems exist to help with this, but I can only conclude that the PM does not communicate the importance to the people on the ground doing the coding and fixing. Like a lot of the 'boring' stuff, no one wants to do it but the organisation needs it to be effective, and the PM is the person who must enforce this (and not just say it).

Work breakdown structure is one of the tools that enables even the biggest projects to be managed comfortably, though I have seen many projects, including beasts of over £100 million, trying to get by without one. It is no accident that it is included in lists of the main reasons for project failure. It is the key tool to show how the different work-packages of the project fit together, where the interdependencies are, and who needs to talk to whom. This is the PM's responsibility, though you may have the support of a planner, and your main focus must be on the big picture rather than on the technical elements of some of the packages. (Seeing the bigger picture while managing the detail is explicitly covered in Part 3.14.)

Planning and scheduling is often left to specialist support, but it must be owned by the PM, as you are accountable for it and must understand the assumptions and constraints that have gone into it. I have seen large projects trying to write plans after the event when they hear that a review is coming up, and very large projects trundling on for over a year without an agreed plan. In my view this attitude is completely unprofessional, as 'failing to plan is planning to fail'. The best plans I have seen have been on the basis of co-construction, that is where the PM, or a facilitator on their behalf, gets the leads for the various work-packages/disciplines/deliverables together and works out how they and the constituent activities fit together. Estimating then becomes a lot more robust when under challenge. So in future, if you don't do so already, get you team together to agree the plan and you will find that they have more ownership of it.

Estimation was always a challenge when working on R&D projects. If people could be persuaded to give an estimate at all, it was invariably hopelessly over-optimistic. Common practice for senior management was to multiply all estimates by a factor of two. (Flyvbjerg proposes more robust means of addressing 'optimism bias'.[57]) I found that the use of 'three point estimation' techniques not only improved the estimates markedly, but also flushed out all the constraints, assumptions and risks. Again, facilitating a workshop is the best way to do estimation, as well as get buy in.

Cost management used to be left to the accountants, or avoided on the excuse that the finance system was not adequate for project accounting. A good PM knows if costs are in line as they put the estimate together and know any key variances from it. They also know what they have committed and what key variations to estimate are. It may be boring but it is part of the job. Reporting upwards, it is your job to turn those pages of accounts into meaningful information to be acted upon. Quite often this translation means turning those pages of numbers into a dashboard's smiley face or a sad face – whatever communicates the message to your particular stakeholders.

Time management has two components that are related – managing your own time and managing that of the project. In Part 3.13 we will look at personal time management, as this is essential in setting the tone for the team. If you turn up late for meetings and deliver on your commitments late then you will find that this is also expressed in the project itself and lateness becomes part of the culture.

Risk and opportunity management, or at least the risk part, is now covered to some extent in most projects. I recently saw the report on the risk management of a large project with a very big PMO which said words to the effect of 'a lot of activity around risk administration but no visible management by the program leadership'. Is this your project? In my book, huge risk logs and complex processes being administered by some centralised PMO do not constitute risk management.[58] What gets talked about in your management meetings is your risk management. Are you getting the leadership to focus on the right things? A question often used by consultants is 'What keeps you awake at night?' During assurance activities this is followed up by checking how many of these 'sleepless night' problems have been captured in the risk log. Thankfully, more attention is now being focussed on facilitation of risk workshops[59] and conferences on soft skills for risk management.[60]

Issue management is something that most of us are good at, as unfortunately we get a lot of practice. The same report that I mentioned above went on to say, 'The default strategy for managing risks would appear to be to wait and see what matures into issues and then deal with them.' Some people love the excitement of fire fighting, and it can be easier to look like a hero, but who let the fire start in the first place? Issues should be kept to a minimum by addressing the precursor risks, and planning contingency for when fires do break out. We are meant to be managing, after all.

Contingency management requires risk management in the first place. Those that we cannot contain or tolerate require a contingency plan, that is, a pre-thought-out set of alternatives that are in place and ready to be actioned. The alternative is to enjoy fighting the fires that we allowed to start. The skill comes in having contingency but not trying to buy our way out of all risk. What is the risk appetite of the sponsor and the organisation for your project?

Stakeholder management to me is key, as success or failure is in the eye of the beholder. Time, cost and quality fall prey to the perceptions of the key stakeholders, who may have nothing to do with the running of the project. Who are your key stakeholders, what do they expect/want, who is responsible for managing those relationships, what activities should you do when? What skills do you need? (NLP techniques for stakeholder management are covered in depth in Section 3.15.)

Much of the OGC's Gateway process is built around the concept that the project will be delivered in the main through **procurement** from a supplier through a bid and tender process. Even when this is not the case, we still have to obtain resources for our project, and this can be a similar process though less formalised. This process, formal or not, should not be left to others. You want to do an excellent job, and you need an excellent team to do that. Work with your suppliers, internal and external, to make sure you get the right team for the job and not the next person off the bench.

Again, **contract management/supplier management** is sometimes left to a contract management department that is basically a set of administrators ticking boxes. The authority for delivering the project has been devolved to you – make sure that you work with your contractors to try to move the relationship as far to a partnership as possible. Win-win is easy to say, but most clients treat contractors in a win-lose fashion, and then wonder why the relationship deteriorates.[61] Try it at home and see if you can guess the results. (Negotiation is covered explicitly in Part 3.18.)

Managing dependencies and interfaces is a job that falls to the PM and no other. Of course it's a good idea to map the dependencies and include them in governance arrangements, but at the end of the day, or better still at the start of the week, the PM still has to make time to check the things that they depend on and that depend on them. Are you well prepared to manage the changes and conflicts that normally arise through associated projects?

Benefits management is becoming increasingly popular to talk about.[62] Some of it is even getting done. When I was serving my time I had a moment of epiphany when my director said, 'The only way to get projects delivered properly is to make the PM accountable for the benefits and stop them focussing on the assets.' Since then I have started out with the end in mind, as we say in NLP, and tried to lose the goggles that wed me to the glamour of the technology. But under some methods, the PM is divorced from responsibility for benefits by the governance framework and roles. It is the sponsor or a business-based change manager who is responsible for these, with the PM relegated to looking after the bits of tin/bricks and mortar. Perhaps in recognition of the limited skills of the PMs they had to hand?

Value management and value engineering is something that I have seen little of since the mid-90s. In this decade of 'more for less', however, it surely must make a comeback. I particularly liked this component as it forced the project to look at where value lay in the mind of the customer. I have facilitated workshops that clearly showed the NLP concept of world-view, where the apportionment of costs and effort by the project were sometimes the inverse of the perception of value to the client. Even if you are not trying to cut budget, it is a great exercise for better understanding what is of value to the client, and what you can trade off when you have to trim time, cost or scope.

Technology management is probably one of the easiest things to do once you know how. Coming from a science and engineering background, I can slip seamlessly into that world, however, and forget that my role is to act as the interpreter between the people with the need and the people with the tools.[63] Some people think that you have to know all the jargon – don't do it ! Make your team stop using any jargon at all and communicate properly. If Stephen Hawking can explain relativity and black holes for the general public with only one equation then you don't really need to hide behind this throwback to the Masonic lodges. My advice is to treat it all as 'black box' – as the marketing people will tell you, focus on 'feature → benefit → value'. And of course, when you go up to the boardroom, don't take your Gantt charts and spreadsheets with you as a shield – it is your job to translate your information into their language.

> 'While it is useful to have a good technical background, it is not essential to manage an IT project. It is more important to have other skills and characteristics'
> Project Management for IT-related Projects, BCS publications 2004

Resource management is not pressing the 'resource smoothing' button on MS Project. Though well done if you have added resources into your plan, especially if you have made them real by giving them names and linked the tasks to their Outlook calendar. Aside from ensuring that you have competent resources on your project, this also means managing those resources. Do they understand their tasks, or at least know about them? Do they have what they need to do the job, including the right tools and training, let alone ability? Do they know where they fit in and where to go when they are not sure? You are the central cog, and if you don't keep moving then it can all grind to a halt very quickly. If you were not a people person to start with, then you had best learn to assume these behaviours, or plan your move back to a technical role. Still, you bought this book, so help is at hand. (Team motivation techniques are explicitly covered in Part 3.19.)

Reporting is something that is usually done very badly, and sometimes not at all. I have seen huge reports, compiled by administrators in PMOs, full of uninterpreted data. What does it mean, and what do they expect the recipient to do with it? As PM it is your job to keep your sponsor and other key stakeholders, including your team, informed of:

- where you are in relation to their expectations;
- what issues have arisen and how you are dealing with them;

- what risks have arisen and how you are managing those;
- your confidence in delivery;
- your own forecast for outturn.

Although we usually have to report these formally, ideally through a scorecard,[64] I prefer to convey the information informally over a cup of coffee to help to build the partnership and trust.

Earned value (EV) is now mandated across large military projects, mainly to give early warning of slippage on projects with long timescales as well as large spends.[65] It has also been introduced as a single subject examination by APM Group. EV forces projects to have detailed cost breakdown in line with schedule, and to report on them regularly. To me, the need to monitor earned value is testament to the fact that, not only were big projects overrunning, but they were somehow failing to make that information clear to stakeholders. Does your project have a big surprise in store for the client, or do you have full and frank exchanges?

I find **Scope management** to be one of the most difficult formal aspects of project management, as we try to adapt to the client's evolving requirements but have to push back, often for their benefit, as things stray into being undeliverable within the resources. I find it best to be firm up-front, but saying 'no' to your customer is a delicate balance. We will cover assertiveness in Section 3.10.

Change control is relatively easy, but often poorly done through lack of attention. It is basically about communication – we might know what has changed and why, but who else does it affect, and how will they find out? Of course, when you move on, or get moved on, someone will have to manually find where you have left your unmarked landmines. In the nuclear industry it was not unheard of for people entering facilities to decommission them to find that the blueprints they were working to had not been updated to 'as built' or 'as modified' when remedial work had taken place. Hopefully, the era when PMs did not enforce a professional culture are behind us. Are your change control procedures enforced?

Project execution is usually regarded as a phase rather than a competence, but how you get people to do what you want them to do, to your timescale, is in my view the defining competence of an effective project manager.[66] Is there a style that works? Do you 'tell' them or 'sell' them? Is it just down to leadership? We will cover a lot on leadership styles in Part 3.

Some PMs may say that **Mentoring and staff development** is not part of their job, as they are only there to deliver the benefits, or at least the assets, and it is the line manager's job to develop the resource pool. The level of competence gained from a sit down five-day course in project management is negligible when compared to professional standards in other industries,[67] and the bulk of development must be achieved on the job. Others will be watching you, following your lead on things like safety and sustainability, and picking up any bad habits that you haven't got around to fixing yet. But since you are a person dedicated to your own professional development, you probably recognise the need to set an example to others and help them on their journey. This may be through structured mentoring, or simply by setting a good example to follow, but I find 'the more you put in the more you get out'. For consultants, the client certainly appreciates you helping to develop their capability and will probably invite you back to help them next time. I have a lot to say on mentoring and development of staff in Part 3.

As we have seen, there are many soft skills even in the hard tools and techniques of project management, and to be effective in them requires a lot more than reading a book about it. Even this one.

1.7 SKILLS AND CHARACTERISTICS OF EFFECTIVE PROJECT MANAGERS

In this section we explore various sources of competence frameworks for soft skills in the field of project management, and compile a comprehensive list of those that help to carry out traditional requirements of project management described in the previous section. Many of these are addressed in Part 3 (illustrated in Figures 3.1 and 3.2).

1.7.1 Competence frameworks and levels

Competences emerged in the 1980s as a way of modelling effective performance and are now an accepted part of human resource management (HRM). A competence refers to **how** a task is achieved. It is measured by observing behaviour at work, using examples of how effective individuals behave to achieve their high levels of performance.

The competence-based approach focuses on the individual's skills, knowledge, attitudes and behaviours rather than on their qualifications and experience.[68] Competences are built up over time and are not innate.[69] Some people hold the view that someone is probably good at something, such as leadership or customer focus, or not, and you just have to select those that show aptitude. This is probably based on the fact that it is difficult to change attitude and behaviours and to learn new skills using conventional classroom training. NLP, however, offers a way of changing all of these aspects.

Even for those of you lucky enough to be competent in those areas that make effective PMs, it is a requirement of the profession that we all undertake continuous professional development. Ultimately, this should lead to improvement in capability through to expert level against those competences deemed most appropriate for the specific role. The table below shows a standard approach to levels of competence with descriptions.[70]

1.7.2 Competence frameworks for project management

We looked at the process and tools-based competences in Sections 1.5 and 1.6, and so in this section we will only be looking at the 'soft skills' types of competence, i.e. those related to traits, skills and behaviours. I will address many of these for improvement using NLP techniques in Section 3.

e 1.18 Levels of competence

Level	**Description**
Stage 1 Foundation	Can demonstrate basic skills that contribute to the activity under direct supervision of competent practitioners
Stage 2 Intermediate	Can demonstrate acceptable performance in the activity, but requires some supervision and guidance
Stage 3 Proficient	Can demonstrate competent performance in the activity to specific criteria without direct supervision
Stage 4 Advanced	Can demonstrate skilled activity with advanced theoretical knowledge and understanding, based on current research/best practice and any relevant policies, procedures and guidelines
Stage 5 Expert	Can demonstrate skilled performance, based on intuition, expert knowledge and established practice

There are a number of competence frameworks for project management, but on review, there is little consistency between them. Extracting the 'soft skills' competences from the APM's list provides:[71]

- leadership;
- communication;
- teamwork;
- conflict management;
- negotiation;
- 'human resource management';
- 'learning and development';
- 'behavioural characteristics';
- 'professionalism and ethics'.

As you can see, some of these are fairly specific, while others such as 'human resource management' and 'behavioural characteristics' are too global to work with. I note that the competences refer to 'leadership' rather than 'management' (or even 'supervision'). Leadership and management, disappointingly, are often used interchangeably in general discussions. (In one assessment I was amused to hear of a candidate evidencing their leadership qualities in their *supervisory* role – it is different.) More on leadership later. The specific ones from this list are all addressed in Part 3.

The list from the International Project Management Association (IPMA) contains some duplication, but introduces the following of note:

- self control;
- openness;
- consultative;
- reliable.

Self control is a new addition (the second part to self awareness – both being addressed in Section 3.5 and 3.7). Being reliable sounds like a good quality for a PM.

BCS, the Chartered Institute of IT, adds the following:

- (leadership);
- (negotiation);
- (motivation);
- reliable;
- responsible;
- approachable.

Reliability is repeated here, and reinforced by the term responsible (though not accountable) – surely a prime requirement for project management?

The highest level of attainment in the BCS is Fellowship, which requires evidence against six components:

- eminence;
- seniority;
- autonomy;
- influence;
- complexity;
- business skills.

If we take eminence, authority and seniority as aspects of leadership, then we are left with complexity and influence.

Turner[72] listed the following traits of an effective project manager, confirmed by practitioners overseas as well as the UK:

- problem-solving;
- energy;
- initiative;

- self-assured leader;
- perspective;
- communication;
- negotiating ability.

I find myself more in accord with this list than that of the APM, and note the useful addition of 'perspective', though this is difficult to pin down. In Section 3.14 I deal with 'Seeing the big picture while managing the detail', which is one aspect.

For a different approach, *Project Management for Dummies* provides us with the following set of tips for being a better PM:[73]

- Be both a manager and a leader.
- Outlook: view people as allies, not adversaries.
- Be a 'why?' person.
- Be a 'can do' person.
- Respect other people.
- Say what you mean, mean what you say (communications/integrity).
- Think big picture/think detail (covered in Section 3.14).
- Acknowledge good performance (covered in Section 3.20).

Most of these relate to outlook, which is covered in Part 3. Personally I think that outlook is more important to success than individual competences.

Covey's 'seven habits of highly effective people' were instrumental in my own development, and since a habit is a repeated behaviour, I think these count too.[74] He adds to the pot:

- Begin with the end in mind (goal setting in Section 3.12).
- Think win-win (outlook/negotiation).
- Creative cooperation (outlook).
- Proactive – the empathy to understand (covered in Part 3).
- Seek first to understand (covered in Section 3.16 on listening).
- Personal management (covered in Section 3.7 as self management and also personal development in Section 3.4).

Again there is a bias towards outlook. In my own work on modelling I have outlook to be the essential first ingredient in the recipe for success. In NLP terms we would say that having an appropriate world-view is necessary to frame our experiences. In project management terms, I cannot think of a more appropriate term than 'Start with the end in mind', and from my own study of entrepreneurs, the ability to visualise and experience the end result is a powerful motivator.

Note that the PRINCE2 method[75] addresses process and does not profess
include skill-based competences.

1.7.3 Research on project management competences

The IPMA funded research on competences for successful PMs that found overwhelming evidence that PMI and other certification systems and project management bodies of knowledge do not measure the most important factors for success in managing projects.[76] The research resulted in defining the following eight behaviours of the best project managers:

- are strongly committed to a clear mission;
- have a long term and big picture perspective;
- are both systematic and innovative thinkers;
- find and empower the best people for their teams;
- are selective in their involvement in project issues;
- focus on external stakeholders;
- thrive on relationships and influence;
- proactively gather information and insist on results (results-focussed).

Of the new elements identified here, results-focussed sounds very much like it should be included in any list of competences for effective PMs. Being selective in involvement in project issues also sounds like a very useful trait, though I am not sure if we can capture this under something like 'management by exception'.

1.7.4 Emotional Intelligence

When Daniel Golman's first book on emotional intelligence entered the public domain it captured what people knew but had not articulated to that point, namely that there are other things than IQ that influence success more strongly. These have been refined over the years and settled down to a consistent set and standard terminology. Looking at the competence frameworks for project management above, although several of them are captured in fairly generic terms, some remarkable ones are not.

The most striking element of this list that is absent from project management competence frameworks is 'self awareness'. Strangely, it was a discussion with the head of capability for one of the largest project management consultancies in the IT sector that prompted me to write this book, as when we were discussing training and development he said that the one competence of his PMs that he wished he could improve was self-awareness. I address it very early on in Section 3.5, as without this all other personal development is doomed. Self management, adaptability (Section 3.11) and initiative are also new additions to the growing list of competences for effective project management. Influence, managing conflict, teamwork and leadership echo previous lists and are covered in Part 3.

Figure 1.19 Daniel Goleman's framework for emotional competences[77]

	Self (Personal competence)	**Other (Social competence)**
Recognition	Self awareness - Emotional self awareness - Accurate self assessment - Self confidence	Social awareness - Empathy - Organisational awareness - Service
Regulation	Self management - Emotional self-control - Transparency - Adaptability - Achievement - Initiative - Optimism	Relationship management - Inspirational leadership - Influence - Developing others - Change catalyst - Conflict management - Building bonds - Teamwork and collaboration

Today, I hope that everyone realises that EI is very important, but the original books only told you what it was and how important is was. Subsequently, measurement frameworks evolved,[78] but after that, probably a majority assumed that it was static like IQ. Anthony Mersino compiled a very useful book on EI for project management, compiled from his articles in the journal *PMI Today*, telling how it helped on his journey to become an even more effective PM.[79] The most attractive feature of NLP to me is that it is very effective in changing behaviours and modelling skills to improve EQ. Most of the aspects in the above table are reflected in Figure 3.2 in Section 3.3 on the same 2×2 EI matrix.

1.7.5 Leadership and Management of Projects

In this section I cannot be comprehensive on the domain of leadership, which I will save for another publication, but will attempt to extract a subset of established competences for leadership in project management to add to those already identified.

Thankfully, leadership was mentioned in most of the competence frameworks for project management. I find that people often use the term leadership when they are actually talking about management, or even supervision. But let's be clear, although we use the term project *management*, the level we should be looking to attain is one of leadership.

Professor Rodney Turner wrote a comprehensive series on leadership in the project context based on research as to whether different leadership styles influenced project success, and whether different leadership styles were more appropriate to different types of project.[80]

Figure 1.20 Schools of leadership (after Turner)

School	Period	Main ideas
Trait	1930s–1940s	Effective leaders show common traits Leaders born not made
Behaviour or style	1940s–1950s	Effective leaders adopt certain styles of behaviours Leadership skills can be developed
Contingency	1960s–1970s	What makes effective leaders depends on the situation
Visionary or charismatic	1980s–1990s	Two styles: 1. Transformational concern for relationships 2. Transactional concern for process
Competence	2000s	Effective leaders exhibit certain competences, including traits, behaviours, styles Certain profiles of competence better in different situations
Emotional intelligence	2000s	Emotional intelligence has a greater impact on performance than intellect

From the Trait school of leadership, Turner identified the following:

- Problem solving
- Results orientation
- Self confidence
- Perspective (big picture/detail)
- Communication
- Negotiation
- Energy and initiative
- Self control
- Openness
- Consultative
- Reliable

Of these, the characteristics of energy and initiative, problem solving, and self confidence are over and above those of the APM competence framework. Results orientation features again.

Turner observes that there is little work setting project management leadership within the context of the emotional intelligence school, but it was observed that there was a significant relationship between project success and inner confidence and self belief.[81] The latter element is what NLP refers to as the self reference meta-program (as against the opposite, external reference. Note also that self reference also tends to make people more resilient). Resilience is dealt with in Section 3.8.

Turner observes that, while some say leaders are born not made, and some people are naturally more suited to leadership than others, everyone can improve their leadership skills. We will cover NLP aspects of leadership in Section 3.11.

1.7.6 A compilation of competences

Putting together the above lists, with a bit of poetic licence, provides us with the following table:

Figure 1.21 A compilation of traits, behaviours and skills for effective PMs

Traits	Behaviours	Skills
• Reliable • Responsible • Self confident • Self control • Approachable • Autonomous • Integrity • Empathy • Big picture • Open • Energetic • Self development (I think many of these are related to leadership)	• View people as allies, not adversaries • Think win/win • Begin with the end in mind • Respect other people • Creative cooperation • Proactively build relationships (Many of these are related to teamwork in its broadest sense)	• Conflict management • Negotiation • Influencing • Listening • Problem solving

Leadership is not cited specifically, as it is a complex competence of many traits, behaviours and skills, as is 'communication'.

To me, however, I think the list is still incomplete. There is still nothing relating to the ability to execute or deliver, and we know that some people are good at it and others not. Even assertiveness (in its true sense) is missing. Time management and ability to meet deadlines is also absent. Decision-making is not present, even though it constitutes one model of project management. Most striking to me is the absence of 'self awareness', as without this it is not possible to recognise one's own weaknesses and start on the path of self development.

1.7.7 Is project management generic and transferable?

I was at a seminar by project management guru Charles Wilbe on 'project management myths' when he asked the question, 'Is project management transferable or sector specific?'.[82] I was surprised when half of the audience of PMs were of the opinion that they could only manage projects in their own discipline. (I would have expected it from buyers of project management services, as adverts for positions invariably ask for very specific sector knowledge.) Closer questioning of those of this opinion soon revealed an answer. Some of the reasons given were: technical assurance, technical design, development of technical staff, etc. There was obvious confusion between the roles of technical team leader and PM at junior levels. As a PM, for reasons of good governance alone, I would never dream of carrying out design and technical assurance type activities on my own projects. It is my job, however, to ensure that there is a competent design authority and process for independent review and sign off. Similarly, it is my job to ensure, in agreement with the project sponsor, an assurance framework. Hence, I attributed this difference to be one of perspective rather than substance, in that people starting out as PMs often come to the role from a technical supervisory position where they are also a subject matter expert (SME).

Figure 1.22 Project management competences, processes and knowledge

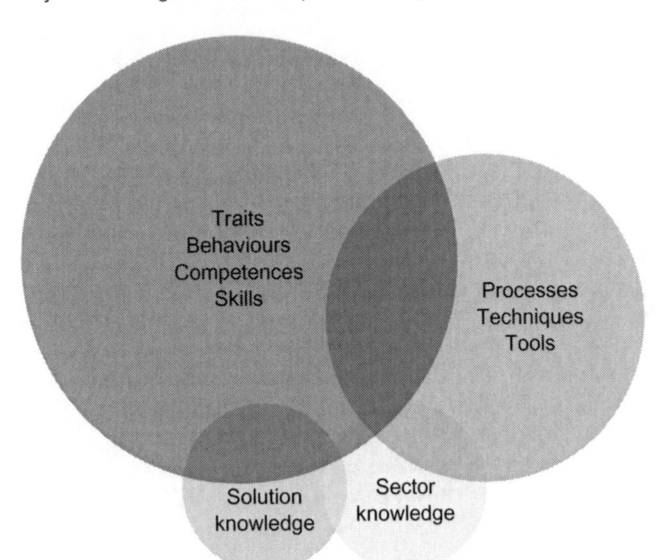

The definitive text for project management of IT related projects,[83] under the section on 'Desirable characteristics of a project manager' says: 'While it is useful to have a good technical background, it is not essential in order to manage an IT project. It is more important to have other skills and characteristics.' Having worked in many sectors and most types of project over the last quarter of a century, I could not agree more. In this section we have been discussing the range of those transferable skills.

I actually found it a real development opportunity to manage projects outside my own discipline for the first time, as it forced me away from my own technical comfort zone and made me focus on processes and behaviours. This is an aspect that has also helped me in my capacity of a reviewer of major projects in that I focus on the processes and competences.

Regardless of examples, there is no part of this book that has been written with any particular sector or type of project in mind. Project management is generic and skills are transferable when a sufficient level of competence has been achieved. This book will help you to improve your competence.

1.7.8 Assessing Competence

> 'Too bad that all the people who know how to run the country are too busy driving cabs and cutting hair'
>
> George Burns (US comedian)

Research repeatedly shows that most of us think that we are smarter/better than we are, apart from the smart ones like us, that is.[84] This is said to be because 'ability' itself includes the meta-ability of being able to assess that ability.

Figure 1.23 People's false perceptions of their own ability

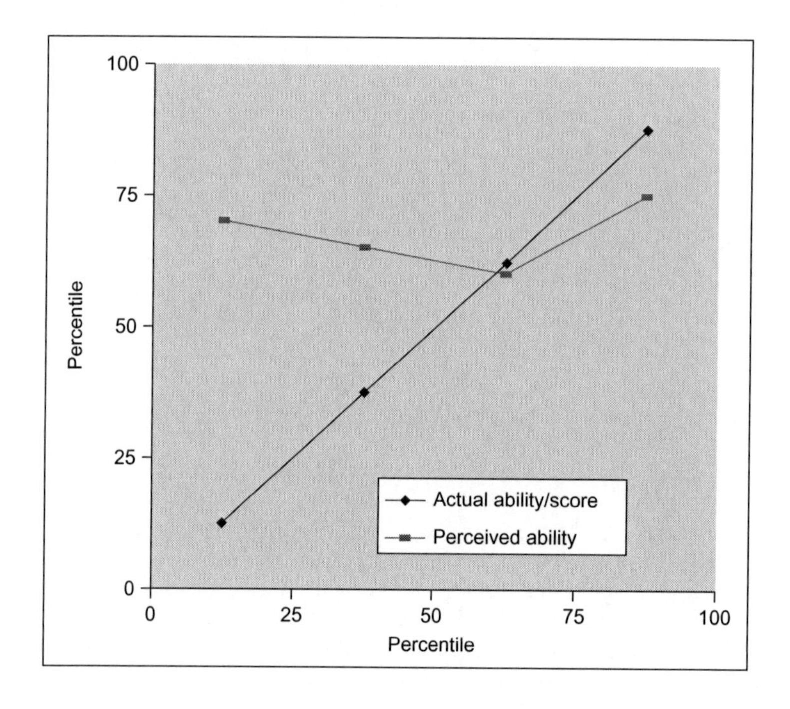

> 'The fool who knows he is a fool is for that reason wise.
> The fool who thinks himself wise is the greatest fool of all'
>
> Shakyamuni

Asking people if they are good at soft skills or even project management is a bit like asking if they are good at driving – we probably all think that we are a lot better than others perceive us. Hence, it is necessary to have a structured and evidence-based approach to assessing behavioural competences, including a panel interview by experts who it is agreed are of high competence (and hence have the meta-competence of being able to assess that competence). Taxi drivers and barbers will not do. The STAR technique is widely used in assessment (situation or task, action, results).

Figure 1.24 The STAR technique for assessing behavioural competences

Situation or task	Describe the situation that you were in or the task that you needed to accomplish. You must describe a specific event or situation, not a generalised description of what you have done in the past. Be sure to give enough detail for the interviewer to understand. This situation can be from a previous job, from a volunteer experience, or any relevant event.
Action you took	Describe the action you took and be sure to keep the focus on you. Even if you are discussing a group project or effort, describe what you did, not the efforts of the team. Don't tell what you might do, tell what you did.
Results you achieved	What happened? How did the event end? What did you accomplish? What did you learn?

In relation to overall project management competence, there is a widely agreed but little used chart of progress through the profession. People still overestimate their own abilities, and it should be noted that the knowledge axis on the chart below would be in terms of thousands of hours of study at high difficulty, similar to postgraduate qualifications at the top end, not a few tens of hours on standard training courses. Similarly, the experience axis is 10 years and beyond at the high levels, and this does not mean 10 years doing the same job, which is more like one year times 10. Usually this experience is only gained by moving through different project types, roles and probably organisations, and possibly sectors and industries.

Figure 1.25 Increasing project management competence with knowledge and experience

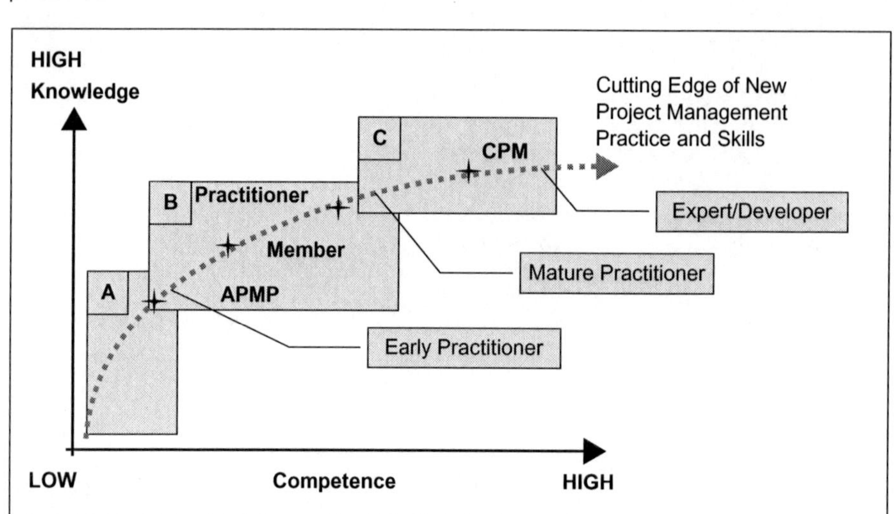

Currently, there is no accepted standard for what constitutes a professional PM. The International Project Management Agency (IPMA), the umbrella body for national project management organisations, recognises four levels of project management maturity up to those capable of managing the most complex programs. This framework aligns with accepted maturity for other professions and general management.

The APM examines four levels, but starting one lower. (The OGC used the same levels as the APM.) As at 2010, however, only about 200 had successfully sought and passed this competence-based assessment from a membership of over 18,000. The APM provides online assessment against its own competence framework as part of the evaluation for higher levels of project management.[85] This self assessment tool has been 'licensed' and was rolled out to project management communities across UK central government departments in 2010. The APM will operate a register of competent project professionals, which is expected to result in the ability to recognise a benchmark 'chartered' status for project professionals in the UK. The level of this 'chartered' status will be at approximately level 3 on the International (IPMA) scale.

The Australian Institute for Project Management (AIPM), on the other hand, takes the view that the only exam of importance to the candidate is the one that they are about to take, and sets out clear criteria and process to move from levels 1 through 5 with post-nominal designation for each.

BCS, the chartered institute for IT, assesses its senior membership level, i.e. Fellow, against the SFIA (Skills Framework for the Information Age.)[86] This is centred around leadership competences which would normally be at level 4 of a five stage model.

Note that most widely available project management training courses, being essentially test of knowledge rather than experience, aptitude or behaviours, would be designated level 1 on the IPMA scale. Currently, over ninety per cent of project management examinations taken globally are at levels 1–2, though many successful candidates apply post-nominals to indicate that they are professional project managers. More worryingly, recruitment agents and employers also treat these qualifications as acceptable for delivery of high risk projects that would be described as levels 3–4.

In my view there is clearly a need to raise the bar in terms of professionalisation. Given that projects and project management organisations are increasingly multi-national, it would be desirable to make global standards practical.

1.7.9 Summary of competences for PMs

In this section we have reviewed competences for project management described by various bodies, relationship to emotional intelligence, and frameworks for assessing level.

Competence is different to knowledge, and many people may not be able to spot the difference between a good project manager and a bad one until it is too late. The competences relevant to your organisation and situation, however, can be identified, defined and measured. More importantly, they can by improved using techniques found in NLP. Tools and techniques for developing these competences are cross referenced in Part 3, Figure 3.1.

1.8 SUMMARY OF PART 1

In this section we started off by looking at the various models for project management and what this means in terms of managing them, particularly the concept of 'delivering through people'. We explored the challenges of managing the temporary organisational structures of projects over and above those for managing business as usual, and the need to develop relationships fast with a wide variety of stakeholders. We looked at the different levels of projects, and how skills changed as we moved up towards oversight of the portfolio, and the need to change our perspective and approach. We covered the range of project types, from small projects to mega-projects, and the increasing need for more soft skills with increasing complexity. A review of trends in projects revealed that they are becoming more complex due to a range of factors from size to the number of organisations involved.

We learned that the reasons for project failure were not strange and unknown, but rather boring and repetitive, and largely down to lack of competence in individuals and organisations. This led us to look at organisational maturity and the need to get not only common systems and processes into place but also a cadre of effective PMs. We read that different phases of projects required different skills and behaviours, which necessitated changing the PM unless they developed appropriate flexibility. Even the wide range of tools and techniques used to manage projects were all shown to require significant soft skills to accomplish, even those traditionally thought of as process intensive such as risk management and planning.

A review of competency frameworks revealed that there were many different perspectives on what constituted an effective PM, but an emotional intelligence framework was a good proxy, especially when combined with leadership frameworks. Current levels of accreditation are currently too low to reduce the levels of failure that are being experienced, but sufficiently high level enables skills to be transferred to other sectors. Methods for assessing higher levels of competence, as against relatively low levels of knowledge, are now lifting the bar for project management, and registers of project professionals will become the norm. And most importantly, the ability of NLP tools and techniques to help us to develop specific skills and effective behaviour was indicated, to be developed in Part 3.

> 'The days of the gifted amateur are over'
>
> Andrew Bragg, CEO of the Association for Project Management

PART 2 THE WORLD OF NLP

2.1 INTRODUCTION

This section is intended only to give an introduction to the underlying principles of NLP, before illustrating application against skills and behaviours for effective project management in Part 3. As such it will not teach you NLP, but it will give you a fairly complete background and sufficient understanding of it to carry out all of the specific exercises described in Part 3.

After originating from the fields of linguistics and cybernetics, through the modelling of leading therapists, NLP quickly found application in counselling and personal change. Through an understanding of the mind-body connection, it has also expanded rapidly into health applications. The mind-body connection also led to growth in coaching for leading sports professionals and athletes. Although there have always been people who take learning across sectors, introduction to the field of management was relatively late, after the modelling of successful business leaders. The body of knowledge around NLP is now huge. Here I will be restricting scope by focussing only on those aspects directly useful to development of skills for effective project management. Given that I personally employ NLP in other spheres of my life, I will give pointers as appropriate to related applications and further study, especially under the concluding section on 'taking things further'.

We will start off by looking at what NLP can do for PMs, which is extensive, before looking at what it is and its scientific origins. The Four Pillars of NLP will introduce the underlying requirements for effecting NLP techniques; outcome thinking, sensory acuity, rapport and behavioural flexibility. Without these basic elements NLP will not work. Underpinning all of these is ethics, or ecology as it is referred to in NLP.

Although it is not unique to NLP, the concept of everyone having different world-views is central to NLP and its communications models. The way these world-views are formed by filtering and coded using representational systems and sub-modalities is shown to give us an opening into our beliefs and values, which are further developed. Being able to communicate with the unconscious mind, both by being able to interpret it through the meta-model for deep structure of language, and communicate to it via metaphor and hypnotic language, will be discussed. But without rapport there can be no effective communication, and ways of establishing rapport by meeting someone on their map of the world, especially by aligning meta-programs, are introduced, before being fully developed in Part 3.

It may sound a bit technical, especially with the over fondness for the term 'meta', but the subject is not intellectually difficult. It just takes application and practice, of which there will be plenty in the context of project management in Part 3.

If you already have a good grounding in NLP and just want to look at the application to project management, then jump straight to Part 3, but please note that some elements such as meta-programs are not usually introduced until Master Practitioner level or beyond.

2.2 ABOUT NLP

NLP is one of those things that can be all things to all men (and women). Here I will define it within the context of my assumed audience and the way we will be applying it.

2.2.1 What is NLP?

NLP is the study of human excellence. It is the science of how the brain codes learning and experience, and can be described as a user's manual for the brain. The memories of our subjective experience have structure. NLP can be used to elicit and replicate that structure through modelling, and so transfer skills. Where learned behaviours are no longer effective in some context, NLP can be used to alter the structure of the subjective experience, changing meaning, and generate alternative behaviours. Thus, NLP provides an excellent toolset for self awareness and personal improvement. Some other definitions of NLP include:

- a form of applied psychology;
- a means of achieving more for yourself and being more fulfilled in your personal and professional lives;
- the difference that makes the difference;
- a means of achieving peak performance.

It has been described as a system, a methodology and a set of processes. More than anything else to me though, like project management itself, NLP is an approach.

2.2.2 What can NLP do for me in project management?

Once you adopt the approach of NLP and start to learn some of the tools that it offers, it will help your development enormously. For a project manager it will:

- give you an understanding of why you do what you do, and what other choices are available;
- help you to control the way you think, feel and act;
- manage stress;
- strengthen your ability to connect with others and develop rapport;

- help you to pick up and decode what is being communicated outside of the obvious – words will give you an edge in everything from negotiation to leadership;
- enable you to communicate more effectively and persuasively;
- help you motivate and lead;
- show you how to develop flexibility in behaviour to match the context and requirements;
- help you to develop new skills;
- enable you to model excellent behaviours from role models that you meet.

2.2.3 Where did NLP come from? The science behind the approach
Richard Bandler and John Grinder are recognised as the founders of NLP in the early 1970s.[87] To me, everything in science has a predecessor, and so you can trace the ancestors of NLP back a long way. I feel that it is important to establish part of this pedigree to demonstrate that NLP is a science, as its early foundation in therapy has led to widespread adoption by those on the fringes of alternative healing, which can cause lack of credibility and resistance in a business context.

Formally, Alfred Korzybyski's work on general semantics is credited with coining the phrase 'neuro-linguistic' back in the early 1930s.[88] His work has breadth beyond NLP, and his maxim 'The map is not the territory', is widely quoted in the world at large. Basically, he was one of the first people to formally make the distinction that words are only an approximation of what they represent.

The TOTE model (test, operate, test, exit experimental cycle), extensively used for modelling (see Exercise 3.18 in Section 3.11), originated from the work of George Miller and co-workers in the late 1950s.[89] Since they are also credited with the famous 'magic number of 7, plus or minus 2', their work was also very influential on NLP's view of filtering of stimuli from the real world to create an impoverished map of reality.[90]

Gregory Bateson's work from the 1950s led to the integration of systems theory and cybernetics, which underpin much of the intellectual basis of NLP.

The idea that people have different 'parts' of their personality was introduced in the 1960s by Eric Berne, and is widely known through transactional analyses.[91] Theory on negotiations using the form of relationships of personalities of 'adult', 'parent' and 'child' originate from this work. The metaphor of parts of personality is widely used in NLP for resolution of inner conflict.

Fritz Perls was one of the first to use the idea of representational systems in therapy. Gestalt therapy, that is the treatment of groups of events as a whole, was introduced from his work.[92]

In the early 1970s Richard Bandler and John Grinder started to integrate the work of their predecessors and use it to model successful therapists. The first of these was Virginia Satir on family therapy.[93] Their seminal work *The Structure of Magic* identified the coding of experience and showed how it could be replicated and altered to model and modify behaviours.[94]

Modelling of therapist Milton Erickson had a huge influence on NLP, resulting in incorporation of hypnotic techniques and development of the meta-model for language that we explore under effective communications.[95]

Further detail of the origins of NLP can be found in, for example, Joseph O'Connor's account of the principal influences of NLP.[96]

Figure 2.1 Evolution of NLP

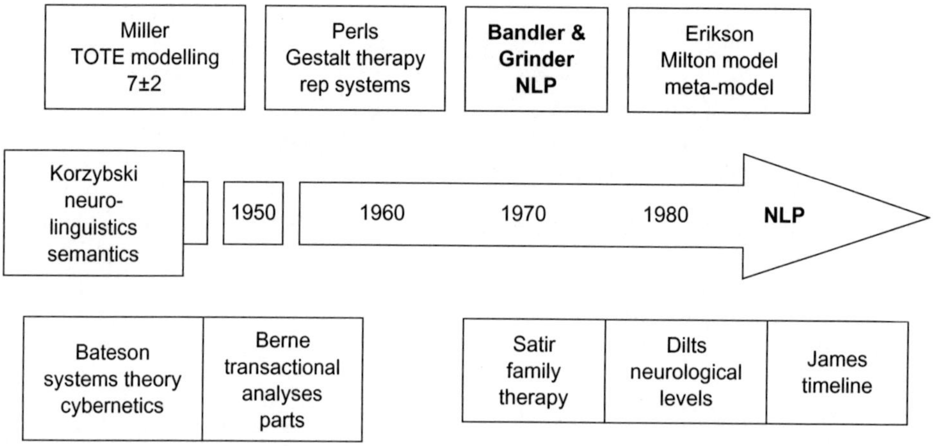

Miller
TOTE modelling
7±2

Perls
Gestalt therapy
rep systems

Bandler & Grinder NLP

Erikson
Milton model
meta-model

Korzybski
neuro-linguistics
semantics

1950 1960 1970 1980 **NLP**

Bateson
systems theory
cybernetics

Berne
transactional
analyses
parts

Satir
family
therapy

Dilts
neurological
levels

James
timeline

These constituents, and many more, went into the melange that Bandler and Grinder created. They are still active, and have been joined by many peers. Of these, Robert Dilts and Tad James have probably been most active, particularly on the introduction of timeline therapies and neurological levels, which I personally make a lot of use of.

Many people were introduced to NLP, particularly in the USA, by Anthony Robbins and his evangelical approach to personal development.[97] He is still hugely popular in print and live performances, attracting several thousand to worldwide venues, often culminating in people overcoming limiting beliefs to 'do the fire walk'.

NLP is now a rich picture, and you can take its learnings and development in any direction you choose. The only limitations are your own beliefs, and NLP can help you to change those, if you choose to.

2.2.4 How to learn NLP

NLP is experiential. No more than you could learn to play the piano from just reading a book on it, you will not learn NLP, let alone change your behaviours, from an intellectual study. You have to do it. This book will, however, open your eyes to new ways of seeing, hearing, feeling and analysing the world and make further practice compelling.

Figure 2.2 NLP requires practice as well as book knowledge

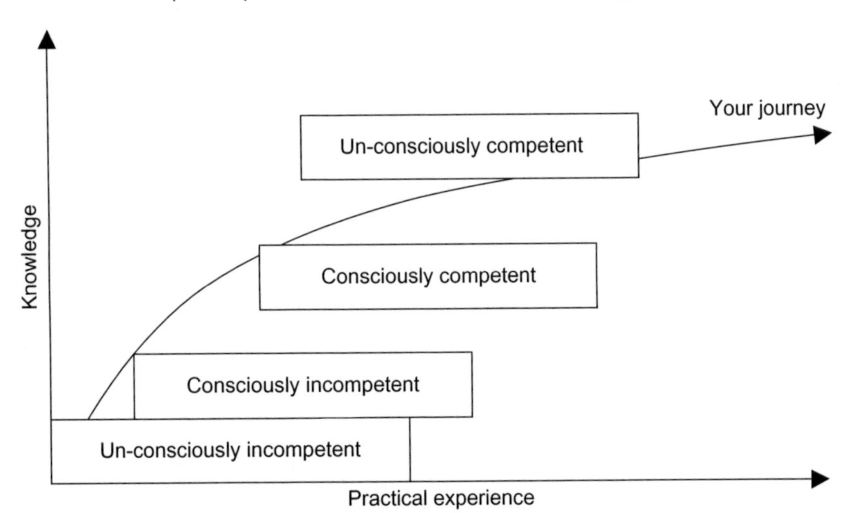

This book gives you some practical examples to illustrate what it can be used for and how it is used. From there, having decided to embark on personal improvement, I recommend some formal training and supervised practice. (See the final section on 'taking things further'.) You do not need to advertise that you are 'doing NLP', as it is only modelling natural processes anyway, and when done elegantly should be invisible. The only visible part will be the way that you start to exhibit more flexible behaviour, build better relationships, and communicate more effectively.

There is a misconception that NLP is what we do to other people, whereas it is principally how we use it on ourselves. We have little impact on changing others, unless we are invited to do so, but we can really make big changes to 'the man in the mirror' when we decide to.

The fact that you have picked up this book and read this far means that you are well on that journey.

2.3 THE FOUR PILLARS OF NLP

One of the reasons that this chapter is included in the book, rather than just launching into applications, is that, being a complete system, there are some aspects of NLP that underpin any and every activity that we use it for. Many tools and techniques have been modelled and developed over four decades, but initially these pillars were all the founders had to work from. They still hold true today.

Figure 2.3 The four pillars of NLP

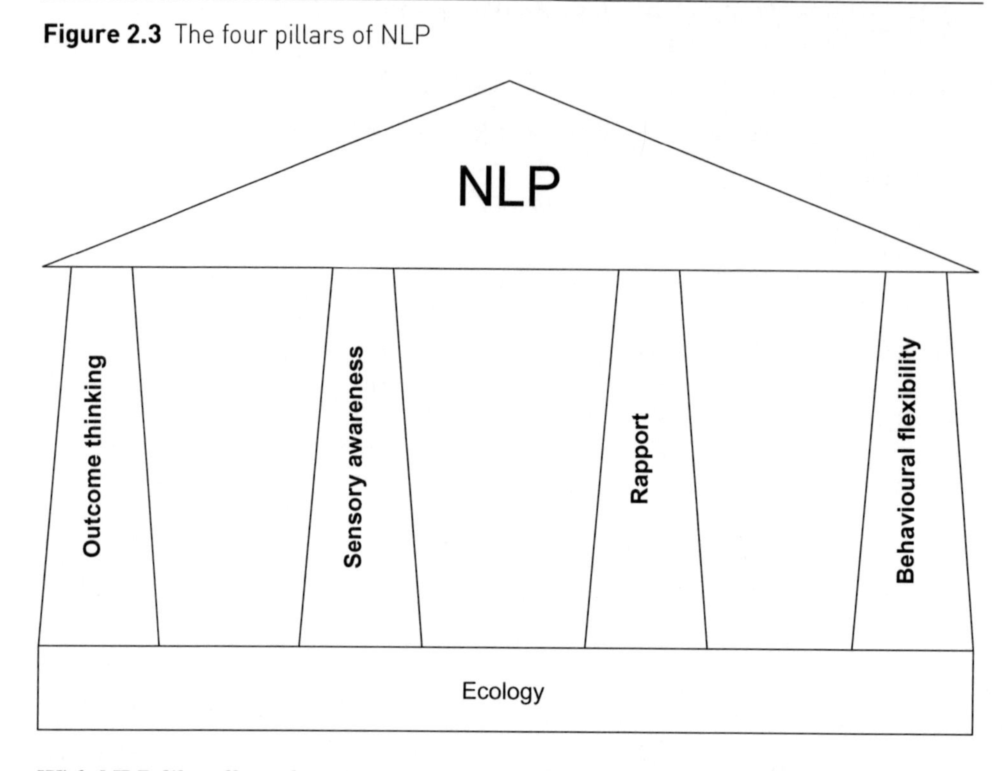

With NLP, like all good projects, we start with the **outcome** in mind. As you will learn, NLP outcomes go beyond even 'SMART' goals that we use in project management.

In NLP we develop **sensory awareness**, not only to tell us what is going on in a situation, but also to give us feedback on the effectiveness or otherwise of our own actions. All processes in NLP should be based on sensory evidence and not guess-work or 'mind reading'.

Rapport underpins not only NLP but all of our relationships. Without first establishing rapport, no NLP technique will work. For counselling work, resistance in a client is a clear sign of lack of rapport. (This should be picked up through sensory awareness, as above.)

Behavioural flexibility is required by NLP and is further developed by it. Aside from not wanting to be a 'one trick pony', insanity has been described as doing the same thing but expecting different results. If what you are doing isn't working then try something else. 'If at first you don't succeed then try again' does not mean to do so in exactly the same way – try again but change your approach if you want to succeed quicker.

I have shown these pillars resting on a base of **ecology**, which in the context of NLP is related to ethics and the appropriateness of actions to all parties. If what we are attempting is not ethical for all parties then it will fail.

These pillars of NLP are described further in the following sections of this chapter.

2.4 PRESUPPOSITIONS OF NLP

Presuppositions are things that are taken as true without further proof. As far as NLP is concerned, however, they are simple statements that have proven to be useful. In effect, they are the belief system of NLP.

Presuppositions originated from the contributing elements of NLP, for example systems theory and cybernetics.

Rather than deal with them as a group here, I have liberally doused relevant sections with them so that they appear in context, but for summary I present them here in the form of a mind map. (I adopted mind maps as they have the ability to satisfy both 'big picture' and 'detail' predispositions in one view, and are also excellent for co-creation by a team.)

Figure 2.4 The presuppositions of NLP

- Pre-suppositions of NLP
  - Modelling
    - Modelling excellence leads to excellence
    - If what you do isn't working then try something else
    - There is no such thing as failure, only feedback
    - The mind and body act as one system
    - People already have all the resources that they need
  - Behaviours
    - Behind every behaviour is a positive intent
    - Every behaviour is useful in some context
    - Choice is better than no choice
    - People make the best choices available to them
    - There is no such thing as an inner enemy
  - Maps of the world
    - The map is not the territory
    - Every person has their own map of the world
    - People create maps based on physical senses (VAKOG)
    - People respond to their maps of the world, not reality
  - Rapport
    - Rapport is meeting someone on their map of the world
    - Resistance in a client is a sign of lack of rapport
  - Communications
    - The quality of our lives is determined by the quality of our communications
    - The meaning of the communication is the response that you get

2.5 WORLD-VIEWS AND FILTERS

> 'If the doors of perception were cleansed then everything would appear to man as it is, infinite. For man has closed himself up, till he sees all things thru' chinks of his cavern'
>
> William Blake

The basic premise of NLP, building on the early work on semantics by Korzybski, is that people make maps of the world, and these maps are mistaken for reality. In fact these maps are only impoverished models that are influenced by a host of factors specific to the individual's previous experiences.

> 'If a man is offered a fact which goes against his instincts, he will scrutinise it closely, and unless the evidence is overwhelming, he will refuse to believe it. If, on the other hand, he is offered something which affords a reason for acting in accordance to his instincts, he will accept it even on the slightest evidence. The origin of myths is explained in this way'
>
> Bertrand Russell

Figure 2.5 We react according to our map of the world, not reality

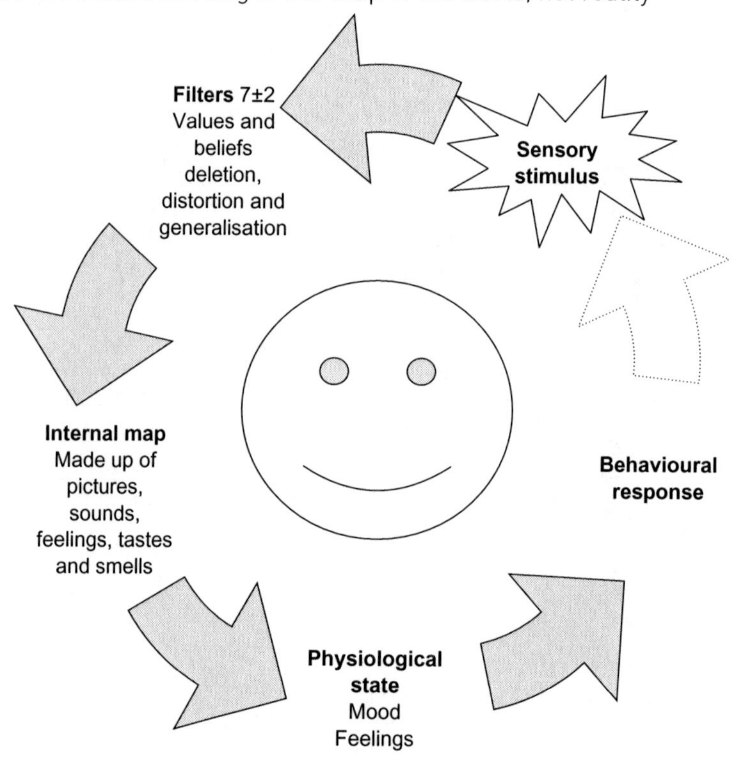

> 'The map is not the territory'
>
> NLP presupposition

Aside from not realising that our 'reality', though seeming real, is a mere internal representation, we do not realise that other people's maps of reality are markedly different from our own. With a huge range of values and beliefs, and combinations of more than 60 behavioural meta-programs acting as filters, the chances of someone's perception matching ours is remote. From a Myers-Briggs Type Indicator I found that only two per cent of the population shared my preferences, and that is from only four pairs of alternatives. Sixty pairs of meta-programs produces the potential for at least two to the power of 60 alternatives, or a enough to fill a hundred million earth-like planets full of individuals. Hence, the person sat next to you is almost certainly different from you.

> 'Everyone has their own map of the world'
>
> NLP presupposition

Our map is also based on our interpretation of past experiences, most of which occurred during our formative years and were lost from our conscious recall. Gestalts, or groupings, of those memories, and our interpretation of them, act as a strong filter on our behaviours, especially in complex personal relationships.

The way individuals react to the same stimulus or situation is also dependent on their physiological state at the time – you do not react in the same way to events when you are happy as when you are sad or angry.

So, we all have different filters leading to us all having different maps of the world which we treat as the only reality. Is it any wonder that we have breakdowns in communications, let alone situations where people are willing to kill and die for what they 'know' is right?

> 'People react to their maps of the world, not reality'
>
> NLP presupposition

The NLP approach recognises that we all have different partial maps and aims to discover the maps of others so that we can have a dialogue on some partial overlap of realities.

Where behaviours are not appropriate in some contexts we can use the tools of NLP to uncover how some of the filters, or emotional states, are producing those behaviours. If desired, we can also use NLP techniques to change internal representations, and hence meaning, such that we can adopt additional behaviours and have more choice.

Where we recognise excellent behaviours that are useful to us, we can use NLP tools to explore the subject's map of the world and emulate their processes and behaviours.

Hence, you could think of NLP as a translational tool for communicating between the languages of different mental operating systems, and of comparing common representations that hold different meanings in different systems. This aspect of bridging the communication divide is developed further through practical examples in Section 3.15 on building rapport with stakeholders.

'Rapport is meeting someone on their map of the world'

NLP presupposition

2.6 THE UNCONSCIOUS MIND – WHO IS IN CHARGE?

'A lot of moves are subconscious. I make them without realising my thought processes'

Magnus Carlson
(Youngest ever competitor in World Chess Championships and ranked world #1 in 2010 at age of 18)

In NLP we view the mind and body as a holistic system; what affects one part influences the other. Our mental state, which is largely subconscious, affects our behaviours, and our physical state affects our emotions. Thus, if we are not performing we can address this by changing our physical state in order to change our mood.

Although we are by definition unconscious of our unconscious, we can have little doubt of its importance. Most obvious is the fact that this engine room runs our body for us, breathes for us and digests our food for us, and manages a biochemistry through hormone and enzyme secretion that the conscious brains of the planet have still to fully explain, let alone mimic.

From an NLP perspective it has many other roles. All of our senses are run by our subconscious, and all information from them is analysed, filtered and interpreted before it ever comes into our conscious awareness.

All of our meta-programs, i.e. learned behaviours, run in our subconscious. The accumulation of these forms our beliefs, values, and identity – no, these are not innate and were not conscious choices. Our experiences are filtered and interpreted by these meta-programs, beliefs and values. The subconscious interprets and groups events and gives them meaning. For traumatic experiences the subconscious may repress memories from our conscious selves until a time when we have accumulated sufficient resources to deal with them. It will usually protect us physically through reactions that it does not even trouble our conscious brain with the illusion of being in control over, and will install involuntary phobias to protect us from perceived danger. Similarly, it will install limiting beliefs by stealth to keep us in our comfort zone and away from risk.

Personal change can only be done through the subconscious mind, whether that is to change a habit, change a behaviour, reinterpret past events and meaning, remove a limiting belief or learn a new skill.

So, who is in charge? Wouldn't it be good to start a dialogue?

2.6.1 Rapport with self

> 'There is no such thing as an inner enemy'
>
> NLP presupposition

Most of us are not practised at being in tune with our bodies or emotions. Our senses have dwindled, we spend large parts of our days in semi-trance like states oblivious of what is going on around us, and we sometimes lose sight of our own identity and values.

Have you ever heard someone say, 'They are their own worst enemy', or wondered why you did things that appeared to be 'self sabotage', like turning up for important meetings late, or not holding your tongue?

I have had several occasions in my life where I have lost direction and been almost completely demotivated. On the last occasion I was lucky enough to spend a month in a remote farmhouse in France studying for my NLP Master Practitioner with a group of delightful fellow practitioners. I came back knowing who I was and what I needed to do. But suppose we don't have such resources to spare?

Firstly, recognise the signals. If you are lucky enough to have made your hobby your job then you don't have to work another day in your life. This isn't the case for most of us, but there are levels of dissatisfaction. If you are suffering illness that may be physiological then this is an alarm bell from your subconscious. Prior to this you will get warning bells of increasing intensity. Lethargy, lack of motivation, depression? It is sometimes difficult to take time out from a hectic schedule to listen to your body, but if you don't then your body will take the time out for you. It's called good risk and issue management.

2.6.2 Speaking to the subconscious – storytelling, metaphor and hypnosis

The reason that I have put metaphor alongside hypnosis here is that they both have a similar method and impact. Both can induce a trance-like rapture that enables the abstracted lesson to be heard directly by the subconscious mind without challenge or interference from the conscious mind.

As described in the history of NLP, hypnotic language was modelled from the therapist Milton Erickson.[98] (From this hypnotic language, the meta-model was back extracted for clarification of language, as described in Section 2.15.) In therapy we spend a lot of effort in distracting the conscious mind to gain direct access to the subconscious so that we can extract meaning and effect change.

Usually we do this through hypnotic language. This can be done without the proverbial swinging pocket watch quite subtly and elegantly with practice. Hypnosis and self hypnosis is outside the scope of this book but is recommended for follow up to give a greater understanding of the workings of the mind. (An introduction to hypnosis is included in many NLP Master Practitioner courses where the trainer has experience.)

A much more widespread method for speaking to the subconscious is the use of metaphor, and more generally in storytelling. Storytelling establishes rapport and delivers a message directly to the subconscious while avoiding resistance from the client. The great teachers, particularly from the religions, have all made use of metaphor and storytelling. Many societies still use the oral tradition of storytelling to preserve history, beliefs and values. Most notable is the Native American Indian sweat lodge ritual. Hence you will find many personal stories in the application section. Famous quotes and sayings are also very effective in presenting views as knowledge, and you will see that I have made liberal use of them throughout this book.

Metaphor and storytelling is widely used as a teaching aid in NLP,[99] and can be for project management too. Many mentoring schemes for professional development have adopted 'fireside chats' with 'elders' in mimicry of these traditional methods. Communities of practice are an extension of these 'tribal' customs.

2.6.3 State management

> 'The mind and body are one system'
>
> NLP presupposition

Before it gets to the state where you are out of rapport and in conflict with your subconscious values, try to get in touch with your body, emotions and subconscious using the following techniques:

- Keep a personal log/diary of your emotions. What did you *feel* today? How is your mood? What emotions aren't you feeling?
- 'Go kinaesthetic', i.e. get in touch with your feelings, at least once a day if this is not your main representational system. Do something physical – it doesn't have to be strenuous. Look down and to your right, drop your breathing to your diaphragm so that you tummy goes in and out like a baby. How are all your bits functioning? How does it feel to be *alive*?
- Make time in every day to go offline. Simple meditation involves no more than taking 10–20 minutes in a calm place and giving yourself time to yourself to let your thoughts and feelings wash over you. If you have distracting thoughts or emotions that restrict your calmness then you might like to visualise them as an object, hold them in your hand, inspect them in a casual way, and drop them to the floor. Do this in turn until the metaphorical gnats around your head have subsided. Now that you are calm, let your subconscious speak to you and raise any concerns.

Self awareness is the key to emotional intelligence and an underlying skill of any professional manager. It is dealt with in detail in Section 3.5.

Practical exercises for state management are included in Section 3.7. Handling stress is an important skill in itself and is covered separately in Section 3.8.

2.6.4 Health and wellbeing

> 'Behind every behaviour is a positive intent'
>
> NLP presupposition

When we see behaviours, particularly anti-social and self-destructive ones, then it is difficult to understand why people adopt them. In fact, in NLP we believe that there is some positive intention behind them all. For example, graffiti and vandalism have been associated with the human need for significance, and many suicide attempts can be seen as cries for help. There are those amongst us who believe that our subconscious will manifest illness when we no longer hear or take heed and fall out of alignment with our internal values and beliefs. Stress, depression and autoimmune conditions are the easiest to imagine in this context, but some have linked specific illnesses to specific problem areas such as guilt, lack of direction, etc.[100] Such inner conflict is manageable when we recognise it as such, seek the source of conflict and address it. I personally suffered with bouts of ill health that had me ambulanced from work on a couple of occasions and nearly had me retired early through ill health. One of the benefits of NLP has been that, since resolving that particular inner conflict, I have been in remission for many years. Now I view those symptoms as the voice of my subconscious, and as such a critical friend, and treat them with respect and take heed. It may not be true, but it is my belief, and as such acts as if true.

Health aspects are outside the scope of this book, and techniques such as 'integration of parts' for resolving inner conflict require expert facilitation. You can find pointers under the end section on 'taking things further'. Before such misunderstandings occur, however, you might like to start getting in touch with yourself.

2.7 BELIEFS, VALUES AND IDENTITY

> '(Excellence is an art won by training and habituation. We do not act rightly because we have virtue or excellence, but we rather have those because we have acted rightly.) We are what we repeatedly do. (Excellence, then, is not an act but a habit.)'
>
> Aristotle (384 BC–322 BC)

2.7.1 Hierarchy of neurological levels

Robert Dilts established a logical hierarchy of neurological levels.[101] Who we believe we are is compounded from our values, beliefs, capabilities, behaviours and environment. If we say, 'I am a professional project manager' (identity), then it is the result of having operated in the context of projects amongst project managers, developed capabilities and competences through appropriate behaviours, and slowly built up certain beliefs about rights and wrongs.

Figure 2.6 Hierarchy of neurological levels (after Dilts)

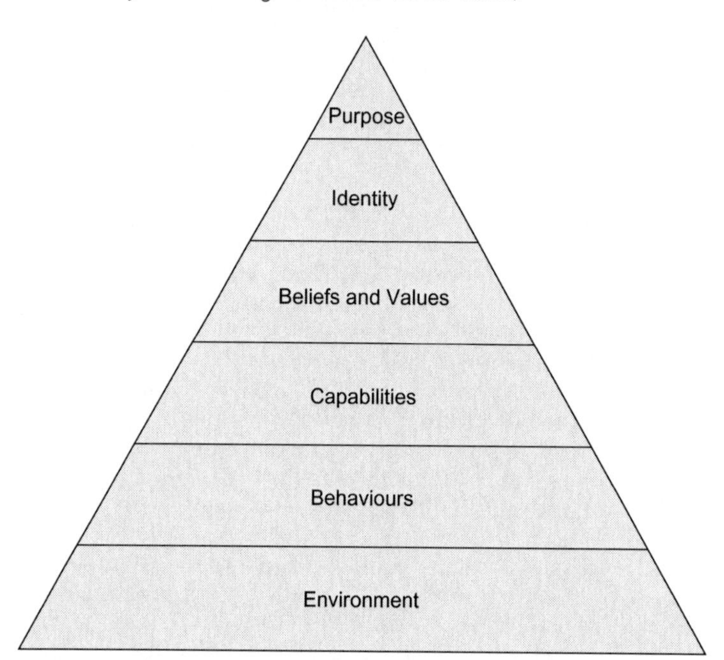

We use these neurological levels as the basis for establishing rapport in Section 3.15.

2.7.2 Beliefs, values and identity

Beliefs can be described as assumptions or presuppositions that you make about yourself and the world around you; that is, taken as true without evidence. In medicine the placebo effect, or sugar pill, has been shown to account for a great part of the efficacy of modern drugs, and all of that for holistic treatments. That is, the belief alone that something will have an impact on us is enough for it to do so. The whole of the power of voodoo is through belief and has been said to be able to kill devotees with a curse. Hence, beliefs are not merely our thoughts, but the instruction-set for our subconscious mind.

Beliefs are invisible to us, and we only become aware of them when we encounter someone with opposed beliefs. Many beliefs are pure, that is without emotion, such as the earth being spherical or that the sun will rise. Some clients believe that all projects run late and overspend – does this become a self-fulfilling prophecy?

Where beliefs have an evaluation attached to them, such as good or bad, right or wrong, then we call them values. Values are unconsciously formed and held but drive our behaviours. If you hand in a lost wallet then it is probably because you value honesty. If you value friendship then it will take precedence over things that you value less, such as money. When you get a strong emotional reaction from someone it is usually because you have transgressed their values, or 'hot buttons'. Hence, if you don't understand someone's behaviour, then that is probably because you do not know their values, and they are probably different to yours if the behaviour looks odd. Everyone has values, but they are not common, and so pressing these hot buttons is usually done by accident, though you soon get to learn where they are if you spend time with someone.

Whenever we use phrases such as 'I am a …' we are expressing identity, whether that is 'I am an expert in risk management', or 'A blonde size 10'. We do not question the validity ourselves as it is how we expect the world to view us. When aspects of our identity are challenged or threatened it has a fundamental impact on us.

2.7.3 Origins of values and beliefs

As you may have realised, you don't get to choose your values. On reflection, isn't that a bit strange, that the things that you might be willing to die or kill for were not chosen by you? The learning machine that is your unconscious brain distilled a set of values for you that it thought would best preserve you in the environment that you grew up in from the models that it had to draw on. By the fact that you are reading this it did a pretty good job of preserving you so far.

Figure 2.7 Creation of values

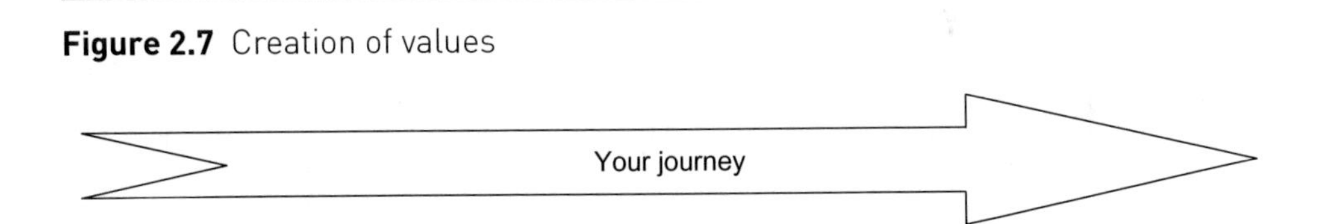

Imprinting	**Modelling**	**Socialising**
0–8 years Unconscious learning from carers	8–13 years Conscious and unconscious modelling from role models. Core values formed	13–21 years Learn values affecting relationships

Belief cycle

> 'People become what they expect themselves to become'
>
> Mahatma Gandhi

If you **believe** that you are not good at gaining qualifications, then you are more likely to focus on all the past experiences where you have failed or had difficulty, and subconsciously delete all the good experiences. This makes you **feel** bad about your ability, which means that you are likely to **perform** badly and play safe, i.e. avoid tests and exams. This means that your **outcome** is that you don't have many qualifications, therefore creating a self-fulfilling prophecy.

Figure 2.8 The belief cycle

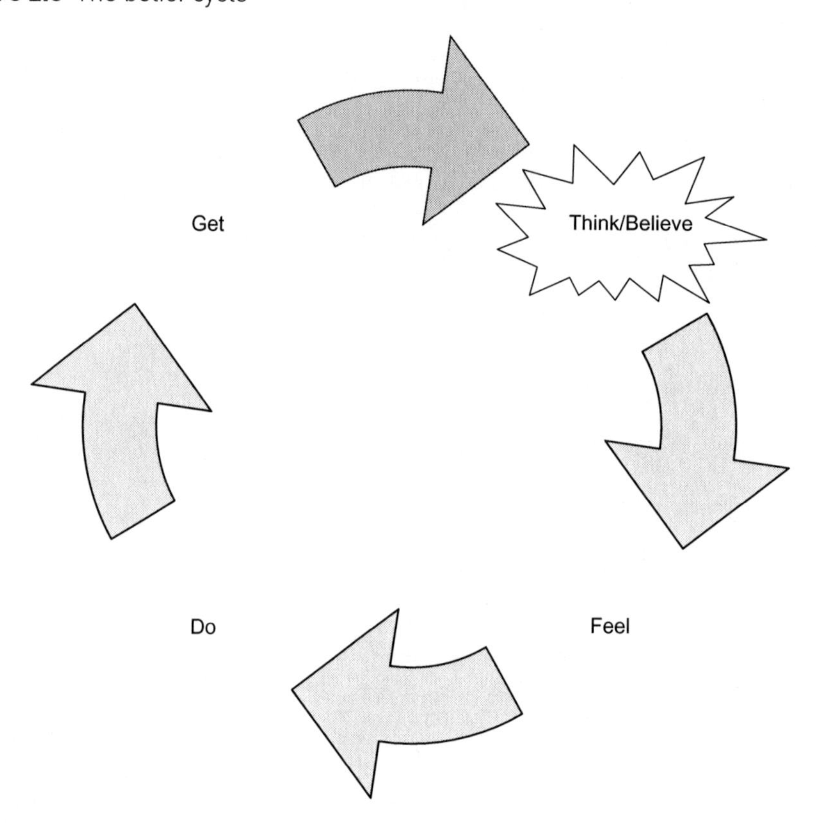

2.7.4 Limiting values and beliefs

Bizarrely, schools are probably the biggest culprit in developing our limiting beliefs and expectation of failure. Are you a good singer and dancer? Most of you will not put your hands up, but you may have done so when you were five years old. Since you started school you may have had belief in yourself slowly but surely trained out by being judged in relation to others day after day.

Aside from the motivational aspects of values, they are fundamental to NLP in that they act as filters, affecting the way we interpret experience and judge things as good or bad. As such, they also give us maximum leverage for change – if you want to change a behaviour then the surest way is to change an underlying belief. Beliefs are not fixed. Some people used to believe in Santa Claus. It is not too difficult to change limiting beliefs if you are motivated to do so, and it does not have to involve a sabbatical with the Moonies and a dose of brainwashing.

A belief change pattern is illustrated in Section 3.4.

2.8 META-PROGRAMS AND BEHAVIOURS

Use of the term 'program' when talking about the human mind originates from cybernetics, which likens the human brain to a bio-computer. According to this mind-as-computer metaphor, the brain is constantly running a complex set of programs. A meta-program then, sitting *meta* or above the program, is the rule that determines which model or set of instructions we run.

Does your glass feel half empty or half full; that is, are you an optimist or pessimist? Do you only want to hear about the big picture, or see the detail? Are you drawn towards opportunity, or do you run away from risk? These are some of the 60+ meta-programs identified to date, and whole books have been written on just some aspects of them, such as matching language to meta-programs.[102] Many of those useful to you in project management are contained in Figure 3.6 and described in Section 3.5 on self awareness, where you are invited to assess your own preferences.

You will meet people with all variants and combinations of these 60+ meta-programs in your career in project management. They see the world differently to you, have different motivational factors to you, and need different evidence to you. Most of this is out of your hands, but being aware of these differences, being able to recognise them, and being able to adjust your language to communicate effectively with them *is* in your hands. Being able to do so will give you a huge advantage in your career and life in general.

I find meta-programs extremely useful in project management for gaining rapport, understanding behaviours and communicating effectively. Rather than discuss the detail of meta-programs in this background section, I have illustrated their application liberally throughout applications in Part 3. How to match language to specific meta-programs in order to gain rapport is covered in Section 3.15, while the best options for meta-programs to help gain rapport are covered in Section 3.15 in Figure 3.30. Motivational aspects of meta-programs are illustrated in Figure 3.37 of Section 3.19.

Specific meta-programs discussed in detail in Section 3 in the context of project management include:

- in time/through time;
- big picture/detail;
- convincer pattern;
- dissociation;
- rule structure;
- stress response;
- same/difference;
- working style (independent/cooperative);
- task orientation (person/thing).

2.9 FRAMES AND REFRAMING

'The meaning of any experience depends on the frame that we put around it'
Anthony Robbins

All of experience is subjective, and the way we frame something profoundly affects our interpretation of its meaning. For example, in projects, having a limited time frame is likely to affect our approach and the amount of stress that we feel. If the frame changes then the meaning changes with it.[103] Jokes are a good example of how a twist of frame at the end transforms meaning.

The figure below shows relevant frames as a hierarchy – they are often used in this way during personal change work to ensure that the change of behaviour is appropriate, real, suitable to the context and permanent.

Reframing is a powerful way of changing interpretation and affecting change and is covered extensively in Part 3, particularly in Section 3.17 on reframing difficult situations (outcome frame, context reframe, and as-if frame).

'I am more and more convinced that our happiness or unhappiness depends far more on the way we meet the events of life, than on the nature of those events themselves'
Wilhelm von Humboldt

Figure 2.9 Frames

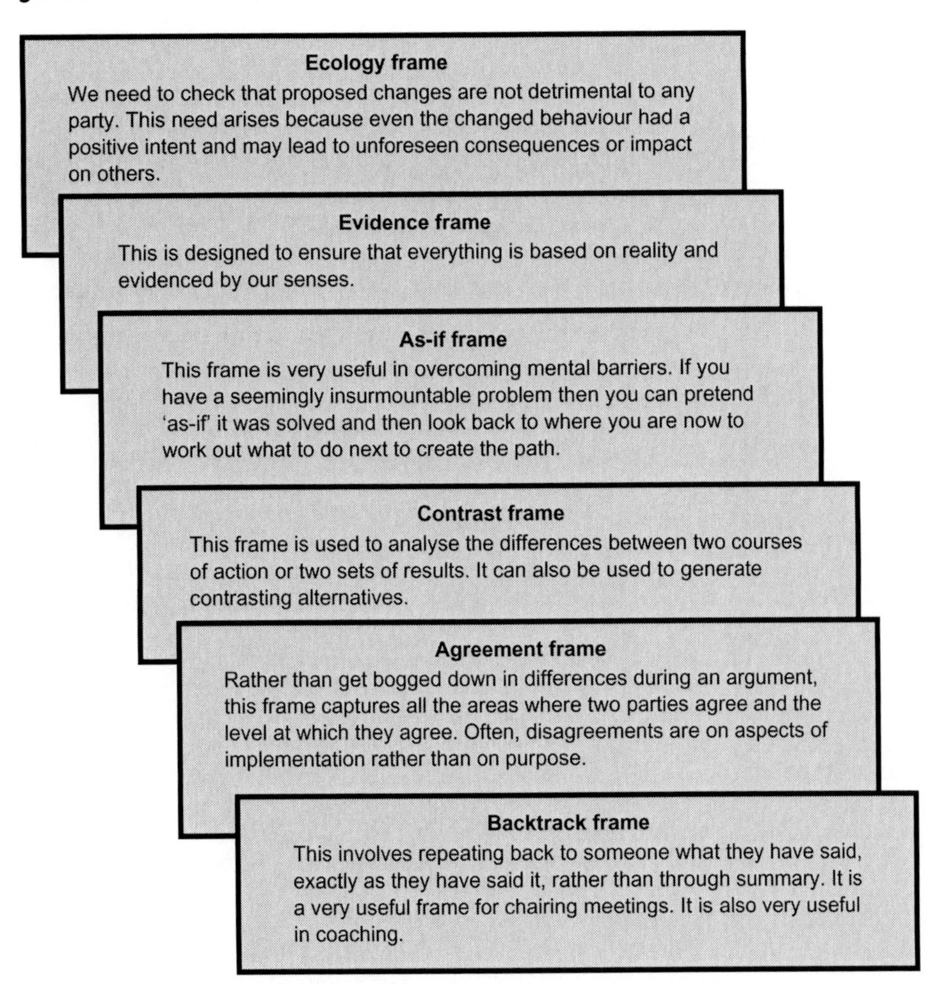

2.10 REPRESENTATIONAL SYSTEMS AND OUR PRIMARY SENSES

As we think about the world around us we do so using pictures, sounds, feelings, tastes and smells, and in NLP these are referred to as the **representational systems**. As we grow up we tend to unconsciously develop a preference for one of these senses, which is called our **primary system**. This may be due to spending a lot of time with music, or images, or in sport or dance, for example.

We unconsciously indicate which representational system we are using at any time by the words that we use. For example, what system would be indicated by:

- 'I like the sound of that'
- 'I don't trust their offer, it smells like a trap'

- 'The future is looking brighter'
- 'Nothing beats the taste of success'
- 'Run that by me one more time'

Exercise 2.1: Determining your primary system through predicates

Complete some more examples of sensory based predicates in the following table:

Primary system	Example predicates	Your examples
Visual	Clarify Clear-cut Focus Hindsight Take a dim view	
Auditory	Discuss Clear as a bell Outspoken Loud and clear Harmonise	
Kinaesthetic	Impact Get a load of this Walk through the proposal Foundation Stir up trouble	
Olfactory (smell)	Sweet smell of success There is something rotten about this	
Gustatory (taste)	Their offer leaves a bitter taste The acid test	

Which one sense did you find it easiest to find words for? This indicates that these are already in your active vocabulary and suggests your primary system for information and memory.

You can tell what other people's primary system is from the predicates that they use. From this book you will be able to judge what mine are, though like a good NLPer, I have attempted to add a smattering of predicates from other systems in order to be better heard by a wider audience.

2.10.1 Matching predicates for rapport

Now that you have gained the understanding that the predicates that people use are not random but linked to the way they filter information and store memories, after expanding your vocabulary to cover a wider set of predicates, you can match those used by your audience in order to gain understanding and rapport more quickly.

Watch situations where a sponsor may say something like, 'Can you talk me through the main sound bites', to be met by the responder with something like, 'I will show you the full report so that you can see as much detail as you like.' Do you think they valued the information that they received? What might they have replied instead?

When someone has a specific preference then they are also likely to have this as their **reference system**, which means that someone with a kinaesthetic preference would want to feel right inside. For visual preference the picture would have to look right, probably vivid or bright, and for auditory it would have to 'sound right'.

Figure 2.10 Being heard through matching of predicates

Expressions of discomfort by client	Matching by respondent
I do not *feel very comfortable* presenting this.	What *support* would you like?
I don't like what I am *hearing*.	What would you like me to *say*?
I don't think you *see* my point of *view*.	*Show* me how you *see* it.
This doesn't *smell* right to me.	How can we *clear the air*?
Are there any *tastier* options?	One of them is really *sweet*.

What were the primary systems being used in the above examples?

2.10.2 Eye accessing cues

We do not use eye accessing cues within application in Part 3, but it is necessary to introduce them as they are a well known part of NLP. Basically, direction of gaze when accessing information can indicate which primary sense is being accessed.

People look up, above the 'horizon', when they are processing visually, and about level when dealing with sounds and voices. Eye movement to their left indicates that they are recalling something (right as you look at them). Movements to their right indicate that they are imagining something or constructing something. Hence, if you ask someone to remember something and they look to their right then it *could* indicate that they are fabricating a reply. It should be noted that eye movements are very rapid, and can be quite subtle, so it is easy to make mistakes unless well trained.

Figure 2.11 Standard eye accessing cues

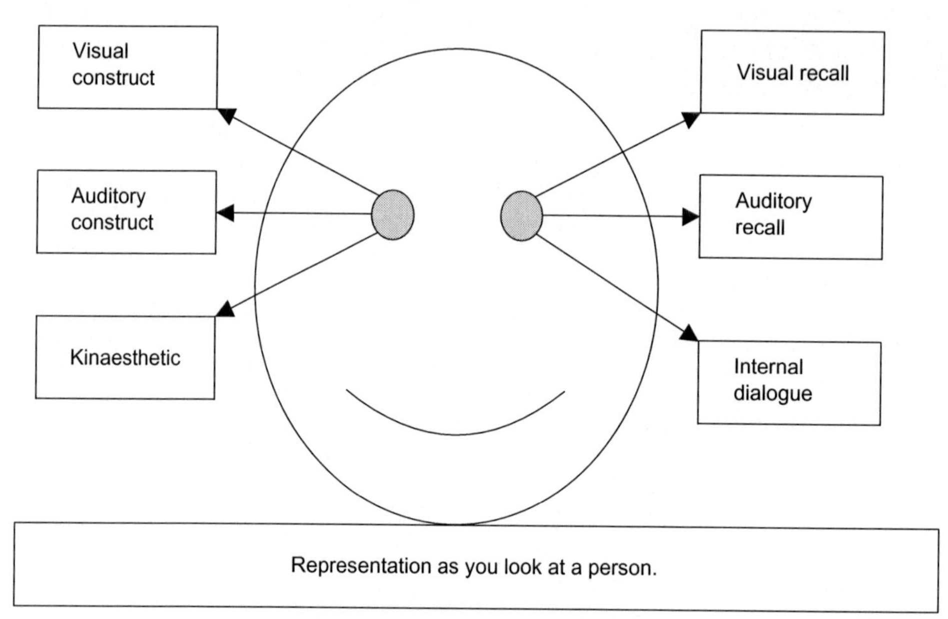

Eye movements down to their right are associated with feelings. Eye movements down to their left indicates that someone is listening to an internal dialogue. I assume that most of us have an internal voice, but some people have a strong preference for internal dialogue, over and above sight and sound, and can appear quite dissociated from their feelings. If you want to dissociate from feeling for some reason then try looking down to your left rather than right.

To test out eye accessing cues try asking questions such as those illustrated below.

Figure 2.12 Eliciting eye cues through questions

	Recall	**Construct**
Visual	What colour is your car?	What would your house look like painted red?
Auditory	What does you mother's voice sound like?	What would an elephant sound like playing a trumpet?
Kinaesthetic	What does it feel like to have your feet tickled?	
Auditory dialogue	Should project managers have to sit entrance exams to the profession and have designatory letters?	

Eye accessing cues are necessary for eliciting 'strategies', that is simple mental processes such as buying behaviour and decision-making. (Strategy elicitation is not within the scope of this book, but is covered in depth under modelling,[104] as signposted in the section on 'taking things further').

2.10.3 Other cues to representational systems
Since the mind and body are one, the way we think also exerts its influence on our behaviours. Personally, I do not use eye accessing cues as I find it much easier to pick up lead systems from more obvious signals in association with vocabulary.

Figure 2.13 Indicators of preferred representational systems

	Visual	Aural	Kinaesthetic
Breathing	Shallow and high in the chest	Even from mid-chest	Deep from the diaphragm
Voice	High pitched	Clear	Low and deep
Speech	Fast	Medium pace	Slow with pauses
Other signals	Usually very smart appearance	Often angle head to preferred ear	Usually dressed for comfort

How you would adapt your breathing to impact your voice tone and tempo to someone from one of the other two styles?

2.10.4 Enriching the world of the project team
An understanding of the fact that people have different preferences for representational systems should be the starting point for the way that you engineer communications to attract a wide variety of stakeholders. Aside from the dry documentation of projects, are there other ways that you can represent the project and present information? Should you stop using teleconferences and email so much? Can you shoot some interviews with key stakeholders and put them on a website? Can you make a poster? Can you do an audio update to the website? And of course, don't forget to walk around and talk to people. (I have seen projects performed as plays and presented as a visual montage – the only limit is your imagination.)

2.11 SENSORY ACUITY, BODY LANGUAGE AND MIND READING

> 'The average human looks without seeing, listens without hearing, touches without feeling, eats without tasting, moves without physical awareness, inhales without awareness of odour or fragrance, and talks without thinking'
>
> Leonardo da Vinci

After most project reviews that I have attended we end up with 'more communication' at the top of the flip chart. Some people may want more, but really I think that we are talking about *better* communication. It is not usually that there has been no communication, but rather that the message has not been received and understood across different stakeholder segments.

> 'The meaning of the communication is the response that you get'
>
> NLP presupposition

It is well established that the bulk of meaning is conveyed, not by words themselves, but by subtleties of voice and body language.[105] The more we train ourselves to be sensitive to nuances, the more meaning we can accurately pick up.

> 'The quality of our lives is determined by the quality of our communications'
>
> NLP presupposition

When you go on an NLP practitioner course you will undoubtedly spend several hours working on ways to develop sensory acuity; that is, the ability to recognise physical evidence linked to emotional states.

> 'Let me not judge my neighbour until I have walked a mile in his moccasins'
>
> Native American proverb

We are all familiar with this saying, but how many of us actually do it? More likely we will imagine walking their journey but in our own shoes, and notice how we would do things differently without understanding why they do what they do in the way that they do it. We are walking on our map of the world, not theirs.

One exercise widely used is called 'walking in someone else's moccasins'. Basically, you pair up and observe each other; for example, walking in a park. You then try to emulate the nuances of stance and gait repeatedly. With practice, the general mood of the other person can be 'read' by emulating them in close detail. Anthony Robbins demonstrates extremes of this with the audience in his 'Unleash the power within' road-show demonstrations, where half the audience report that they have successfully 'guessed' what the person is thinking about after being physically manipulated into an exact mirror.[106] Television 'mentalist' Derren Brown uses sensory acuity to 'mind read' his audience, noticing minute leakage from thoughts to muscle, especially being able to guess names and words people are thinking about from tiny unvoiced movements in the throat.[107]

For matching and mirroring, discussed in Section 2.14 on rapport, you will need to be very accurate in your reading of slight changes in other people's posture. Personally, I like to match breathing, which when shallow as when seated and resting can be barely perceptible.

We have already talked about the eye-accessing cues in Section 2.10 on representational systems. The ability to spot these fleeting, sometimes subtle, eye movements takes a lot of practice, especially doing it without staring into people's eyes like you just escaped from a secure mental unit.

Matching of tone and tempo are not so difficult, especially for those who are aurally biased, but it takes intent and practice to do so.

Whatever you believe, being more observant will help you to work out what is going on. For change work on others, being able to recognise tiny shifts in physiology is essential, as all outcomes must be evidenced based, i.e. observed changes in physiology and not guesswork.

You can practise you own sensory acuity by, well, practising it. Pick a regular time and use it to be more aware. On your commute to work, for example, you could use 5–10 minutes each day to run through your senses and make a mental note of what you pick up. What can you see, big things first and then details of things that catch your eye? What sounds beneath the clatter of rails and iPods? Each day you will notice more layers even for a common scene. As you practise more it will become less conscious and you will find yourself noticing more detail as a matter of course. The rest is elementary, my dear Watson.

Another way to practise is to get a colleague or friend to think of a strong memory, happy or sad, and make a note of all the details of their physiology. Hopefully you can guess which emotion they are experiencing without too much difficulty, though people who tend to be dissociated and internally referenced can be fairly well masked (see Section 3.8 for association/dissociation). Make notes for other experiences – what physical evidence is different? What is beneath your radar?

One definition of NLP is an attitude of curiosity, and that is nowhere truer than in developing your sensory acuity. Perhaps Sherlock Holmes was a trailblazer for NLP and sensory acuity?

2.12 SUB-MODALITIES – THE CODING OF OUR MEMORIES

We covered the primary senses under representational systems in Section 2.10. Each of these basic five senses, or modalities, stores memory with sub-modalities, examples of which are shown in the table below.

Figure 2.14 Sub-modality check-list

Visual representations	Auditory representations
Dull/bright	Stereo/mono
Colour/black and white	Volume (loud/soft)
Near/far	Pitch (High/low)
Clear/blurred	Tempo (Fast/slow)
Associated/dissociated	Near/far
Moving/still	Rhythm
Location of image	Melody
Size of image	Clear/muffled
	Whose voice?
Kinaesthetic representations	**Auditory Digital representations**
Hot/cold	About self or other
Heavy/light	Simple or complex
Rough/smooth	Constant or intermittent
Strong/weak	Volume
Dry/wet	Location of voice
Static/moving	Pitch
Large area/small area	Whose voice?
Internal or external	

One of the presuppositions of NLP is that experience has structure, and the sub-modalities used to store the experience are part of that subconscious structure.[108] It has been found in practice that the impact and meaning of a memory is affected more by the sub-modalities used to code it than the actual content. Changing the sub-modalities changes the memory of the experience. This is widely used for curing phobias, but can also be used for less dramatic changes.

Exercise 2.2: Experiencing sub-modalities

The best way to understand sub-modalities is to practise experiencing them.

1. Think of a time when you were happy, perhaps a recent holiday or event.
2. Close your eyes and try to associate with the experience and relive it.
3. What do you see? Use the table of sub-modalities checklist above to help to extract the sub-modalities for vision. Is it bright? Does it have colour? Is it vivid? Moving?
4. What can you hear? Are there voices? Near or far? Deep or high pitched?
5. What do you feel? Where do you feel it? Dull or intense?

6. What can you smell and taste?
7. Write it all down.

Now think of a bad experience. Perhaps something that didn't turn out the way you planned it, but nothing too traumatic. Run through the same exercise, exploring the sights, sounds and feelings of the experience. Note them down.

Now compare and contrast the way these good and bad memories are stored using sub-modalities. You may find, for example, that good memories are brighter, more vivid, with voices coming in different tones from a different place, and different feelings in a different part of the body. It is how these memories are coded that determines whether they are considered good or bad, rather than the actual experiences themselves.

Now think of something that went well at work, something that you can associate with. Run through the same exercise, again noting down the sub-modalities.

Think of something at work that went really well, perhaps where you were highly praised or felt really good about achieving a deliverable. Associate with the experience and again note down the sub-modalities for each of the senses.

Figure 2.15 Differences in sub-modalities for good and for bad experiences

Sub-modalities of happy experience	**Sub-modalities of bad experience**
Sights Sounds Feelings Thoughts Smells and tastes	
Sub-modalities of good work event	**Sub-modalities of poor work event**
Common sub-modalities for good experiences	**Common sub-modalities for bad experiences**

Now, compare the sub-modalities used for each of the four examples. What are the common sub-modalities for the good experiences, what are the common ones for the bad experiences, and what are the key differences between good and bad experiences?

By swapping over the way you store these memories through sub-modalities you can change your subjective experience of them. This is the basis behind phobia cures, which can neutralise debilitating fears.[109]

Changing sub-modalities is used in Section 3.4 for changing limiting beliefs and 3.6 for taking away the power of our inner critical voice.

2.13 ANCHORING OF STATE

Anchoring is the association of mental states and memories with sensory stimulus. When the alarm bell went off at school or the jingle of the ice cream van sounded it elicited a response based on our association with it. As we grew up, new anchors were installed, many against our will, for example by advertising campaigns. Other anchors or associations are more subtle and outside our consciousness unless we dig for them.

2.13.1 Conditioning

From school biology you are probably familiar with the story of Pavlov and his dogs, whereby he demonstrated that a stimulus of food, which elicited a response of salivating, could be associated with another stimulus such as a bell and achieve the same response. It seems quite unremarkable to us now, but the demonstration that you could get a dog to salivate at the sound of a bell opened up a whole new avenue of behavioural science and earned Pavlov a Nobel prize in 1904. (Subsequent research has established the biochemical mechanism for establishing pattern recognition using the hormone dopamine.) Marketing and advertising have been keen to associate our buying behaviours with their products through simple stimuli of jingles and logos.

Conditioning of behaviours goes a lot further than simple responses. If you travel through the streets of India you may be shocked that full grown elephants are expected to remain tethered and controlled by thin pieces of rope or even string. Elephants have a leg tethered by rope from a very early age while they are small and relatively weak to condition them that a rope means they are immobile. Long after they have the resources for this to no longer remain true they remain constrained by this limiting belief. And all discovered by village people long before Pavlov got his Nobel Prize. What limiting beliefs have been conditioned into you, and what are the anchors for them? What flimsy pieces of string stop you going where you might dream of being?

2.13.2 Installing anchors

Before we go into exercises for anchors, there are several parameters to bear in mind to make them most effective:

- Anchors have to be **unique**. During training it is easiest to use kinaesthetic anchors. Touching points on the wrist is common. Anchors on the hands can be contaminated through regular handshaking and use of the hands. In setting my own anchors I use, for example, pressing my thumb and forefinger together or pinching my ear lobe. (When I used them in martial arts I would press my tongue against the roof of my mouth for resourceful states when fighting.)
- Anchors have to be **timely**. You need to activate the anchor at the same time that you elicit the emotion that you want to anchor. Start a second before the peak intensity of the emotion and exert peak pressure to coincide with full association. An anchor should not be triggered for more than 5 seconds otherwise it might become contaminated with secondary emotions.
- Anchors have to be **consistent**. You need to be able to replicate the exact trigger in terms of position and pressure if you are using a kinaesthetic anchor.

2.13.3 Choosing your mood

Wouldn't it be great to always be able to choose our mood, and select the best resources for the task in front of us. Well, with NLP and practice we can.

> 'We have all the resources within us to achieve what we want'
>
> NLP presupposition

While I was leading a transformation program in local government I was also offering some personal counselling for those personally affected by changes. One lady was assisting us in the PMO and asked for some help with a job interview as she became very nervous in such situations. Bearing in mind the presupposition above, I looked for a resource within her to help through the exercise below. I asked if she had ever been in a situation where some people may have been very nervous, but she managed to stay calm. 'Oh yes,' she replied, 'I used to be an international gymnast'. This lady had managed to remain calm and composed as she was about to do a back flip on a 10 centimetre bar but was experiencing nerves going for a secretary's job in her own department. An extreme example of a common occurrence. We had the resources we needed.

Exercise 2.3: Anchoring positive resources

1. Identify a problem or situation where you would like additional resources. An example might be when you are presenting to a group of strangers.
2. Think of a resource that might help you in the situation. For example, you may want extra confidence when you are presenting.
3. Now, think of situations where you have experienced this resource. Think laterally. Do you have a hobby where you feel very confident? Did you have an achievement that made you feel really confident?

4. Now, shake off this state by thinking of something completely different, for example, the smell of your favourite food. This step is called breaking state.
5. Identify three types of anchor that you could use for this resource. For example, one might be kinaesthetic like pulling your right ear, one might be visual such as looking at a projector, and one might be a word such as 'confidence'.
6. Recall the situation where you had this resource. Fully associate with the feelings, images, sounds, memories etc of this experience, and while you do, trigger your anchors.
7. Break state by for example thinking about the sound of a fire engine.
8. Now, fire your anchors and relive the associated experience of confidence. How vivid was it?
9. Repeat with other examples of experiencing this state until your anchors trigger an experience as vivid as when they actually occurred.
10. Think of a time when you might need this resourceful state.
11. Imagine the situation.
12. Now fire your anchors and experience this state of confidence.
13. You now have additional resources to perform at your peak.

Anchors become stronger the more they are used, so don't save them for a rainy day. It is also good to reinforce anchors. When I experience a very positive mood or achievement I add it to my 'fist of power', where I clench my fist while mentally saying 'yes'. When I need a very resourceful state for some new challenge I can call on this anchor to put me in peak performance. This process is known as **stacking anchors**.

Think about situations where you feel that you could use more resources. Examples might be for making presentations, listening in meetings, or chairing workshops. What kind of state might you like to be in and what mental resources would you need? Can you think of situations where you have had these emotions in other parts of your life? What resources might you like to support you in being assertive?

2.13.4 Don't shoot the messenger

Have you ever wondered why the kings of old used to kill the bearer of bad news? They became a visual anchor for the emotion (and hence it was wise to send a messenger instead of delivering bad news in person). We can become associated with negative emotions in others by accident. If someone has received some bad news or experienced a bad event then don't stand in front of them, especially if it is a regular occurrence; for example, repeatedly reviewing all the risks and issues with key stakeholders. Keep the focus on something inanimate such as the log itself or a flipchart and don't put yourself directly into the field of view. (Another good reason not to sit directly opposite someone unless they are in a particularly friendly mood.)

2.13.5 More about anchors

An exercise known as 'circle of excellence', where we stack up several positive resources for a challenging task, is illustrated in Section 3.7 on state management. There are several techniques on variations of anchoring, including: **chaining anchors, sliding anchors** and **collapsing anchors**, which I have not included as they are refinements and are better done with facilitation. Anchoring of resources is part of the process of changing personal history and timeline therapy, which are outside the scope of this book.[110] Phobias are extreme forms of anchors; for example, severe reaction to even the image of a snake, but can be removed through NLP.[111]

2.14 RAPPORT – THE DOORWAY TO BETTER COMMUNICATION

> Rapport: a close and harmonious relationship in which the people or groups concerned understand each other's feelings or ideas and communicate well
>
> Oxford dictionary

Rapport is one of the pillars of NLP, as without it you will not be able to lead, communicate or negotiate. It is natural, and the best leaders all exhibit it, but it can be learned.

While you would naturally tend to spend the bulk of your time with people who are more or less like yourself, the world of work is filled with people who are even more different to you than they would at first seem. In order to deliver your projects you will need to learn to get on with a wide variety of people. Don't worry, this doesn't mean that you are going to have to start liking your boss or the guy from accounts and going down the pub with them, but you do need to foster an atmosphere of trust, mutual respect and understanding of each other's worlds and ways. NLP can help you with all of this.

It may sound like extra work up-front, but it will certainly save you a lot of rework downstream in not having to keep hammering out similar messages and trying to get people to do things that they either don't understand or don't want to do.

Practical approaches to building rapport are illustrated in Part 3, particularly Section 3.15 on stakeholder management and 3.19 on motivating the project team.

2.14.1 Matching, mirroring and mimicking

Neurological levels were introduced in Section 2.7. Ideally, by finding out about the person that we are trying to relate to, we should be building bridges with identity, values and beliefs. Practical ways of doing this are illustrated in Figure 3.22 of Section 3.15 on rapport with stakeholders. Before we manage to do that, however, we must initially develop some rapport in order for them to trust us enough to give us their time and reveal something about themselves.

If you watch people, it is not difficult to notice from their body language who gets on and who doesn't. People who get on are 'in synch', and flow together. Their body language, though not identical, is complementary. People who are not getting on seem awkward with each other. Recall, for example, images of ex-Prime Minister Tony Blair in awkward stances next to his Chancellor Gordon Brown. Compare with those of a confident Blair at ease with President George Bush. People immediately believed newspaper stories of animosity between Blair and Brown, and a special relationship between Blair and Bush, because their eyes told them as much. Recalling images of Brown with Bush, how do you think they got on?

When done elegantly, matching and mirroring can get you to a point of open communication much quicker than fumbling your way through the process. Deliberate matching requires sensory acuity to notice details of the other person, not only the inclination of their torso and limbs, but also their gestures, energy, breathing, pace and tone. Experience of crude matching and mirroring, on the other hand, is what puts some people off NLP. This is what we call **mimicking**, and like the person on the playground who used to copy everything that you said, it can be very annoying, and definitely doesn't build trust or rapport at all.

Mirroring is where you literally act like a mirror to their posture. It happens naturally when you are in rapport. When you accurately mirror someone's body language it is surprisingly easy to get into tune with their thoughts. It is not at all subtle, however, so most people use matching, where you pick some elements and match those. Matching of the torso is quite unobtrusive.

If people remain standing then you probably want to do the same, and if people take their jackets and ties off then you probably want to comply. For a very important meeting with a blue chip company, I called in the day before to get a feel for their HQ and how people were dressed so that I could blend in on arrival the next day. No need to take it too far, but turning up in jeans to a room full of pinstripes, or vice versa, is not a great start, though it can be rescued by doing some of the other stuff.

2.14.2 Matching through energy and pace

Irrespective of people's posture, and whether you are sitting and they are standing, they will have a natural energy and pace to them, and particularly if they are under the influence of a strong mood such as anger or excitement. In order to be heard, you should match their pace and energy. Personally, I am primarily visually oriented and my pace is fast. When I talk to someone who is kinaesthetically oriented it can feel like I am watching a slow motion film, so to adjust the energy and pace I drop my breathing from my chest to my diaphragm and look down to my right to associate with my body and feelings, naturally slowing my pace and dropping the tone of my voice. We now have a much better chance of having a meaningful conversation, rather than just talking at each other literally on different frequencies.

2.14.3 Pacing and leading

At one time I thought that when people were angry or excited then the answer was to stay calm, but this risks mismatching them and failing to communicate. Instead it is better to match their energy until you have established a measure of rapport. Once you have an effective dialogue going on you can start to set the pace and slowly lead them back to a less excited state.

Successful change management projects effectively use pacing and leading at an organisational level. First you must show people that you are listening and trying to understand their view. Once they feel like they are valued and being listened to you can start to introduce some of your drivers and ask them what impact these might have and how they could be accommodated. Ideally, only then do you co-construct a solution, balancing gain against minimising resistance. Once an agreed amount of change has been achieved, often called a meta-state, you go into another round of matching before agreeing the next set of outcomes. As you work with and pace the organisation they become acclimatised to the new culture of continuous change. (But please don't consult with them on changes that you have already decided in a closed room – better to just implement these rather than insulting their intelligence by pretending to listen and then doing what you were going to do anyway.)

2.14.4 Matching through language

Although most information about personal interaction is predicated by body language and tone, beyond this we must get our actual message through. Many of us fail at this hurdle because we do not match our language to our audience. Most effect is achieved by matching predicates to our audience's lead representational system, as illustrated in Section 2.10. Practical examples of matching to individuals' meta-programs is covered at length in Section 3.15 on stakeholder management.

2.14.5 Noticing and using mismatching

I have had my wife stand on my foot at parties, where afterwards she tells me that my unfortunate audience was looking for the door as I bored them with some tale of matching meta-programs or similar topic. I don't know how often I do it at work when my wife isn't there to stand on my foot, but hopefully less often than I used to. Do you know anyone at work who bores the pants off everyone, droning on while everyone else tunes them out and doodles in their notebooks? How can they not notice all the negative body language and absence of any type of rapport? When we are absorbed in what we are talking about we sometimes get lost in the story, especially for visual types, and drop out of the moment into a mini storytelling trance. In such circumstances you need to mismatch in a strong way, by adopting very different body language, energy, tone and movements. Having your hand on the door handle just won't do as they will fail to notice. (Read Section 2.11 on sensory acuity for more ways to notice if you ever bore your audience.)

For less extreme cases, for example when you have to be somewhere else for another meeting, a single change of body posture or tone should be enough to break rapport and signal the end of the conversation.

2.15 SURFACE AND DEEP STRUCTURE OF LANGUAGE USING THE META-MODEL

The meta-model is the heart of NLP. It was the first model, developed when the founders of NLP, Richard Bandler and John Grinder, modelled successful therapists Virginia Satir[112] and Fritz Perls. They observed that certain types of question had a therapeutic effect. These were summarised into 12 language patterns in the first NLP book, *The Structure of Magic* in 1975.[113]

> 'Wisdom is not in words; wisdom is meaning within words'
>
> Kahlil Gibran

Basically, below the surface structure of the words that we hear, which is the grammar element, is a deep structure of our coding of meaning. The meaning is distorted by our internal filters through deletion, distortion and generalisation. The deep structure or meaning can be reinterpreted from our words, as was done successfully by leading therapists, by applying the meta-model. Hence, the meta-model is a coding of successful language patterns that help to uncover deeper meaning, and in the process reveal the internal filters, or world-view, of the subject.

On the face of it the meta-model can at first appear to be an academic study, but as you start to use it you will realise how pervasive these filters are, and when you realise that these statements are not random, but reflect actual beliefs, you will understand the power that understanding of the meta-model can give. Milton Erickson made a career out of it, and made many people well.

Have you ever had a run-in with a project accountant and come away believing that '(all) accountants are unhelpful', or found '(all) sponsors don't tell you anything'?

Figure 2.16 The 12 patterns of the meta-model

Pattern	Example	Response
Simple deletion An important object has been left out of the statement	'I am disappointed'	'Disappointed about what?'
Comparative deletion A comparison is implicit	'Its better to go along with things'	'Better than what?'
Lack of referential index Subject or object isn't specified	'People won't support me'	'Who won't support you?'
Unspecified verbs Verb is not adequately defined	'I explain things badly'	'How do you explain things badly?'
Cause and effect A causal relationship is implied	'The supplier drives me crazy'	'How do they drive you crazy?'

(Continued)

Figure 2.16 *(Continued)*

Pattern	Example	Response
Mind reading Inference of intent from behaviour	'The sponsor thinks that I am incompetent'	'How do you know that?'
Complex equivalents A relationship is implied	'I didn't pass my PMP exam – I am a complete failure'	'How does a test make you a failure?'
Lost performatives Opinion presented as fact	'Its not right to have to work overtime to complete the project on time'	'Not right according to whom?'
Nominalisations Verbs expressed as nouns	'There is not enough communication'	'What communication aren't you getting?'
Universal quantifiers Broad generalisations, e.g. every, always, never, no-one	'His reports are never on time'	'Never?'
Modal operators of necessity and possibility Statements that limit behaviour	'I cant delegate'	'What would happen if you did?'
Presuppositions An implied belief	'If they respected me they would behave differently'	'How do you know that they don't respect you?'

2.15.1 Listening skills

This model is extremely useful as a listening skill, and is covered in Section 3.16 on listening. Examples are also illustrated for clarification in the negotiation process in Section 3.18. Obviously, you would not reel off a series of these challenges as written and expect to remain in rapport. Hear them in your head and follow the conversation, only intervening when you really do need to check meaning. Practise listening in your next project board or team meeting and keep a score of meta-model distortions by type. Try to frame appropriate questions to challenge.

Check your own language – which of these patterns regularly fall out of your mouth?

2.15.2 Meta-model and hypnosis

When people employ hypnosis, they reverse procedure and introduce generalisation, distortion and deletion to confuse the conscious brain in order to directly access the subconscious mind.[114]

If you listen to politicians speaking, including those that play office politics, you should pick up on extensive use of deliberate meta-model violations.

To avoid being confused into a waking trance by people using this type of monologue, concentrate on the meta-model violations and insert your own clarification questions to stay focussed.

2.16 TIMELINES

We spoke about different maps of the world in Section 2.5. One might think that time, however, being linear and measurable, is fairly constant. In fact, the way we code memories in time is arbitrary, and the meaning of time to individuals is as individual as they are.

Do you know anyone who is so 'in the moment' that they miss appointments, meetings and deadlines more often than not? What about people who seem to live in the past, and constantly hark back to how things used to be, and how things were done differently on earlier projects? And what about those who seem to live only for tomorrow, constantly planning for the future with little heed of the past or association with the present? Time means different things to all of us.

2.16.1 Meta-program for time – in time and through time

People who are good at managing to time generally have a 'through time' bias for this meta-program; that is, are largely dissociated and objective. You may think that this would be ideal for PMs. For building relationships, and general communication, however, it is better to be 'in time'; that is, living in the moment. Hence you will need to develop flexibility, or at least recognise what tasks require which behaviour and delegate appropriately. An exercise for elicitation of your timeline is described in Section 3.13, alongside an exercise for developing flexibility in your approach to time.

2.16.2 Gestalt memories

> Gestalt: 'an organized whole that is perceived as more than the sum of its parts'
> Oxford English Dictionary

When we code experiences, we tend to do this as an association with similar memories in a gestalt. Thus, when we experience a situation that our filters decide belongs to a gestalt then it triggers all the associated memories at the same time.[115] Hence, we sometimes completely overreact to some situations, because in fact we are reacting to a long history of situations that our subconscious has associated for us. 'The (extra) straw that broke the camel's back' would be an appropriate metaphor. Sometimes, these associations can be tenuous in the light of day. Not only that, but the associations are often long forgotten and hidden from our conscious awareness. As you may have realised, the triggers for these gestalts are mood dependent.

2.16.3 Timeline therapy

There is a whole discipline in timeline therapy, developed originally by Tad James,[116] which is extremely powerful for changing behaviours by revisiting the earliest incident that created the gestalt and reinterpreting its meaning in order to diminish the associated emotion. They are particularly useful when dealing with traumatic experiences and suppressed memories. These techniques use the metaphor of timeline regression. As they are mainly associated with therapy, I do not cover them in the scope of this book, but I personally make extensive use of timeline techniques for behaviour change in myself and in others.

> 'It is never too late to have had a happy childhood'
>
> Anthony Robbins

2.17 MODELLING OF EXCELLENCE

People are natural modellers, and most of our early life learning is from implicit modelling. But as we get older we seem to develop an aversion to trying new things out of fear of 'failure'. This trait would not have served us well when learning to walk and talk by modelling those around us, where we learned from our 'failures'. To model and learn you have to be involved in the process – you could never learn to play the piano or football by reading a manual. Modelling is already extensively used in top level sports.[117] Fran Tarkenton, NFL Hall of Fame quarterback, said 'Most of my learning has come from modelling other people and what they do.' Similarly, Dale Carnegie set out to 'model' excellence, and Covey sought to identify 'the difference that makes the difference'. Here, we present a more structured NLP approach.

2.17.1 NLP and modelling

NLP has several presuppositions relating to modelling, including: '*If one person can do something then anyone can learn to do it*', and '*Experience has structure*'. It is the latter that NLP focuses on, viz uncovering the deep structure or meaning. It led to the first treatise on NLP, *The Structure of Magic*.[118]

NLP was originally developed by John Grinder and Richard Bandler by modelling the shared cognitive, linguistic and behaviour patterns of exceptional psychotherapists such as Fritz Perls (Gestalt therapy), Virginia Satire (family therapy), and Milton Erickson (hypnotherapy). Modelling of techniques used by these eminent counsellors explains why there remains a strong focus on counselling and use of hypnotherapy, though we do not cover those aspects in this book.

What is now taught in NLP courses, and sampled in this book, is a collection of models of excellence. The first NLP model was the meta-model for language.

The second NLP model was representational systems. The third NLP model was the Milton model (after the hypnotic language patterns of Milton Erickson).[119]

An example of modelling of a simple skill is illustrated in Section 3.21.

2.18 SUMMARY OF PART 2

In this section we have learned that NLP is an approach with a long pedigree of familiar ideas and concepts than can help PMs to communicate more effectively and develop flexibility in behaviour to match changes in context.

We learned about the pillars of NLP: outcome thinking, sensory acuity, rapport and behavioural flexibility, which are required to support any NLP technique, and the fact that everything is underpinned by ecology of the human system as a whole.

The familiar concept of different 'world-views' was explored, and the way in which our world is filtered by our prior experiences, beliefs and values was introduced. Coding of memories, and hence beliefs, via the representational system of our primary senses was shown to be dependent on the sub-modalities of those senses – the qualities of brightness, colour, sounds and feelings. The NLP technique of changing beliefs, including limiting beliefs, by changing the way that we code our memories was shown, enabling us to develop much more flexile behaviour.

We introduced meta-programs to help explain our different thinking patterns and to show that these had structure and reproducibility. Although meta-programs are not usually introduced until Master Practitioner level, I make extensive use of them as a working tool in Part 3, as effective PMs must develop flexibility in behaviours to suit different tasks.

The meta-model, which describes the deep structure of the meaning of language, was introduced. Although appearing quite academic at first, it is a powerful tool to assist listening skills and establish hidden meaning. The origin of the meta-model in hypnosis and therapy was explained.

Of great importance to project management, timelines were discussed. Despite time being linear, our experience of time is not, and the concept of gestalt memory and reinterpretation of meaning was explained. More practically, a way of moving from being time focussed to situation focussed was introduced, as PMs must switch between orientation depending on task.

You now have all the background and underpinning tools that you need to understand and carry out the project management focussed exercises in Part 3. These exercises will help you to communicate even more effectively and develop flexible behaviour that can be used in all aspects of project management.

PART 3 BRINGING THE TWO WORLDS TOGETHER – PUTTING NLP INTO PRACTICE FOR PROJECT MANAGEMENT

3.1 INTRODUCTION

This is the section where we bring it all together, and put some NLP theory into practice to help develop skills for effective project management. In Appendix 2 I go further to describe a typical week in the life of a PM who has taken on board the learnings described in this chapter to become an even more effective manager.

3.1.1 Approach and scope of coverage

It is not my intention to address the total potential skill set, or even to be comprehensive on each skill or behaviour chosen, as that approach would require a huge volume. Instead, I will give an NLP perspective on a selection of skills and then provide a few exercises for each to show practical application of NLP techniques.

More to the point, a huge volume would be counterproductive. It is unlikely that you will become masters of the skills here from reading alone, as they require a shift in behaviours, which are largely ingrained and subconscious. Rather, this section is intended to whet your appetite so that you undertake practice and facilitation in this NLP approach. It is, in my experience, the most effective toolset for effecting personal change and improvements in key soft skills required for management of projects. (In Appendix 1 I give pointers on where and how you can take things further with NLP, including other directions not covered in this book such as health and wellbeing.)

These skills are very important and transferable to other domains. In fact, 13 of the top 14 most searched topics in People Alchemy for Managers[120] are included here (which include project management, change management and NLP – the number one searched topic is leadership). There are huge bodies of knowledge surrounding these topics in the general literature, and it is not my intention to duplicate this general information. I do, however, use poetic licence to include what I consider to be *NLP by another name* from guidance that predates awareness of NLP. After all, one definition of NLP is 'doing things that work', and we also seek to model effective strategies from the wider world.

The skills selected here do give a good coverage of basic NLP approach and tools, as can be seen from the figure below.

Figure 3.1 Summary of skills and NLP techniques used

Skill	Main NLP technique
2 Ethics	Ecology Well formed outcomes Hypnosis
4 Continuous development	Belief cycle Changing limiting beliefs
5 Self awareness	Meta-programs Language and behaviour profile
6 Self coaching	Representational systems Positive language Sub-modalities (inner voice)
7 State management	Mind/body link Circle of excellence
8 Handling stress	Anchoring Meta-program for working stress response Mind-body link Meta-mirror Dissociation Rapport with self
9 Presenting yourself	Congruence and body language
10 Being assertive	Three part assertiveness strategy
11 Flexibility	Models of leadership T.O.T.E. model
12 Goal setting	Well formed outcomes Same/difference meta-program
13 Time management	Timelines In time vs through time meta-program Future pacing
14 Big picture/detail	General/specific meta-program Chunking
15 Building rapport with stakeholders	Rapport Hierarchy of neurological levels Maps of the world Meta-programs for rapport Convincer meta-program Matching language to representational systems Matching language to meta-programs

(Continued)

Figure 3.1 *(Continued)*

Skill	Main NLP technique
16 Listening skills	Meta-model (surface and deep structure of language)
17 Handling difficult situations	Blame frame/outcome frame Context reframe As-if reframe
18 Negotiation	Negotiation Strategy Meta-mirror Perceptual positions Meta-model Chunking
19 Motivation	Identity, beliefs and values Modal operators Presuppositions Matching meta-programs Rule structure meta-program Working style (person/thing) meta-program Use of metaphor
20 Feedback	Sandwich feedback model
21 Modelling excellence	Modelling

3.1.2 Doing things *even better*

It is important that you do not consider the following sections to be a guide to 'how to do things properly'. To have got where you are, you are probably already doing things well. These are suggestions for doing things *even better*. And remember the NLP presupposition *'All behaviours are appropriate in some context'*, i.e. what you do already works in some situations. Many suppliers have met the 'Mr Angry' PM caricature that only has one behaviour, e.g. shouting. We are just trying to improve our range of behaviours so that we can better match them to context, situation, individuals and their motivators. As you will read in Section 3.11, flexibility can be everything.

3.1.3 How to practise

> 'A little knowledge that acts is worth infinitely more than much knowledge that is idle'
>
> Kahlil Gibran

With regard to 'doing' the exercises, as I keep repeating, learning is experiential and cannot be gained from just reading a book, otherwise we would already 'win friends and influence people',[121] have the 'habits of highly effective people',[122] and have perfect scores on our emotional intelligence.[123] So you understand that you have to 'do' the exercises, ideally with a facilitator, or at least with a partner. The good news is that you can do all NLP exercises 'content free', i.e. you do not have to tell your facilitator any details of the situation that you are imagining. Some counsellors find that it works even better content free, as the client is less inhibited, and the facilitator finds it easier to stay dissociated from the story, which is less draining emotionally as well as making for a cleaner process. (This is particularly important when doing personal counselling, especially when working with deeply traumatic experiences, to prevent people reliving bad experiences and reinforcing negative anchors.)

3.1.4 Do, don't think

You will read more under the section on being your own coach (Section 3.6), but my final comment on the following sections sounds counterintuitive – when trying exercises like these, disengage your brain! What we are trying to change are behaviours/meta-programs long-embedded in the subconscious mind. I wasted many years trying to intellectualise myself into changing. (As do many smokers – note that I do not say '*ex*-smokers'.) It may come as a surprise to many on reading Section 2.6 that our conscious mind is not actually in charge of what we do. I think of it as the GUI (graphical user interface) to the big complex biological computer that sits behind. As facilitators/mentors/counsellors, many of us spend a large proportion of our time and effort trying to distract/disengage the oaf at the front of our heads that controls our voice in order to get direct access to the engine room behind. And a lot of NLPers, including myself, end up becoming certified hypnotherapists to facilitate this process, i.e. render the volunteer amenable to suggestion. In summary: Read, do, don't think. Do again.

3.2 ETHICS AND WELL FORMED OUTCOMES

Ethical behaviour is returning to fashion in society and to the professions.[124] The popular backlash to the near failure of the global banking system in 2008 is likely to accelerate the pace of change. The move towards chartered status by the UK's Association for Project Management has brought to the fore the need to demonstrate that it is 'acting for the good of the public', and this requirement cascades down to professional project managers. Professional bodies, like the APM and BCS, have ethics and standards committees that have the power to 'strike off' individuals who do not act in the public good in the same way that medical doctors or lawyers can be struck off and prevented from practicing.

3.2.1 Congruence in word and deed

NLP, when done well, can achieve incredible personal change. Therefore, it must be done with due care and in an ethical manner. One of the cornerstone publications to bring NLP into the domain of management in 1983 was the well-named *Influencing with Integrity*.[125] What we refer to as 'well formed outcomes' (Section 3.12) means that the goals we set for personal change must be in the best interests of *all* parties. If we are naive enough to attempt to effect change that is not in the interests of all parties then we are not likely to succeed as we will lack 'congruence'. That is, our words and actions will be out of synch. This is evident when we see some people trained in NLP-like sales techniques subverting the process by trying to persuade potential customers to buy things for which they have no use. This results in them coming over as desperate, and the victim suffering from buyer's remorse.

NLP can be used effectively for sales by using techniques to establish; if the prospect has a need and is likely to buy, where they are in their buying cycle, and what their buying strategy is. If they do not have a need then a good salesperson quickly moves on to the next prospect without wasting time of either party. NLP can also be used to model excellent behaviour from successful peers in sales.[126]

Similarly, when people try to manipulate matching and mirroring of body language in order to gain rapport for some selfish end, it comes over as creepy and can actually break rapport. In my opinion, 'mirroring', as illustrated so well in courtship display rituals in the annual kingdom such as with swans, is best used as an output measure to test whether rapport has been achieved, rather than as an input to artificially effect rapport. If you take an honest and active interest in people you will naturally achieve rapport without the need to try to fake it.

3.2.2 Look into my eyes

Some people are distrustful of hypnosis, perhaps fearing that they will reveal something personal, be made to jump on a table and impersonate a chicken, or generally lose control.

> At one of the business schools where I offered to speak on modelling of entrepreneurs, the promotional flier mentioned that I was also a hypnotherapist and jokingly promised that 'everyone will go away believing that they learned something and had a great time'. At the end of the main session I offered to do a short motivational hypnosis session and asked those who wanted to be led through a trance to close their eyes to signify consent. More than half the room sat with their eyes firmly wide open. Maybe I should say this at the start of future sessions to stop people dropping off, and just tell those that do close their eyes what they need to know at the summary while they are still in trance.

Hypnosis can only be achieved with 'permission' from the subject. This is usually implicit, e.g. you turn up at the doctor's for hypnotherapy, or you step onto the stage when volunteers are asked for. Once you have given your permission, if you think that you can't be hypnotised then you are mistaken. It is in fact much more difficult to be out of trance, i.e. 'present' or 'in the moment', than in a trance-like state. In NLP we refer to being out of our daily trance-like state as 'up-time'. This is similar to the state of total unemotional awareness sought through intense meditation.

We actually spend most of our lives hypnotised, i.e. in trance-like states where we do not notice our environment or the passage of time. Have you ever driven home from work and realised that you cannot remember any of the journey from getting in the car to getting out of it, or switched off the TV and wondered why you sat transfixed through such rubbish and are now late for bed? World class athletes develop the ability to go into a focussed trance, often called 'flow', where all extraneous information is filtered out and time seems to run in slow motion. (NLP is sometimes used to induce or anchor such highly resourceful states for athletes.)

What do you think the key meta-programs might be for people most susceptible to hypnosis?

3.3 WHY THESE SKILLS?

We saw in Section 1.8 that there are many skills and competences required for effective management of projects. Rather than slavishly follow a long compound list, I decided to follow my own process for managing stakeholder requirements – ask them what they want! Hence, I met with a cross section of my stakeholders, including: the publisher, heads of PM profession, people responsible for competence frameworks in professional bodies, project sponsors, executives from recruitment agencies, trainers and of course project professionals. I asked them one of my favourite NLP questions – 'If I had a magic wand and I could give you/your PM any skills that would make a real difference, what would they be?'

The emergent list of skills surprised me, in a good way. I was expecting to see things like planning, risk management etc., i.e. PM processes. Instead, I got a list that is more in line with where my own personal and professional development has been focussed in the latter half of my career. A compounded list of these collected stakeholder requirements, plus a couple I added for completeness, are covered in the contents of this section and shown in Figures 3.1 and 3.2 below. This list also covers most of those compiled from the various sources of competence frameworks described in Section 1.8. There is also a good overlap with the components of emotional intelligence (EI) frameworks, which have become synonymous with 'soft skills', as described in Section 1.8.4. The EI framework can be divided into groups of: self awareness, self management, social awareness and relationship management, which are all covered here to significant extent, as can be seen in the table below. Hence I believe that this part of the book will make a significant contribution to further improving the emotional intelligence of people who study and apply it.

Figure 3.2 Skills for knowing and managing self and others

	Self (Personal Competence)	Other (Social Competence)
Recognition	Self awareness Feedback Self coaching Presenting yourself Self confidence	Sensory acuity Listening Rapport
Regulation	State management Goal setting Continuous development Handling stress Flexibility Big picture/detail Time management Modelling	Reframe Conflict management Negotiation Motivation Feedback

3.4 ADOPTING AN ATTITUDE OF CONTINUOUS DEVELOPMENT

'When you encounter someone greater than yourself, turn your thoughts to becoming his equal. When you encounter someone who you consider lesser than you, look within and examine your own self'

Confucius

3.4.1 'Sharpening the saw'

In Covey's book *The 7 habits of highly effective people,*[127] his last habit was what he refers to as 'sharpening the saw'. I put it as my first behaviour, as if we cannot motivate ourselves towards personal improvement then the rest of the book is a waste of time. I relate it by paraphrasing his story:

A man walks to work and notices another man sawing a tree. On the way home he sees that the man is still sawing the same tree. He suggests, 'Have you thought of sharpening your saw?' To which the man replies, 'I don't have time to sharpen my saw, I am too busy sawing this tree!'

In my professional life in project management, I often see people who are too busy with the day job to invest in making the day job easier, i.e. by developing themselves in parallel through new skills and tools.

In my work with the professional bodies, especially during my time as Chairman of the London Region of the Association for Project Management, we spent a lot of voluntary effort bringing a wide range of quality presenters to pass on their substantial experience, but statistics across professional bodies shows that engagement with members is consistently below ten per cent. Ninety per cent are always too busy sawing the tree. Bearing in mind that membership of professional bodies is low in the first place where it is not a de facto standard, this means that only a small percentage are actively seeking ongoing development. But don't worry, you picked up the book and so are in the ten per cent who want to sharpen the saw. NLP is sometimes called the search for 'The difference that makes the difference', so here is the opportunity to really sharpen your saw!

3.4.2 *You* are the project

Having spent so much time in project management and change management, I often think of *myself* as a change management project. This also fits well with the NLP view of the world. As with many change management projects, it is a journey rather than a destination, with many 'meta-states' along the way where we pause to consolidate improvements, having achieved our outcomes for the current phase.

Figure 3.3 The DIY change project

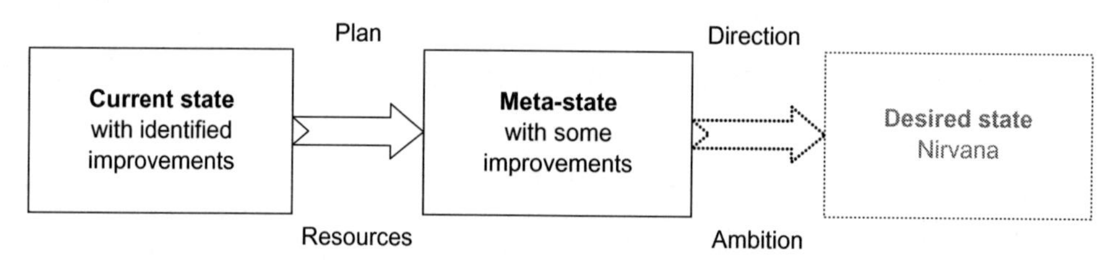

"What you get by achieving your goals is not as important as what you become by achieving your goals"

Zig Ziglar

3.4.3 Gain the competitive advantage

We know that when companies don't invest they become inefficient and uncompetitive, and perhaps insolvent, with their customers won over by their competitors.

While inside the PM department of one of the big banks, I saw a room full of people all scribbling away at desks. When I asked what they were doing, I was told that they were all doing a common PM exam. I expressed my delight that people were pursuing professional development, especially being supported by their employer. My host replied that they had in fact all been made redundant after a takeover, as they did not meet professional standards. As part of their release they had been offered training to help get a new job. My outlook on professional development is to do it before I need it, and avoid being one of the candidates in that room.

The figure below illustrates a standard model for improving competence. The International Project Management Association (IPMA) ascribes four levels of competence for PM, with the top level being the likes of people in charge of mega-projects similar to Heathrow Terminal 5, Beijing Olympic Park, the Space Shuttle etc.

Figure 3.4 Competence requires skills and experience as well as knowledge

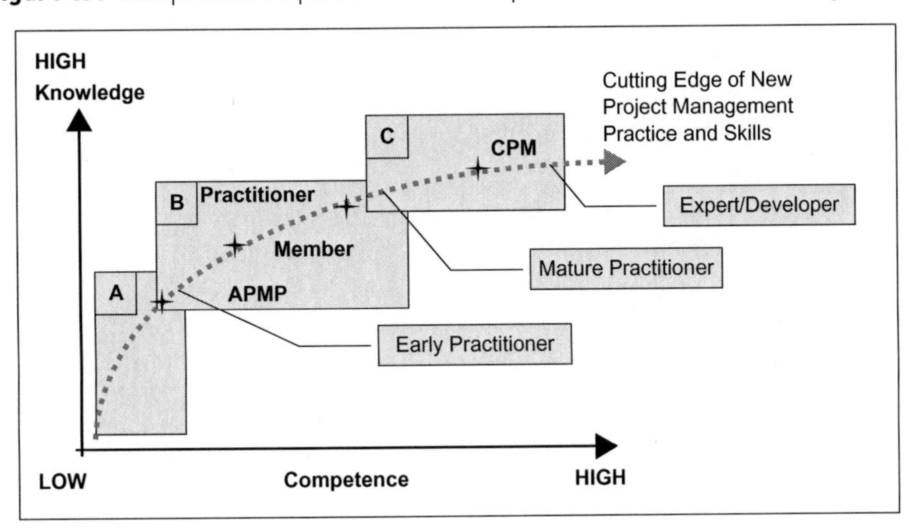

3.4.4 Become the professional

In project management, there seems to be a reluctance to be what I consider a professional. In NLP we talk about people being polarised by the *meta-program* of 'towards or away from' – popularly referred to as 'the carrot or the stick' (to motivate the donkey). In order for PMs to become 'professional', there need to be drivers *and* attractors in place.

When I completed my Certificated PM examinations through the APM in 2000 (IPMA level 3), I was about the 100th person to pass from a membership of about 15,000 at the time. Although it was a very testing process, I doubt that this low number was because the rest were not capable. More likely they did not have sufficient motivation. Introduction of the PRINCE2 method vastly increased the number of people taking formal training and examination in PM. Was this because people suddenly got motivated to become professional? I doubt it. More likely it was the fact that it was mandated by the UK's Office of Government Commerce (OGC), which used to oversee a high proportion of the UK public sector spend, which also led to it becoming a prerequisite minimum standard for most employment and interim agencies for PMs. Similarly, the Association for Project Management is introducing a new higher standard for project professionals against a widely used competence framework.[128] It is recognised that this will have limited impact on motivation unless it is coupled with a Royal Charter for the UK, whereupon it becomes both a motivator and a de facto standard.

But anyway, you are reading this book, so you are one of the minority already inclined 'towards' excellence.

3.4.5 Believing in yourself

> 'If your mind can conceive it, and your heart can believe it, you can achieve it'
> Jesse Jackson

Dale Carnegie said, 'In order to get the most out of this book[129] you need to develop a deep, driving desire to master the principles of human relations'. That is good advice, but how do we 'develop a deep desire'? Reading that statement on the page won't change our identity, beliefs, motivating values, behaviours or meta-programs. So how do we cross the start line and develop that motivation and take away our limiting beliefs?

3.4.6 Changing limiting beliefs

In section 2.7 we discussed beliefs. These are usually buried very deep in our psyche and we are not aware of them ourselves. They are often evident to others via our language and behaviours. Expressions like 'I am bad at exams', 'I will never be a good project manager', or 'I am just an IT project manager', do not just fall out of our mouths, but actually represent deeply held beliefs. We all have these types of thoughts in our psyche to a greater or lesser extent at some time or other. These beliefs, originally designed to keep us in a zone of safety, are often reinforced during our formative years by parents, siblings and rivals.

Exercise 3.1: Changing limiting beliefs

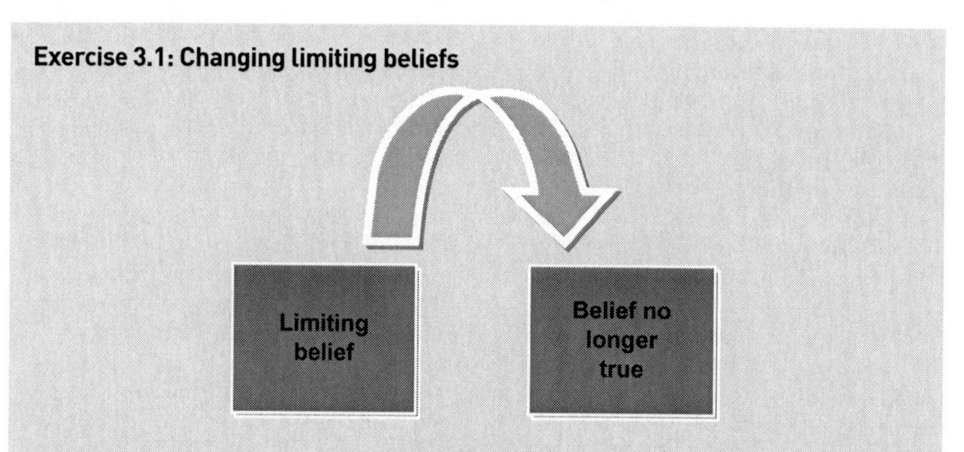

Sub-modalities were introduced in Section 2.12. The activities in this exercise, that is changing sub-modalities, are analogous to the very successful fast phobia cure that many of you may have seen on TV carried out by the likes of Paul McKenna, and which were the professional starting point for NLP guru Anthony Robbins.[130] The exercise is based on the NLP presupposition that we can change the meaning of memories by changing the way we store them and the way that they are represented.[131]

1. Think of a recent scenario where the outcome has not been satisfactory. What were you believing about yourself that created the outcome that you got?
2. Think of the limiting belief that you would like to change.
   a. Close your eyes. Create a picture as you think about it.
   b. Explore all the sub-modalities (pictures, sounds, feelings).
3. Open your eyes and note down the sub-modalities of the limiting belief. (A check list is shown in Figure 2.14).
4. Think of a belief that you once held but that is no longer true for you.
   a. Close your eyes and bring up a picture of this belief. Concentrate until it is vivid.
   b. Explore all the sub-modalities (pictures, sounds, feelings).
5. Open your eyes and note down the sub-modalities within this belief.
6. Work out which sub-modalities are different, and make a note of what needs to be changed.
7. Close your eyes and bring back the picture of the limiting belief.
   a. Change the sub-modalities (from 3 and 4) in turn by making the changes to the picture.
8. Open your eyes.
9. Now think about the old belief that you used to have and notice how it is no longer limiting your behaviour.

There is also an exercise in the appendices which illustrates a counselling session to remove limiting beliefs around professional development.

3.4.7 Oiling the machinery

There is another aspect of sharpening the saw, which is akin to oiling it and looking after it. In my experience, many in the world of project management are highly driven and tend towards being workaholics. For short bursts this is OK and sometimes necessary. Over long periods of time, however, it is detrimental to our wellbeing, and often those around us. As others will be taking a lead from our behaviour, it also tends to dysfunctional behaviours across the team. Over a long project it becomes counterproductive, as our performance deteriorates. It is our duty to turn up, in life as well as work, appropriately rested and with a clear head. This means that we need to set aside time for family and friends, hobbies and interests, holidays and relaxation. It is also extremely beneficial to build a contemplative activity akin to meditation into our daily routines to help clear our mind of 'dwelling' and other negative thoughts that affect our performance.[132] In computer programming terms, this is akin to clearing all the background processes out that slow down our mental processes and take up chunks of our active memory, thus making us less efficient. Don't be too busy sawing the tree!

Exercise 3.2: Putting priorities into perspective

What is *your* order for the following priorities?

- getting today's 'to do' list/activities out of the way;
- achieving the next milestone;
- project deliverables;
- project benefits;
- wellbeing of project team;
- managing stakeholders;
- reputation in the organisation;
- professional reputation;
- ethical behaviour;
- professional development;
- promotion at work;
- financial reward;
- material things such as cars;
- status;
- personal development;
- own health;
- wellbeing of family;
- emotional wellbeing.

Is this how you proportion your time and energy?
What are you going to change?
How are you going to change it?

3.4.8 Same difference

As a final note on this section, most of us work in projects because we like variety. In NLP terms, this means that we have a 'difference' bias rather than 'sameness' for that meta-program. Conversely, the more naive recruitment agencies usually ask for 'PMs' who have done exactly the same project in exactly the same sub-sector, using the same vendor etc, i.e. people who prefer sameness to difference as a meta-program. Such people demonstrating preference for sameness make good operational managers but not good PMs as far as I am concerned. (Perhaps the PMs are being requested by operational managers who value sameness!) If you can help it, don't do a project unless you can learn something along the way, and don't get stuck in a rut. People sometimes say they have ten years experience, but in reality they may only have one years experience but have been doing the same thing for ten. It is not necessary to change sector or even employer to get variety, just seek out novelty and set yourself personal development objectives at the start of every project. Active engagement with professional bodies and communities of practice helps.

3.5 KNOW THYSELF – DEVELOPING SELF AWARENESS

> 'He who knows others is wise; he who knows himself is enlightened'
>
> Lao Tzu

Self awareness means understanding ourselves and our emotions and is the fundamental step to gaining emotional intelligence. Unless we have deliberately studied them, we are mostly unaware of most of our own core behaviours/meta-programs, or the fact that people have markedly different ones to ourselves, as we usually develop them subconsciously at an early age.

'Know thyself' said Socrates. But how many of us do? 'Know thyself? If I knew myself I would run away', said Von Goethe.

Here are a few descriptions for effective PMs from various texts on project management that relate to self awareness:

- reflective, i.e. learning from experience;
- open to candid feedback;
- open to new ideas and perspectives;
- aware of our strengths and weaknesses;
- know our limitations, and know when and how to ask for help;
- able to admit mistakes;
- able to laugh at ourselves (before others do it for us).

In the straw poll of stakeholders that I referred to at the start of this chapter, self awareness was rated the number one characteristic for effective PMs. Without it you do not know where to start on your development, or where your starting point is. Hence it sits here, before any other aspect of personal development. If you don't appreciate it yourself, know that people who pay for your services do appreciate it. So don't run away.

> I visited the Head of PM Capability at one of the big global consultancies several years ago, and rather than attempt to sell myself, I used a tried-and-tested consultancy technique. Since something had already got me through the door, they had obviously seen something of value in me, so I asked, 'What is it about me that you see of value to you?' (Incidentally, this is a very good technique for convincing a potential client, as they will not resist their own assertions, whereas there will always be resistance to you making your own claims – a sort of one-up on the principle of using third-party advocates and references.) They replied, 'You are very self aware, and I want to develop that into my people.'

3.5.1 To see ourselves as others do

One of the techniques used in projects, as well as other business applications, is JoHari Windows.[133]

Figure 3.5 JoHari Windows

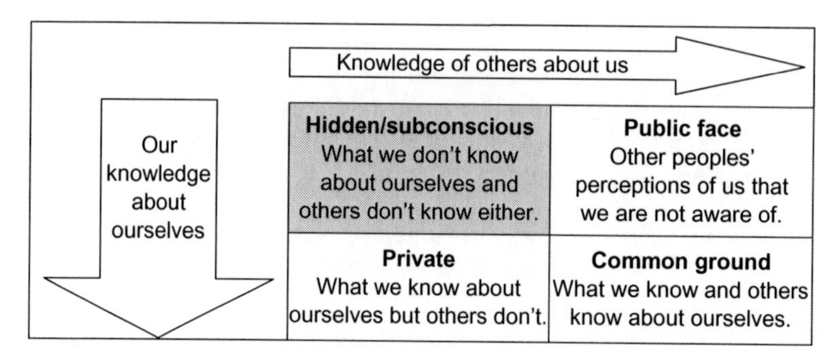

In one of the four boxes, we have what we and others agree about ourselves, i.e. largely factual. Then we have the stuff that only we know about ourselves, some of which we may want to keep private. Now we have the more interesting area of what people know or think about us but we do not know or realise ourselves. In projects, this would be what our stakeholders know or think, but want to keep to themselves, or we haven't got around to asking them. Companies spend a fortune on market research to find out what people think about them and their products. You may think that a company should know everything about its own products, but most realise that 'the only reality is perception'. Companies also spend a fortune on consultancy, many to confirm what their own employees could have told them. Why?

> 'Oh wad some power the giftie gie us
> To see oursels as others see us!
> It wad fra monie and blunder free us
> An foolish notion'
>
> Robbie Burns

Many projects are subject to layers of third party assurance for the same reason.

But what about ourselves? Well, aren't we supposed to get feedback from our managers? How many managers loathe the annual ritual of giving feedback for fear of causing a scene, and often resort to selecting the middle performance marking and writing something mundane. Why? Because they assume that we don't know how we come over. And this is often the case. It is much better to get into the routine of seeking feedback at the end of each piece of work rather than waiting for the dreaded annual review.

I was fortunate enough to be in a large multinational that adopted 360 degree appraisals for senior staff. This is where you ask peers, subordinates, managers and customers to give feedback via a standard process/tool and the results are fed back in a structured form. The results can be most illuminating, especially if you treat the exercise as a development opportunity and choose people to respond that you have had misunderstandings with, rather than only people you get on with in order to engineer a flattering high mark. (Hence it is a bad idea to link 360 appraisals with performance pay, as it ceases to be a development tool, which was its original purpose.)

There are many other tools that can help us to understand ourselves which all have value, including: Myers-Briggs Type Indicator,[134] OPQ (occupational personality questionnaire), de Bono's Thinking Hats,[135] etc. There are also a number that are useful to understand our natural role in teams, including Belbin.[136]

When I was interviewed as a program manager for a Swiss airline company, part of the interview was with an occupational psychologist. (I was told that this was routine in Switzerland for senior posts, but maybe they just thought that I looked dodgy.) They ran a number of tests, and I agreed with the results of all of them. Most surprisingly, the handwriting expert was able to give a very detailed analysis of my inner workings that I agreed entirely with. Interestingly, I never went through any of these types of personality or behavioural tests when I went to high level clearance in the nuclear sector, let alone as a project manager.

3.5.2 Nature or nurture?

One large company sat me down with a Myers-Briggs Type Indicator (MBTI) as part of their selection process. When I told them my profile, as previously assessed, they replied, 'Good, you are through to the next stage then.' As they explained to me, a study had been done relating MBTI to PMs that had successfully delivered major projects, and said that eighty per cent of successful major projects were delivered by people with MBTI of 'X'. Since this was one combination from a possible 16, with a natural occurrence of only two per cent, it was quite compelling for them and they were shortlisting on this basis. At a conference in 2010 there was a panel discussion on behaviours for effective PMs and I related the story. At the end of the session the other party, program director for a large government department, revealed that she was also type 'X'. I commented on the coincidence to a colleague on the taxi ride back to the hotel, a director of another professional association. He replied that it was his profile too. For those who are familiar with MBTI, which profile do you think it may have been? Is there a unique profile for an effective PM?

When 'world class performance' for project management was introduced at one large corporation where I was a senior manager, delivery made a major improvement when we profiled our most successful PMs and shortlisted candidates with similar profiles. A lot of these candidates had no previous experience in projects, but the method aspects of PM were much easier to teach than the desired behaviours. Subsequent performance improved dramatically.

Years later, I jokingly asked an organisation specialising in soft skills for PMs for our money back when we had to let go one of our PMs that they had been coaching. They responded with a northern expression that, 'You can't polish a turd', apparently meaning that the person's core style and behaviours were diametrically opposed to being suitable to work with projects (or people). I think that the coaches were wrong, and the PM just had limited resources and tools at that time. This was not surprising, since his professional background was quite different from project management. I did not get the opportunity to test if NLP could help on that occasion, but I think it would have if the candidate accepted the approach.

3.5.3 Behaviours as meta-programs

But what does NLP have to contribute to all of these different types of assessment? Fundamentally, tests such as Myers-Briggs are assessing some groupings of behaviours/meta-programs. Over 60 meta-programs have been identified from composite behaviours. The basis of meta-programs was introduced in Section 2.8, but to recap a few points:

- Meta-programs are one of the sets of filters that we use to create our world-view and deeply affect how we interpret things, e.g. whether the glass is half empty or half full.
- They are systematic and habitual, not random.
- They can be context specific; that is, different in work or in the home environment.

Exercise 3.3: Meta-programs for project management

The following are a selection of the most relevant meta-programs to project management. Although shown in pairs, they are analogue rather than binary. Think about your work context and score yourself – do you sit at one end or nearer the middle? Remember, like MBTI, there is no right or wrong, just an understanding of your natural inclination. And unlike in the earlier story, it is possible to develop flexibility in your meta-programs if you choose to, as covered later.

Figure 3.6 Scoring your meta-programs

1	→ 10
Proactive Initiates action.	**Reactive** Analyses first then follows the lead from others.
Towards Focussed on goals. Motivated by achievement.	**Away from** Focuses on problems to be avoided.
Internal Has internal standards. Takes criticism as information only.	**External** Gets reference externally. Likes direction.
Match Notices points of similarity.	**Mismatch** Notices differences.
General Likes to take a 'helicopter view' and gets bored with detail.	**Specific** Likes to work with detailed information and examples.
Options Likes to generate choices. Good at developing alternatives.	**Procedures** Good at generating logical flows. Likes to have processes documented.
Associated Feelings and relationships are important.	**Dissociated** Detached from feelings. Works with information. Task oriented.
In time Lives in the moment. Creative but poor with deadlines.	**Through time** Good at keeping track of time and managing deadlines.
Self/Introvert Need to be alone to recharge batteries. Few relationships with deep connections. Interested in a few topics but to great detail.	**Other/Extrovert** Relaxes in the company of others. Has a lot of surface relationships. Knows about a lot of things, not in detail.
Sameness Likes things to be the same. Doesn't like surprises.	**Difference** Likes challenge. Looks for opportunities to try new things.

(Continued)

Figure 3.6 *(Continued)*

1 → 10

Independent Wants to work alone. Wants sole accountability.	**Cooperative** Wants to work as part of a team. Likes shared responsibility.
Person Oriented towards people and focuses on feelings and thoughts. People are the task.	**Thing** Focused on tasks, systems, ideas, tools. Getting the job done.

Exercise 3.4: Uses of different meta-programs

There is no 'best' option for a meta-program, but some options work better for a particular task than the alternative. For the above examples, think of a management situation, project phase, or discipline such as risk management where each of the options on the left might work better.

Now repeat for the options on the right.

So, you have worked out your natural bias for several important meta-programs, and also identified tasks where an opposite bias might be more effective. Now, what are you going to do to develop flexibility in behaviour?

3.5.4 Using knowledge of meta-programs

Having discerned what our preferred meta-programs are, which helps us to understand our likely behaviours under different situations, and what the alternatives are, we can use this information to develop more flexible behaviour (Section 3.11), or model excellent behaviours noted in others (Section 3.21).

Note also that we can usually recognise another person's meta-programs from signals in their language and behaviour. This helps us to frame our own language and behaviour in a more appropriate way for the recipient and aligned to their world-view, which significantly helps with rapport and communication. This aspect of meta-programs is covered in more detail under Section 3.15 on building rapport with stakeholders.

Aside from understanding our underlying meta-programs, however, we also need to be able to understand our emotional states, as this greatly influences our behaviour.

3.6 BE YOUR OWN COACH

It is expected in sports that you need a coach to achieve your potential, but it is relatively new to business, and usually confined to those in senior positions. Although PMs may have the future of the organisation in their hands, I have yet to meet one with a coach, though I am told that they exist. (I have had mentoring, and been a mentor, but that is something different.) But we can all be our own coach with the help of a few techniques and a bit of NLP.

3.6.1 From knowing to being

In Section 1.8 we talked about competences and becoming competent, and how this was achieved through a combination of knowledge, experience and ability. The figure below is a popular model of this process.

Figure 3.7 Towards unconscious competence

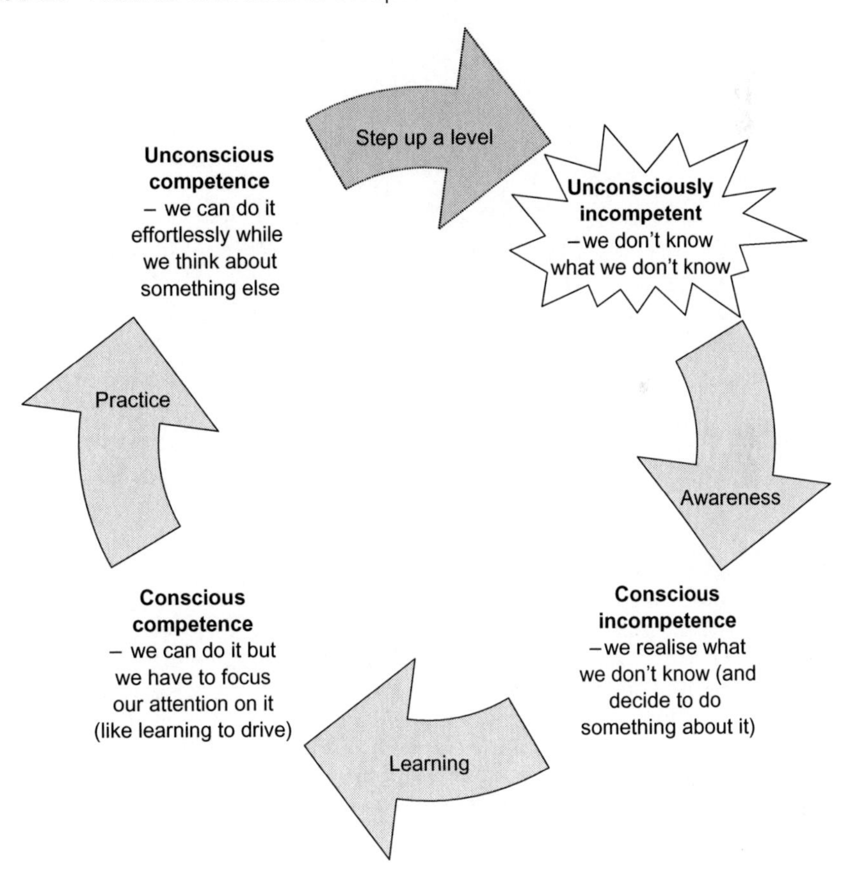

I have shown it as a cycle as, hopefully, like top tennis and golf players, we continue on the cycle until we reach out ultimate target.

A similar model to this, which I have seen promoted in recent years to assist in sales, suggests a progression from 'just do it', to 'being it'. I think it better represents the journey for PMs, from understanding, to practising, to feeling fully comfortable in the role.

Figure 3.8 Being there

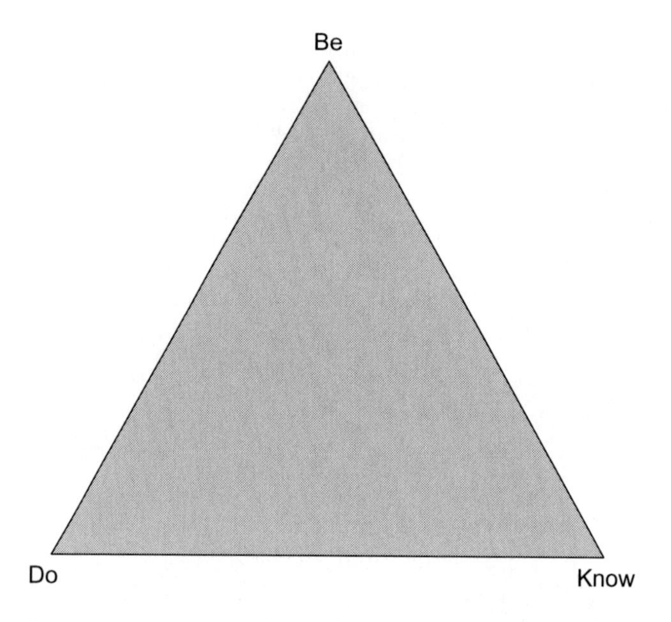

> 'We are what we repeatedly do. Excellence then, is not an act, but a habit.'
>
> Aristotle

3.6.2 What is your preferred style of learning?

The education system in the UK used to be geared to separating out those who learned from books and those who learned from doing. Education establishments are now better at taking into account that people have different learning styles, as credited to Honey and Mumford,[137] and they try to address all of these styles in the one environment. This learning preference has been termed a meta-program. If you have not experienced this yourself, does this account for your relative success or difficulty in learning to date? As a comparison, I have shown these styles alongside the main representational systems as introduced in Section 2.10.

Figure 3.9 Learning styles and preferred representational systems

Preferred learning style	Main representational system
Activists Like to be involved in activities Like to seek out new experiences Active supporters of change	**Kinaesthetic** Like doing physical things Use the language of doing
Reflectors Like to collect all the facts and look at things from all angles Risk averse	**Auditory** Like to hear and tell stories Listen to the sound of word Use words related to hearing
Theorists Logical and dispassionate Perfection not pragmatism	**Audio-digital** Led by a constant internal dialogue The language of logic
Pragmatists Full of ideas but little patience Happy to go with the first practical idea rather than search for the best	**Visual** Like to see things Like words relating to seeing things

Unless they have been trained and have developed flexibility, a trainer is likely to deliver in their own preferred learning style and preferred representational system. As a consequence, that can lose some of those students with whom they don't develop rapport and communicate with effectively.

Where do you fit in? When you are learning or self-coaching be sure to bear in mind your own preferences for learning style. As a leader and coach to others, of course, you should try to understand the learning styles and primary representational systems of team members that you are developing.

3.6.3 Compassionate coaching and the inner game

We sometimes make the mistake of thinking that the – sometimes harsh – inner voice is 'me'. It is not, though it is a part of us. We have the most effective learning machine ever developed between our ears, and yet when we try something new we tend to over-rationalise it. Our inner voice didn't teach us to crawl or walk, and certainly wasn't around to teach us to speak, so put it aside. Top athletes have learned 'the inner game' of practice without judgement.[138] This results in the ultimate experience of what has been referred to as 'flow', or 'up-time' in NLP speak.

As described in Section 2.6, the subconscious mind is what drives us. If you want to put an internal voice to good use then let it be 'your compassionate coach',[139] and be gentle and encouraging with yourself. Know and repeat your goals. The more solid they are and the more you can visualise them and experience them with all your senses, then the stronger will be the compulsion of you subconscious mind to attain them. (Visualisation techniques and the use of mantras can be very effective but are beyond the scope of this book.)

Exercise 3.5: Conquering negative language

Look at the table below. Do you recognise some of the negative words there? Negativity puts us in unresourceful states and holds us back, and that affects both you, and the people that you influence. It is easier to start with what we write, so check what you put down on paper/screen and edit out that negativity. Now that it is in your conscious mind, catch yourself if you use a negative word and correct it. It will start to affect your outlook and put you in a more resourceful state. Others will also start to see you as a much more positive and competent person and have more trust in you.

Figure 3.10 Using positive language

Negative language	Positive language
Can't	Working out how to
Difficult	Stretching
Problem	Challenge
Have to	Want to
Failure	Learning
Complaint	Feedback

Next time you catch yourself or one of your team saying something like, 'We can't get the supplier to deliver on time', use the rephrase, 'We are working with the supplier to deliver on time'. We are not talking about putting a positive spin on things here – it may sound like just words but it will frame how you behave and what you do subsequently. Similarly, lessons learned are not about looking at what went wrong and attributing blame as we see on a TV episode like *The Apprentice*, but a time of reflection on how we will do better next time.

What are your 'favourite' negative words? Add them in the space in the table. What would be a more positive way of expressing them?

Note the forward for this book penned by Mike Nichols. Mike refuses to acknowledge any negative language or talk of failure in whatever he says or writes. To my mind this is one reason why his company has been so successful, for example being a family business that leads on a mega project like Crossrail in London and also operates globally. It is also a reason why he is energising to be around and often picked to chair board meetings.

Exercise 3.6: Taking control of your inner critic using sub-modalities

Does a voice in your head sometimes hold you back? Don't worry, it is part of the human condition. As you have heard, with NLP everything that we experience is subject to the way our brains code it. Making subtle changes to the language of our code can cure people from severe phobias, and we can use the same technique to quieten our inner force if it misbehaves. Here we will be making use of sub-modalities, as described and illustrated in Section 2.12.

1. Call up that negative inner voice.
2. What does it sound like? Anyone's voice that you recognise? What are the sub-modalities (volume, pitch, near or far)?
3. If you can locate it, e.g. on your right ear or behind you, then move it to the opposite place.
4. Turn down the volume.
5. Change the pitch.
6. How about giving it a new character? Daffy Duck?
7. Now, let it say some stupid negative thoughts, but in that stupid little voice.
8. Now, that's easier to ignore, isn't it?
9. Imagine the future where you are going to do something where the voice used to hold you back. Now see yourself successfully doing it, with that funny little voice keeping you amused.

That was easy, wasn't it?

3.6.4 The virtual mentor – imaginary friends for grown ups

Before the 're-engineering of corporations',[140] there used to be multiple tiers of managers, and people stayed in their jobs for a long time. Nowadays, a few years in a job seems to be a long time, and many people freelance. Hence we have fewer opportunities to 'learn on the job' through informal mentoring. I would strongly advise you to find mentors for all aspects of your life wherever you can. Sometimes you may really wish that you had one there and then. Well, with a bit of imagination you can. I have a collection of virtual mentors that I use in different kinds of environment. I am using Genghis Khan a lot less than I used to, and relying more on Mahatma Gandhi to do things a bit more elegantly. I think of it as a metaphor to put a bit of distance between me and the situation to allow me to be more creative (rather like 'as if' reframing). For this exercise imagine a mentor called 'John' – perhaps someone that you have encountered and admired in your career.

Exercise 3.7: The virtual mentor

1. When you find yourself in a situation where you feel you need more resources, ask 'John' to come and help you.
2. Imagine John next to you and get into his character.

3. Ask him what he thinks about the situation and imagine what he would say.
4. Ask him for some options.
5. Have a think about them – do any sound like they might be promising?
6. Ask for some tips on what to look out for.
7. Note down a plan and the first steps.
8. Thank John and ask him to look over your shoulder until you are comfortable and back on track.
9. Remember, John and his friends are there whenever you need them.

3.6.5 Action learning sets and communities of practice

Action learning is essentially where you agree a common development aim as a group and agree to work on it individually and share experiences.[141] It also acts as a support group. I have been involved in action learning sets as a senior manger, but have not yet come across these in project management. A related principle is that of communities of practice,[142] which are covered in the APM's Body of Knowledge for the first time in the 6th Edition. A number of large organisations are now setting up PM communities of practice to share resources and support. In large government departments I found the take-up of these to be poor. Without the opportunity of doing a proper investigation myself, I assigned this low take-up to be down to lack of trust, in that the organisations were relatively new to project management and the groups were too large for people to be comfortable to share their problems and lack of knowledge. Instead, individual PMs relied on support from external contractor PMs and some limited mentoring. A focus on sharing successes rather than failures, however small, could have proved more motivational. What do you think, do we learn from success or failure?

I have set up an online community as part of this endeavour to discuss application of NLP to project management, which you can access via the supporting website www.nlp4pm.com.

3.7 STATE MANAGEMENT

'A man's greatest battles are the ones he fights with himself'
Ben Okri (Nigerian poet)

State management is called self management under emotional intelligence (EI) frameworks. It is defined under EI as, 'The ability to remain in control despite our emotional state.' In the world of NLP, however, we prefer to refer to it as, 'The ability to control our emotions so that they do not control us.' The difference is that in NLP we choose to change our state once we have become aware of it being detrimental to desired outcome, rather than trying to control our anger, for example.

> 'Anyone can become angry – that is easy. But to be angry with the right person, to the right degree, at the right time, for the right purpose, and in the right way – that is not easy'
>
> Aristotle, The Nicomachean Ethics

3.7.1 The emotional hijack

Projects can be like pressure cookers and bring out the best and worst in us. Have you ever been emotionally hijacked, or sent an email response in anger only to regret it on the way home? We naturally resort to primitive neurological systems under stress. When we are scared we tend to be overly pessimistic and risk averse, which limits opportunity and future benefit. As many in the banking fraternity now realise, when we are optimistic we can also make poor decisions by disregarding risk. Wouldn't it be great to be able to control our emotions so that they didn't control us?

In projects we live in a space between different and often conflicting world-views, and people, often accidentally, press our 'hot buttons'/emotional triggers. What separates us out as high performing individuals is what we do next. Our subsequent actions are largely determined by the context that we put the event in and how we control our emotional state.

> I was employed as program director for an IT-enabled transformation project in an organisation that was going through turmoil after a scathing audit report. Most of the organisation's leadership had been removed and were in the process of being replaced. Morale was as low as I have seen in an organisation. To cap it all, the head of IT had been suspended for bullying, and the impact was obvious on the behaviour of the staff, who were reacting from a place of fear and anger rather than logic. I was asked to take charge of the IT function as the deputies were seen as 'uncooperative' with the new management. Fortunately, I had been offering some out of hours counselling to individuals in the organisation and, after one of the deputies had another brutal run-in with the new director, I managed to persuade him to take some coaching. When we ran though a standard approach of asking, 'Is your behaviour having the desired effect, or would you like to start doing something that does?', we got some movement. The angry reactions, rather than protecting his department, were actually putting it in peril of being downsized and outsourced. His retort of, 'It's all right for you, you don't get angry' was met with my response of 'I can show you anger if you want, but only in a situation where it gets results'. We then agreed behaviours that were supportive of his desired outcome of protecting the department and its services, and at the same time his job. We used some of the techniques described below. At the same time I spoke to his director, saying that I was doing some counselling with X and he would now start to see some fundamental changes in his behaviour, including more cooperation. (You may recognise this as being suggestion.)
>
> At future meetings X would smile as he thought about nice things and, rather than argue with the director, would reply with the likes of, 'Thank you for pointing

that out. Good point. We will have a look at that and get a short report back to you before our next meeting.' A virtuous circle ensued, with lack of anger enabling a more cooperative relationship. X kept his job, the director got his results, and I got satisfaction from seeing someone being in control of themselves rather than reacting from primordial reflex. No one wants to follow a leader who is not in control of themselves. Isn't it good to be able to choose?

'Don't panic'

Douglas Adams[143]

We go through most of our days 'too busy' or too numb to be in tune with our own emotions. Fortunately, emotions have a physical manifestation in our bodies that can help us to recognise those emotions in ourselves and others. The key to successful interaction with others is to become more aware of the state you are in and step out of it if it is un-resourceful. You will make good choices and decisions when you are in a resourceful state (e.g. confident), but more likely to make poor choices and decisions when you are in an un-resourceful state (e.g. angry, upset, irritated, frustrated, fearful, depressed). A resourceful state is not the same as being dissociated, though that is another useful tool if not overdone.

Figure 3.11 Being in control is about choice, not power

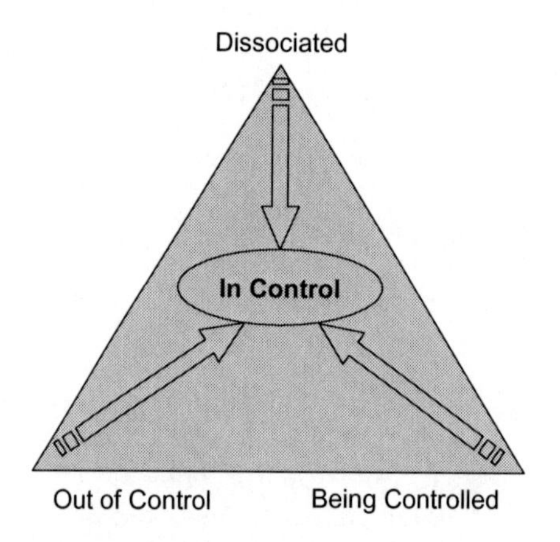

Exercise 3.8: Motion is emotion

This exercise demonstrates the principle of our mood manifesting itself in our physiology.

1 Remember a sad time from recent events that you can associate with. Can you feel it as if it is happening now?

2 Now accentuate the physiology. Stoop your shoulders more. Crumple your chest. Let your mouth curl down more. Let your head drop down until your chin touches your chest. Sink into your seat. How sad does that feel?

3 Now try to remember a happy recent event, but try to keep the same physiology. Go on, keep trying.

What happened? Did you manage to feel happy? If so, you would have had to have changed your physiology. Hence, to manage your state, manage your physiology first.

Exercise 3.9: Manifesting resourceful physiology

Now try the opposite experience, i.e. imagine a happy time. What is the physiology you need to accentuate for Step 2? Remember it (or even anchor it, as described in Section 2.13). And do it more often, especially when you are feeling like you did in the previous exercise but don't want to any more. (There is more under Section 3.9 on presenting yourself.)

Exercise 3.10: The circle of excellence

In this exercise we are going to be using an NLP technique known as 'The circle of excellence.' It will use sub-modalities (Section 2.12), anchors (Section 2.13), and future pacing (Section 2.16).

1. Identify what would be a useful resource as the opposite to your particular un-resourceful state (for example, if you tend to react angrily to a supplier, you might want the feeling of calm).
2. Imagine a spot in front of you.
   a. Step into that spot and think about a time when you have had 'X' resource (e.g. calm, confident).
   b. When you feel really associated into that feeling, anchor yourself by squeezing together your thumb and forefinger (for example).
3. Step out of the spot.
4. Repeat the process to add any other resource states that might be useful to manage your state by stepping onto the spot each time, accessing the resourceful state, anchoring it in exactly the same way, then stepping out of it. Repeat with as many resourceful states as you can think of (as more resources makes it more potent).
5. Finally, step out of the spot and imagine a situation in the future where you might need to manage your state and access the resourceful state. When you think about that situation and feel yourself becoming un-resourceful, fire your anchor and notice what happens. Your state will shift. (Go back and reinforce

the anchors if necessary.) You are now equipped with an anchor that you can use any time, any place to help you manage your state from an un-resourceful one into a more resourceful one. (This step is known as future pacing, i.e. imagining some future event and putting it to an imaginary test.)

Any time that you think that it would be useful to have those resources, fire your anchor by squeezing your thumb and finger together (assuming that this was your anchor for this state). The more you practise using it, the stronger the anchor and the trigger will become. It can also kick start a positive/empowering belief cycle.

Exercise 3.11: Exploring state management

1. Pick two opposite states and notice what they are and what situations or people tend to cause them.
   a. Pick one un-resourceful state that you often find yourself in that you wish you could change. For example, if a particular person or situation often causes you to be stressed/sulky.
   b. Think of that person or situation and notice the image, sound and sensations associated with that state.
   c. Then think of the opposite, resourceful state (in this case calmness or being upbeat) and access that state by thinking of a person or situation that often makes you feel that way and notice the image, sound and sensations associated with it.
2. Compare and contrast the two states.
3. What are the differences?
4. How do the different states affect the way you feel and act? (Refer back to the belief cycle in section 3.4)?

Exercise 3.12: Experiment with moods

Think of a situation that would normally get you stressed, e.g. reporting to your project sponsor, but this time you are going to get yourself into the opposite state and notice what is different. See how it affects your perception of the experience (again referring to the belief cycle). For example, you can replace the relaxation state with a stressful state and observe your feelings and inner perception of the experience.

As you have seen, your mental state affects the way you behave, as well as the way you are perceived, and it is worth investing the effort up-front to manage your state to achieve a better outcome.

From now on, the phrase *'look at the state you are in'* should take on a whole new meaning.

3.8 HANDLING STRESS

> 'How much pain have they cost us, the evils which have never happened'
> Thomas Jefferson

Projects can be very tough environments, especially when things do not run to plan or in turnaround situations, and there is a strong correlation between mental toughness, or resilience, and management seniority. The good news, however, is that NLP means that you can deal with the stress at source rather than trying to develop a thick skin, though it can help you to do that too. Indeed, there are popular authors on NLP with whole books on the subject of controlling stress.[144]

3.8.1 About stress, triggers and effects

In small doses, stress provides a useful stimulus. Stress is a natural response built in humans as a 'flight or fight' response to danger. It increases the heart rate to pump blood to the limbs so that we can either stay to fight or run away quickly. In today's society we often involuntarily invoke this 'flight or fight' mode in response to social situations. The problem is that, unlike the historic dangers that the response evolved to meet, these social situations can be prolonged and ongoing. For projects, and other time pressured jobs, the result can be chronic stress, which results in strain, i.e. where we do not return to our original state after prolonged and cumulative stimulus. This is sometimes referred to as burn-out. Stress and burn-out have been cited as the principle health concerns of project managers.

Long before burn-out occurs, primitive responses triggered by stress hormones result in many decisions being routed to the primordial part of our brain, the part dominated by fight and flight, rather than the higher functions more suited to social interaction. It focuses our senses on a single issue facing us, to the detriment of wider social interactions.

I have often felt stressed in certain situations, and sometimes in anticipation of them, such as before difficult meetings with suppliers or clients, before presentations, etc. Sometimes our response can be so extreme that it is called 'emotional hijacking', where our mental faculties are not in control of the situation but we are reacting to our hormones. This has occurred to me where my values and beliefs have been transgressed. This usually happens unintentionally, as others have different values and beliefs and are not cognisant of ours. (In sport particularly, some individuals specialise in pressing these 'hot buttons' in others to get them to react in an inappropriate way and lose their focus or even get sent off the pitch by the referee.)

3.8.2 Working stress response

NLP regards response to stress as a meta-program. People with a 'feeling' pattern respond to stress at work by going into their emotions and then getting stuck there, making it difficult for them to function normally. At the opposite extreme, people with a 'thinking' style do not have a strong emotional response to stressful situations. Great for leadership, you may think, but unfortunately this means that they are not good at empathising either. These two extremes account for perhaps a fifth of the working population each, with the majority being in the continuum between and having some natural ability to choose whether to empathise or stay detached as the situation dictates. (Note the similarity to the feeling/thinking category in Myers-Briggs Type Indicators).

3.8.3 Reframing stressful situations

The good news is that **stress is triggered by the *thought* of a situation, not by the situation itself**. The brain processes these thoughts, equates the stimulus and context as danger, and triggers the stress response. Once the threat passes you tell yourself that you're safe and in response to these new thoughts, your body returns to its natural state of balance. We can use NLP to reframe the context and also manage our state so that we either avoid triggering stress or make it pass quickly.

Given that the bulk of projects are probably delivered later than the original estimate, one of the most stressful constraints on project managers is time, especially when faced with complex interdependencies. Not only can we not control time, but people also have different attitudes to time, with only a few focussing on the now and most living in the past and future. But can we reframe time? Well, we can reframe our attitude to it. I used to think of time on a project as being like an egg timer, filled with sand that was running out. When a precious resource is 'running out' it is bound to cause stress. But time will never run out – it is abundant and infinite.

In planning we are only dealing with an abstract mathematical summation of third party estimates based on imperfect data. By law of averages, the estimate should be under as many times as it is over, and that is making the risky assumption that the estimate was not unduly influenced to be on the short side. Ideally, we will have used three-point estimates (duration that activity will definitely be complete, likely to be complete, and possibly be complete – taking into account the optimists, pessimists and pragmatists). What we can do is track progress against assumptions, monitor risks that may affect planned duration, and address mitigating actions for issues that are impacting the plan. I have yet to see a project manager getting stressed over a risk log, but maybe I haven't seen enough projects yet. Do not mistake this for meaning that I think that time is unimportant, just that stressing about it does not lead to a resourceful state, and reviewing risk and issues logs is likely to be more beneficial to the completion date than looking at a stopwatch.

3.8.4 Removing the source of stress

> 'If you are distressed by anything external, the pain is not due to the thing itself, but your estimate of it; and this is your power to revoke at any moment'
>
> Marcus Aurelius

In NLP we say that every action, emotion and behaviour has a positive intent, no matter how bad the actual consequence.

In my early career I would sometimes get stressed about project boards to the point where I felt unwell. When I 'had a chat with myself', I realised that I was coming from a place of fear as I was not in control of the board and hated surprises. I recognised that this feeling had started after I had been 'ambushed' at one board by someone with a hidden agenda. Instead of gritting my teeth and continuing as I had done, I started to visit key stakeholders ahead of board meetings to see what issues might come up and get their views on them. As a civil servant at this time, like in the armed forces, it was not usual to arrange meetings with people who were senior to you unless it was via your boss at their grade. Individuals turned out to be quite welcoming of chats outside the floodlights, and said things that they would not have at minuted meetings. This gave me the confidence to relax more at the actual project boards and operate from a state of resourcefulness. Fortunately, it got me into the excellent practice of active stakeholder management, which was not widespread at that time.

Exercise 3.13: Look for the positive intent of the emotion

1. Think about the thing that you are feeling stressed about. Close your eyes and associate with the feeling.
2. What are the feelings, sounds and images attached to this stress response?
3. Ask yourself: 'What is the positive intention of this worry? What does it give me?'
4. Notice what answers come to mind and keep asking this question until you have at least three. You may be surprised at some of the answers.
5. Now, ask the creative part of your brain to come up with at least three new ways of achieving the same positive intent as your stressful behaviour.
6. Check with yourself that you are happy with these new ways to stress.
7. Visualise how it will feel to do those new behaviours instead of stressing out in the future.
8. Keep doing this until it feels like a natural response.

3.8.5 Use of dissociation

One of the recognised NLP meta-programs is association/dissociation. When associated, we are in touch with our feelings and this is a very resourceful state for working with people. It is also the state most sensitive to stress. Conversely, the dissociated state is useful in potentially stressful situations. The real skill is being able to switch between the two according to context.

In Section 3.5 on self awareness we discussed the need to be in tune with our emotions in order to achieve greater self awareness, and the fact that people can often be very dissociated from their feelings. They are not particularly happy or sad but just go about their allocated tasks much like an automaton. (Strangely, some people resort to various drugs to help achieve this unresourceful state. TV works for many.) Often it is the result of some trauma or depressing event in the past, but it becomes a way of life. People in this state are easy to spot for NLP practitioners as their eye movements are very limited and they often adopt a slightly off-centre, out of focus look into the middle distance, making it almost impossible to determine visual sensory information and queues from their body language.

Figure 3.12 The dissociated mental state

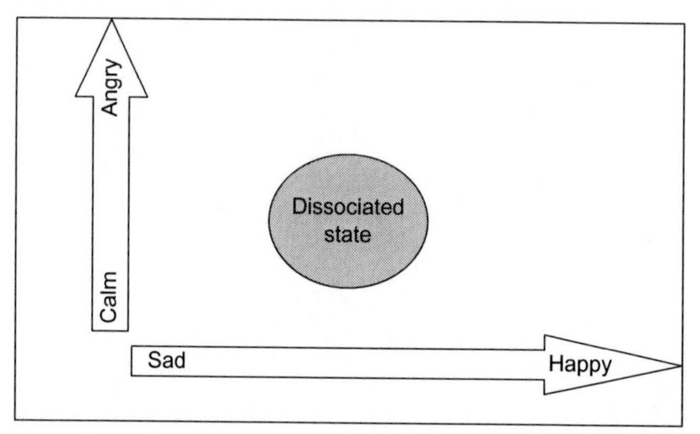

On the other hand, being able to dissociate from events in a controlled way is a very powerful technique. In another arena where mental control and calmness can be the difference on the podium, the world champion snooker player Jimmy White is attributed with the quote: 'Play like it means nothing when you know that it means everything.' (He won the World Cup three times with England and scored the maximum possible break of 147 points at the World Championship.) The skill is being able to switch in and out of this state, and not living your life in it.

Exercise 3.14: Dissociating from stressful situations

This technique uses sub-modalities to affect our perception of events. (Note that this exercise is very similar to effective cures for phobias.)

1. Think of a situation that previously made you feel stressed and notice the pictures, sounds and feelings associated with the situation.
2. Imagine stepping out of the picture and sending it, with its associated sounds and feelings, way off into the distance and watching it play out on a cinema screen far away.
3. Make the picture black and white, make it smaller and smaller and switch off any sounds and feelings.
4. While you're looking at the picture in the distance, notice if there are any new insights. There may not be, but if there are then make a note if they have given you a new or different perspective on the situation.
5. Keep sending the cinema screen further and further away (ensuring there are no sounds or feelings there and that you are looking at yourself in the black and white picture) until you have no emotional response when watching the picture.

6. Think about a similar situation in the future that may have previously caused you to feel stressed and notice how you feel now. You should be feeling calm. If you don't then repeat the exercise until you do feel calm. Alternatively, run the 'movie' backwards and add some 'keystone cops' music alongside it.

3.8.6 The mind body connection and rapport with self

'We never obtain peace in the outer world until we make peace with ourselves'
Dalai Lama

You may be one of the lucky ones that always seem to be in harmony with yourself. Some describe it as being 'grounded' or 'centred'. For the rest of us, there is usually some measure of internal conflict going on. This can manifest itself in self sabotage, and in the extreme can progress through bouts of ill health, depression, stress-related illness and worse. Some of us who work with NLP and health issues believe that this is because the conscious and unconscious mind fall out of rapport, and communication between the two breaks down.

The role of PM is not for everyone. It is not for the shrinking violet or thin skinned amongst us. I myself had bouts of internal conflict when I was managing corporate downsizing projects. I have worked with individuals where their identity and behaviours were clearly in conflict with their role as a PM. One of them wanted the role of PM, which was seen as a fast track route to promotion, but she actually liked working independently rather than in cooperation or even proximity (this has an associated meta-program that is covered in Section 3.19 on 'motivating the team'). She became a recluse, emailing instructions to the people sitting across from her. Her mood and health suffered, as did that of her team. While she tried to battle on through pure resilience, the end result was inevitable and she left the project for another role.

Exercise 3.15: Handling stress in the moment

1. **Breathe slower and deeper:** usually we breathe shallowly in the top of our lungs when we feel stressed (especially if we are visually oriented). Build up of carbon dioxide in the lungs makes the heart race faster and can bring on a sense of panic without even trying. One of the first things to do, therefore, is to slow down your breathing by dropping your breathing all the way down into your diaphragm, using the whole of the lungs to breathe. (For extreme panic attacks, sufferers are advised to breathe into a paper bag – try this to begin with if you like to get the hang of it, but probably best not to do it in public, as the image of a PM with a panic attack does not foster confidence.) Keep doing this until your breathing is deep and slow.
2. **Anchor calm state:** Repeat the 'circle of excellence' exercise (Exercise 3.10 in Section 3.7) but use a different place to anchor states of calmness and add anything else that you think would be an antidote to your stressed state.

Exercise 3.16: Meditation and self hypnosis

'Tension is who you think you should be. Relaxation is who you are'

Chinese proverb

Invest in a calming hypnosis track to listen to before you go to sleep and listen to it regularly. (I have several on my iPod and listen to them when I am travelling on the train to meetings.) Paul McKenna has a hypnosis tape dedicated to controlling stress that accompanies his book of the same name.

Exercise 3.17: Get the juices flowing

'Lack of activity destroys the good condition of every human being, while movement and methodical physical exercise save it and preserve it'

Plato

'Motion is emotion', as NLP guru Anthony Robbins says;[145] that is, our physiology affects our mental state. Hence, to change your mental state over time, make big changes to your physiology, e.g. through exercise. Make time in your life for regular exercise that gets your heart pumping and lungs breathing more deeply.

- It will act as a 'pattern interrupt' technique to break long lasting cycles of negative thoughts and emotions.
- It will keep you healthy (which can be a problem in relatively sedate office environments).
- It will stimulate your hormones in a natural cycle, i.e. stimulants and then relaxants, rather than letting your body marinade in stress hormones topped up with artificial stimulants.
- The exercise itself will give you a dose of endorphins as a reward, which will counteract stress hormones.

3.8.7 Avoid passing stress on to others

People who run the 'away from' meta-program for motivation often feel that they need stress around deadlines to motivate themselves. At the extreme, some of these are the people who 'heroically' manage to complete things at the last minute, from homework as a child to deliverables on major projects. The PM, often being more resilient, may cope with this unnecessary stress, but the team are likely to suffer. As the T-shirt says, 'I don't suffer from stress, I am just a carrier.' In my view, panic around deadlines is poor project management and should be rectified by better planning and better self management. If you feel that you need the pressure of deadlines to be motivated then make sure that your plan has plenty of intermediate deliverables and milestones so that pressure is not all loaded onto the back end of the project when there is no contingency to use.

As managers, it is our professional duty to make sure that our staff return home as they left it, and not suffering from stress-related illness as a result of our style or failure to manage the work environment. Regulation around health and safety at work is also coming into play now and classifying avoidable stress-related illness as an industrial injury. Use the techniques above to keep your team functional as well as yourself.

A common reason for people getting stressed is that they are being aggressive or passive rather than assertive. We need to develop our assertive behaviour to avoid stressing ourselves and others (see section 3.10).

3.9 PRESENTING YOURSELF

'Presence'
1. The state or fact of being present
2. The impressive manner or appearance of a person

Oxford English Dictionary

The term presenting yourself implies being 'present'; this means more than physically being somewhere, but rather having 'presence'. Under emotional intelligence frameworks it is classed under the grouping of self awareness as 'self confidence'.

3.9.1 Being the professional

Aspiring professionals realise that every time they interact with others they have the opportunity of projecting a positive image, or diminishing it. Hence they make efforts to demonstrate in all of their communications a person who is likeable, respectful, positive, committed and professional.[146] They understand that they are always on show and behave accordingly.

For project managers this means that not only do you have to know the technical stuff and do the right things, but people have to believe that you are a project manager. When you hear a sponsor dismissing someone saying 'he is not a real project manager', they are not likely to be talking about the quality of their Gantt charts.

3.9.2 Achieving congruence in word and deed

Congruent: in agreement or harmony.

Oxford English Dictionary

One of the NLP presuppositions is, 'The meaning of the communication is the response that you get', i.e. you are responsible for ensuring that meaning has been understood. Studies have shown that the words we use account for less than ten per cent of the message that we deliver.[147] The tone alone counts for far more, while body language accounts for over half of the message *as received*. Saying, 'I'm not angry' through gritted teeth is not congruent behaviour.

Here are some tips for aligning words, voice and body language:

Figure 3.13 Congruence in words, voice and body language

Body language	Voice	Words
• Stand/sit straight with shoulders back • Engage your core muscles (if standing, stand feet hip width apart with weight evenly spread between both legs (i.e. no leaning) • Maintain appropriate eye contact (varies between cultures) • Dress appropriate to the situation • Move towards people (but don't get too close and cause discomfort) • Avoid fidgeting and tapping	• Steady • Paced • Fluid • Audible • Avoid 'ums', 'errs', 'you know', etc. – slow or pause instead	• Simple • Never use jargon • Avoid abbreviations • Match key words to recipients vocabulary where practical • No swearing

It's not that you have to do these things all the time, just when you need to deliver important messages or when you need to convince people of your authority. The more you practise, however, the more natural it will feel and the less you will have to think about it.

3.9.3 Self-confidence and feeling good about yourself

> 'If you think you can do a thing or think you can't do a thing, you're right'
>
> Henry Ford

One of the traits of 'the human condition' is that we lack confidence in some situations. As seen in the belief cycle, the behaviour is self fulfilling. But no one wants to follow a leader who lacks confidence in themselves. So how to appear confident even if you don't feel it inside? Don't worry, NLP can help by using change techniques based on the way we code beliefs. Revisit 'Beliefs' and 'Belief change' in Sections 2.7 and 3.4.

The way we view or frame a situation also affects the way we feel, which in turn will affect the way we behave. Look at the table below. Keep yourself in the outcome frame to make the most of your internal resources and look confident.

The 'circle of excellence' technique in section 3.7 can also be used to 'anchor' confident states.

Figure 3.14 Feelings associated with Blame and Outcome Frames

Blame frame	Outcome frame
Stagnant	Moving forward
Limiting	Choice/opportunities/possibilities feels
Frustrating	Freeing
Negative	Positive
Disempowering	Empowering
Pessimistic	Optimistic

3.10 BEING ASSERTIVE WHILE AVOIDING CONFLICT

> 'In difficult and desperate cases, the boldest counsels are the safest'
> Titus Livius (59 BC–17 AD)

There is a large body of work on assertiveness that I will not reproduce here,[148] but the basic process and skills can be easily covered with an NLP approach. The linguistic part of NLP means that we know how to use precise language, avoid 'mind reading' other people's intent, and avoid meta-model distortions such as gross exaggeration. Using these techniques we can build confidence so that we tackle situations early and head-on by practising assertive behaviours.

3.10.1 Finding the sweet spot between submissive and aggressive behaviour

Submissive behaviour is appealing because it seems to avoid conflict. Being submissive, however, usually builds up with bad consequences. Similarly, being aggressive will have that effect blow up in your face one day. People who are overtly aggressive can become submissive and compliant after a certain amount of stress. Assert early before you get angry, as anger starts to pass command from the higher brain functions to the primitive brain functions and our abilities with language start to diminish. Of course, if you set and communicated your boundaries in the first place then there wouldn't be the need to assert yourself so often.

> In my early career, I would become quite aggressive when challenged, though I often felt bad about it afterwards, especially as 'good will' vanished and some tasks became onerous in terms of monitoring and control. After one clash with a newly appointed superior we rightly had our heads banged together by a director. I licked

my wounds and bit my tongue in future meetings, which allowed my protagonist to reign free. My resentment built up until I felt like I would explode while we sat in project meetings together. I didn't explode, but I was eventually stretchered off site in an ambulance with a stress-related illness. As I lay on my back in a hospital bed I had time to reflect. Although I was not NLP trained at the time, I found the resources and model that I needed within me. From my martial arts training we had the motto, 'The samurai remains outside the battle'. Rather than meaning that they led from the back, this refers to attaining a state of total unemotional awareness, i.e. without anger or fear. From then on I took pride in never losing my temper at work and also never backing down from any situation. I reframed the situation from being some personal conflict to being just a job that I was being paid to do.

Figure 3.15 The submissive, assertive, aggressive continuum

Submissive	Assertive	Aggressive
→		←

I like this continuum model of assertiveness:

- Submissive behaviour is about ensuring everyone else's thoughts/feelings/ rights etc. are taken into consideration. 'Don't worry about me.'
- Aggressive behaviour is about ensuring your own thoughts/feelings/rights etc. are taken into consideration. 'Forget everyone else.'
- Assertive behaviour is about ensuring your own and the other person's thoughts, feelings and rights are taken into consideration – part of what NLP considers as the 'ecology' of the situation.

3.10.2 Beliefs

'He who finds Fortune on his side should go briskly ahead,
for she is wont to favour the bold'

Baltasar Gracian

We all carry around certain beliefs about appropriate behaviour that limit our repertoire. In some cultures, organisational as well as national, even assertiveness is frowned upon, especially where rigid hierarchies are in force. Let's tackle a number of general beliefs that many of us carry around with us:

- Despite appearances, none of us like confrontation. By the time we feel we have no other option, however, we are usually so angry that we overreact and end up regretting it and having to sweep up the damage.
- Mostly we don't like to hurt other people's feelings, and we go to great lengths to avoid the possibility of upsetting people.

- We make the assumption that we won't get what we want by asking for it directly. Instead we often assume that we have to be Machiavellian and use subterfuge. In fact, you will get more respect stating expectations clearly up-front.

In terms of beliefs around your role as a PM in relation to asserting yourself, these are some that came up in a workshop with a major consultancy:

- I think I know but I'm not sure.
- It's not my place to say/do that.
- I'm *only* a grade X.
- I'm not really part of their team.
- I can't challenge clients.
- I can't challenge more senior members of staff.
- Someone else will already have thought of this and I will sound ignorant.

If you are carrying around beliefs like these then it is unlikely that you will assert yourself. Therefore, you can either change these beliefs (as in Section 3.4) or you can act 'as if' you are assertive by following the models below.

> 'When a resolute young fellow steps up to that great bully, "the world", and takes him boldly by the beard, he is often surprised to find it comes off in his hand, and that it was only tied on to scare away the timid adventurers'
>
> Ralph Waldo Emerson

3.10.3 Assertiveness models

> 'Most of our obstacles would melt away if, instead of cowering before them, we should make up our minds to walk boldly through them'
>
> Orison Swett Marden

Some assertiveness models don't take into account the thoughts and feelings of the other person and border on aggressive behaviour in my opinion.[149] Steps would be:

1. factual description of behaviour you want changed;
2. disclosure of how the behaviour makes you feel;
3. description of tangible effect on you;
4. (description of behaviour that you want to see instead).

An NLP model, taking into account the thoughts and feelings of all parties, would be:

1. Find out what the other person's thoughts about the situation are; for example, 'I have noticed that you don't submit your project report on time. Is there any reason for this?' This is about listening to their side of the story.

2. Listen and empathise – 'I understand that (repeat their key words to show understanding).' Then say 'I *feel* (because no one can disagree with what you feel) annoyed because it creates extra work for me.' This is about you putting your side of the story forward.
3. What next: 'From now on, I would like you to hand in your project report on time.' Or you can ask them to 'decide what they can do to ensure that they hand in their project report in on time'. It depends what is most appropriate to the situation.

This model needs lots of practice. Submissive and aggressive behaviours are primitive and automatic, which is why we can demonstrate them even as children, whereas assertiveness doesn't come naturally and has to be learned. I had to try the structure out many times at home before I got the hang of it at all, but found that it reduced needless arguments. Of course, when something touches our 'hot buttons' and challenges our values, the natural reaction is to react from the primitive centre of the brain. Practice makes those incidents less frequent. Try it in everyday life before you try it out on your project sponsor at a project board.

Figure 3.16 Do's and don'ts in assertive behaviour

Do	Do not
• Assert yourself on the real issue, not the symptoms. For example, rather than pick someone up on being late for meetings, if you actually feel someone is not respecting your authority then deal with that. You must, of course, give factual evidence of the behaviour (being late) that causes you to feel that they don't respect you rather than assuming it was their intent. • Separate the behaviour from the person. • Write down what you intend to say and check it. Like most things in projects, it's more difficult to recover from a bad start than to do a bit of preparation. • Pick your place and time. Although you may like an audience, if you cause the other person to lose face then they will not forgive you. Ever.	• Do not let small issues build up into big ones. • Do not try to force your values onto someone else, e.g. 'It is *wrong* to...' • Do not assume that someone is 'bad' because they do something that doesn't match your values. If you treat the other person with respect you are much likelier to get a positive result with the minimum of defensive behaviour. • Do not assume other people's motives as you are probably not a mind reader and hence are likely to be wrong. • Do not 'wait for the right time'. Arrange it and do it. • Do not use code or 'think' that people got the message – be explicit. • Do not exaggerate (e.g. 'every time'). • Do not use sarcasm, blame, or put down – you may feel smart but they will react badly. • Do not hang around afterwards or ask them to go for a drink. Move on.

(Continued)

Figure 3.16 *(Continued)*

Do	Do not
• Use assertive body language, i.e. o face them square on, but avoid looking aggressive; o maintain eye contact, but don't try to stare them down; o breathe from your diaphragm to enable you to speak with a clear voice in mid-tone. • Pick your battles wisely.	• Do not feel responsible for the other person's reactions. Their reaction is their choice. • Remove aggression from your tone – easier done by tackling things before there is too much pent up emotion.

'Be bold and mighty powers will come to your aid'
Basil King

3.11 DEVELOPING FLEXIBILITY IN APPROACH AND STYLE

'Insanity is continuing to do the same thing and expecting to get a different result'
Albert Einstein

One of the presuppositions of NLP, based on the field of cybernetics, is 'The person with the most flexibility in a system controls the system.' Another presupposition is that 'Choice is better than no choice.' By becoming more flexible, we are increasing our range of choices, not taking established behaviours away. As another presupposition states, 'All behaviours are useful in some context', otherwise we would not have adopted them in the first place. When we have problems with behaviour, it is usually that we are transferring a strategy that was successful in the past to a context where it is no longer useful.

3.11.1 Adapting style to situation

Many of us deal with a range of projects, sometimes in different sectors, for different clients, with a wide range of internal and external stakeholders. One strategy, which I was an early exponent of, was what I call 'The Genghis Khan school of project management.' At times I was so forceful, and aggressive, that I effectively bludgeoned dissent and got my own way without taking any prisoners (including the client on some occasions). This might kindly be referred to as an extreme of the 'directive' style of leadership. The directive style can be useful in turnaround situations and projects where there is no clear plan and lack of direction. When I moved on to change management projects, however, this strategy was the opposite of effective. I had to learn to do things more elegantly; that is, develop more flexibility in style and approach. If we do not adapt our style to the situation, aside from achieving limited success, we are liable to suffer excess strain and early burn-out.

Figure 3.17 Adapting style to context

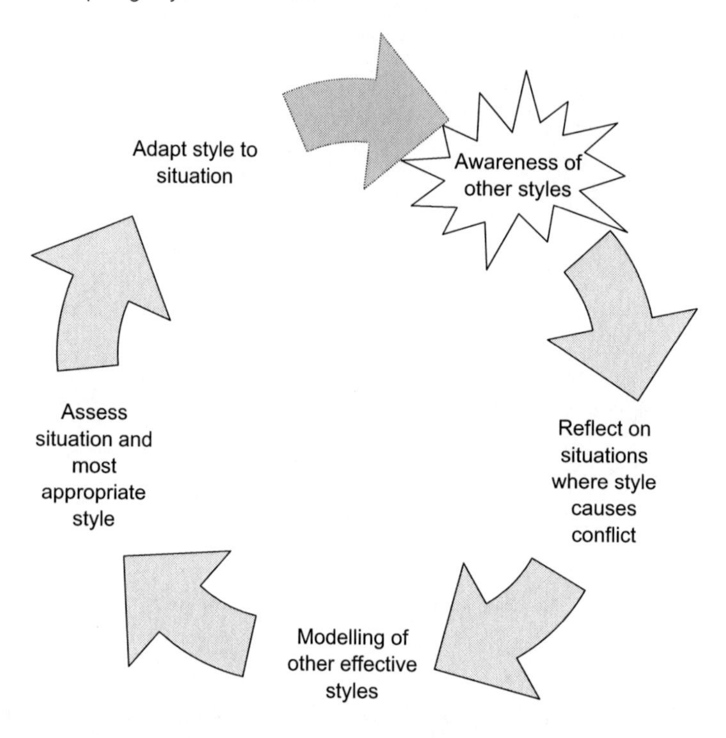

3.11.2 Models for leadership in project management

There is a large body of literature on leadership, which need not be reproduced here, but 'The six styles of leadership', as shown in Figure 3.18, gives a succinct overview of range of styles that are useful from a PM perspective. There is no right or wrong style, only in the wrong context. I think each of these styles has use for some types of project in some situation or other. What is your preferred style?

In Professor Rodney Turner's series of articles on leadership in projects, he says, 'Some people are more suited to leadership than others, but everyone can improve their leadership skills by taking the personality they were born with, and using it to develop leadership styles and behaviours appropriate to the projects that they are working on.'[151]

3.11.3 Flexibility and meta-programs

I am happy to tell you that some of you will find changing style and behaviour a lot easier than others. In Figure 3.6 of Section 3.5 on meta-programs we discussed some aspects of our nature, and one of these was the options/procedure meta-program. Those preferring options always want to have several potential ways of

Figure 3.18 Six styles of leadership[150]

Style	Defining characteristic	Useful when	Harmful when
Directive	Tell employees what to do and expect them to do it.	Organisations are going through a crisis, a period of turmoil or significant change.	The bureaucratic, imagination-stifling nature of the style means that it's inappropriate in situations where staff need to be creative or innovative.
Visionary	The objective is providing long-term direction.	Use it when you need to galvanise people and get them to see the bigger picture or motivate them for an unpleasant phase.	Don't use it in a crisis and it would not be effective if the person articulating the vision did not have credibility.
Affiliative	The primary focus is about creating harmony in the team so that they all like one another.	To get a group of creatives or scientists to overcome egos long enough to perform as a group.	Don't use in a crisis at any time when performance issues need to be addressed.
Participative	Likely to hold a lot of meetings and ask people for their ideas and opinions on what should happen next.	Good way of getting fresh ideas from a team of people who know what they are doing.	Terrible in a crisis. Asking for people's input on a decision that you've already made will damage trust and credibility.
Pace-setting	The underlying concern is about getting work delivered to a high standard, but what it looks like in practice is leaders effectively showing people how to do things.	Effective when in charge of a competent, achievement-focused and highly motivated team of people, for example in consulting or professional services.	Poor for long-term results as lack of delegation limits development of the team and creates clones. Burns out the leader.

(Continued)

Figure 3.18 *(Continued)*

Style	Defining characteristic	Useful when	Harmful when
Coaching	Try to understand the strengths and abilities of each member of the team and look for ways to help them to grow and develop over the long term.	One of the most effective long-term styles.	Not useful with a team that lacks confidence, drive or ambition.

doing things, whereas those preferring procedures like to have a set process for things that they use time and again. The good news is that NLP has a procedural tool for installing new options!

3.11.4 The TOTE model – a strategy for change

'Time to change the man in the mirror'

Michael Jackson

As human beings, we have strategies for doing everything in life, whether it's motivation, learning, relaxation or indeed love. When things don't work, it means that our strategy isn't working in this context. For example, most of us wouldn't talk to our boss the same way we talk to our kids, as the context and purpose is different. The TOTE (test, operate, test, exit) model can help understand the current strategy you have, and if it isn't working in this context, how you can develop a new strategy. The strategy may be one that is successful for you in another context, e.g. dealing with your spouse, or from someone that you observe as having success in this area. You may recognise that the TOTE model is widely used in scientific and technical fields for testing, e.g. whether the code in a computer program actually achieves the desired outcome in real life situations. Here we are applying TOTE to your own strategies/programs to see if they are effective in the context.

Exercise 3.18: The TOTE model for internal strategies

1. Think of an outcome that you want to achieve and are having problems with. Maybe you don't seem to be able to get on with your sponsor, or maybe you have had a series of miscommunications with one team leader in particular.

2. **Test:**
   a. Notice what is happening in the situation. What do you think about the other person? What do they think of you? Are there any peculiarities? Does it remind you of similar situations from your past?
   b. What would be the desired outcome?
   c. What are key differences between what happens and what you want to happen?
   d. What will you notice to be different when things happened the way that you want them to?
3. **Operate:** The idea here is to generate different ways of doing things.
   a. Think of another area of your life where you deal with similar situations or where you have achieved similar outcomes.
   b. What were key features of the successful behaviour?
   c. What are the main differences in behaviour? Maybe what you thought about the person, maybe tone of voice, maybe use of language such as motivation style, or even choice of words.
   d. Identify some aspects of your behaviour and actions in the problem situation that might be changed.
4. **Test:**
   a. Ideally in a non-threatening environment or situation, test whether the revised approach has got you nearer to achieving your desired outcome.
   b. If the approach works to some extent, continue to cycle through the TOTE model until you are happy with the results.
   c. If the approach does not work then consider looking for external resources, i.e. modeling people who do achieve success in this area (see next example).
   d. Future pace. Think about a time in the future that you will have to deal with the same person in the negative situation. Imagine that you have all the new resources from (d); notice how you act differently and, therefore, how the situation will turn much better.
5. **Exit:** When you are happy with the results then the TOTE model is complete.
   a. Were your success criteria met?

I used to clash with the finance department on a regular basis. 'Why did they need all this information from me, and why don't they give me reports like I want them?' The finance department can be a strong ally to a PM, and they can also make a bad adversary. Things had to improve.

I realised that I didn't appreciate the role of 'bean counters', and was going along to meetings expecting a fight in order to put them right. It had not even occurred to me to explore their map of the world, or understand why they were asking me to fill in forms. Outside of this minor conflict, relations with others were generally OK.

I decided that the desired outcome was that both parties had been listened to (rather than me ending up shouting at them). Both parties smiling would be a good indicator of this, followed by common courtesies and show of appreciation for help.

When I thought about the '**test**' part of TOTE, I realised that the present state was vastly different compared to the desired state, i.e. neither side was smiling.

I considered how I could reduce the difference between the two states and used the strategy that seemed to be successful for other requests for information, such as with railway enquiries or customer services. On comparison, the two similar situations could not have been approached more differently. My body language, use of words, tone, expectations, etc., were all at opposite ends of the spectrum.

To put this idea into action (**operate**), I translated the strategy across situations and made a non-urgent enquiry with accounts. (Fortunately, I was able to see a new member of the department, so the relationship was not tainted by previous experiences.) I merely asked for help on how I would go about getting financial approvals, how they could help me, pitfalls to watch out for, etc. I hope you will not be surprised that the meeting took a completely different tone (**test**). Having given them personal and professional respect, we had a constructive conversation. Asking for help, instead of telling them what I wanted, removed barriers and built bridges instead.

I could **exit** as there was no difference between the present state and the desired state.

It was easy to visualise future meetings, where I would go to ask for help, and at worst being redirected (future pacing).

When I was later managing implementations for finance systems, I got to know the world of accounts, processes and financial governance. This gave me an understanding of why they were forced to act as they had. Even later, I ended up as program director with one of the major firms of 'bean counters', so we in fact became friends. (Mind you, I seem to have kept the old strategy for dealing with my own bank.)

3.11.5 Modelling excellence from others

A more elegant way to achieve flexibility is through direct modelling, which is my favourite. Here, once I have identified an area that I am having problems with, or am not sure how to do, then I identify someone who has achieved success. Ideally, I will look for several people that have solved similar problems in different contexts and different ways and try to identify common elements to form a new strategy. We can then feed this new strategy into the TOTE model, test if it works in a non-threatening environment, and go around the loop until we have sufficient improvement. As we shall see in Section 3.18 on modelling, it is something innate in our nature – NLP just makes it a bit more explicit.

3.12 SETTING YOUR OWN GOALS AND ACHIEVING WELL-FORMED OUTCOMES

'Everyone needs to keep learning. Everyone needs goals'

Richard Branson[152]

Desired outcomes are central to NLP. To effect any change, whether it be personal effectiveness, change in others, or in an organisation, we need to be targeting the desired outcome rather than subordinate activities. If you want that outcome, NLP can help in many ways. On the other hand, it is said that if you don't want anything then NLP has nothing to offer you. But obviously you picked up this book, so you had some desired outcome at the back of your mind.

3.12.1 Beliefs and values

All the things that you *want* to do are ways of actualising your values. That is, in some way you are trying to reflect your nature. Of course, there are some things that are imposed on us, and these may conflict with our inner nature and could result in some internal sabotage, or at least a lack of enthusiasm. People who have a strong sense of what's important to them, i.e. are in tune with their values, usually have a real sense of purpose that acts like a propulsion system that moves them towards it.

At the turn of the decade (2010) there was a resurgence in the power of belief, evidenced by books and films such as *The Secret*, which advise that the universe is like a cosmic ordering service, and you only have to wish for it and believe it and it will come true. While NLP supports the idea that being in tune with your own beliefs and values will help you to get what you need, NLP gurus like Anthony Robbins are quite clear that to get what you want you have to take action. In fact in his terms, massive action, i.e. if you want big outcomes then be prepared to put in big efforts, not sit on the couch waiting for your lottery ticket to win or the project to come in on time and delight the stakeholders. Sorry to break the bad news.

Exercise 3.19: Values elicitation

What is important to you in work? Don't write down the things that you put on your CV or say at interview just because you think that it is what people want to hear in order to give you the job. What do you *really* like doing?

1. Just jot them down for now.
2. What aspects of work don't you like?
3. Again, just jot them down.
4. Is there anything that would help to make these things that you don't like more palatable?
5. Jot them down too.

6. Now put them all in a list, or write each one on a sticky note and start to put them in order of preference, with most desirable at the top and least liked at the bottom. Here are some examples:
    - challenge;
    - recognition;
    - working with a team;
    - telling people what to do;
    - working with data;
    - solving problems;
    - managing a budget;
    - writing reports;
    - working with customers;
    - working with stakeholders;
    - coaching;
    - planning;
    - variety;
    - working up a business case;
    - negotiating;
    - working with suppliers;
    - developing specifications;
    - writing reports;
    - being home by 5:30;
    - etc.
7. How does this list measure up to what you are currently doing?
8. Do you know anyone who likes the things that you don't?
9. How could you do more of what motivates you and delegate more of the things that you don't like, e.g. accounts?
10. Ask people what it is that they like about the things that you don't like (hint: they probably have a different view of the world and different values).

3.12.2 Meta-programs and goals

In terms of achieving your outcomes, you have probably found that some people seem to be real achievers, while others never threaten the finish line. Perhaps the section on meta-programs in the section on 'know thyself' gave you a clue. Which options do you think might lend themselves to setting and achieving outcomes?

- active/proactive;
- towards/away from;
- options/procedure.

What was your natural preference? Don't worry, with NLP even outcomes like changing these meta-programs are achievable. (See sections on flexibility and modelling.)

When giving yourself and others tasks it is much more effective to allocate them to people who are naturally inclined – a bit like running downhill instead of up.

3.12.3 Sameness or difference?

Some meta-programs will influence the kind of goal that you will naturally be aligned towards. We have mentioned several already; for example, whether you are naturally inclined to a high level view or detail, or towards options or procedure.

Another meta-program is for 'sameness or difference', and this will greatly influence your own career path and goals. Some people like sameness to an extreme and they do not deviate from a schedule. I know one man who has been sitting in the same seat in our local pub every night for 60 years. He is an extreme exception, as only about five per cent truly prefer sameness, but of course you will meet five in a hundred on your next change project. At the other end of the spectrum about twenty per cent like out and out difference – change for change sake. These are easy to get on board, but as soon as you have implemented your change they will want to keep changing it. Some of these people ran R&D in the nuclear sector in the early days, resulting in only two of the nuclear reactors in the UK being to the same design, the rest all requiring different fuel production lines, etc., at great expense. Incidentally, the only two that were the same were under the Ministry of Defence – quite a conservative bunch in comparison. Most people are in the middle and like same-with-difference or difference-with-same. Some people are comfortable doing the same kind of project over and over again, while others like to take on new roles, new sectors and new industries. What about you? What about your team members?

3.12.4 Outcomes and goals

For those working in change management, and particularly those working to frameworks such as managing successful programs (MSP),[153] the term outcome will probably have replaced the more popular 'deliverable' from the project management lexicon. The focus moves from the asset, e.g. build a school, to something a little more abstract, e.g. create a teaching environment, all the way through to full alignment of goals with 'well educated children'. For most of us, programs such as that probably exceed our tenure, if not our scope, but it is always good to start with the outcome in mind and work backwards.

Some of you may be more used to working with objectives, goals, targets or even deliverables. Let's take New Year's resolutions as an example. Most of us set goals, but they just don't seem to get implemented. Outcomes, on the other hand, look at the complete context around change. Management courses teach us to set SMART objectives, that is specific, measurable, achievable, realistic and time-based. NLP outcomes capture these facets, include a few behavioural bits, and round off with a few more.

Exercise 3.20: Achieving well-formed outcomes

1. Think of an outcome that you would like to achieve. (If you don't have any problems or things that you wouldn't like to change then drop me a line and I will give you some of mine.)
2. State the outcome in the positive. 'Don't think of an elephant' doesn't work, as the subconscious brain doesn't process negatives. You don't want to *stop* smoking; you need to focus on some positive attribute such as to have fresh breath/hair/clothes.
3. Scale the challenge. As you learned in the section on 'know yourself', some of us have a meta-program for big picture, while some are into the detail. You need to chunk up or down until you get some something that is meaningful to you. Like any project, you may want to break a big change down into a number of smaller ones and deal with them in turn. After all, even the great pyramids were built one stone at a time.
4. Be specific. What is it exactly that you want to change, and how? When you have it what will it give you? How will that make your life better?
5. Evidence – how will you know when you have it? Would others be able to tell, and if so, how?
6. Is the outcome congruent with your beliefs? Do you believe that *it is possible*? Do you believe that *you are able*? If not, go back to the start (or consider the NLP belief change techniques). Do you think that *you deserve it*? Many people are thought to 'self sabotage' because they have some inner conflict and a part of them that believes that they do not deserve to be successful/rich/happy/loved etc. (Self worth is a common part of the human psyche and most NLP practitioners visit and tweak their subconscious values and revisit their limiting beliefs).
7. Is the desired outcome largely within your control? We used to laugh about bonus-related targets based on things outside our direct control but we would be foolish if we set achievement of our own desires on things outside our own control.
8. Resources – is it worth it? What is the opportunity cost, i.e. what could you do instead? (A bit of value management creeping in?)
9. Ecology – what might be the impact on self and others? Are we happy to give up watching the football to make the time to get that qualification? What impact might those extra hours have on your relationship? Is it who you are and congruent with your beliefs, or are you just doing what other people tell you that you should be doing? If so, don't worry, you will probably fail along the way. On the other hand you may succeed and be unhappy.
10. Action – you should be good at this part. Make a realistic plan. Pay particular attention to the first step – what, when, how. **Now JDI!**

'The journey of a thousand miles begins with one step'

Lao Tzu

When you set your goals, reflect on the full picture and balance those of work and play. Personally, I am successful in achieving professional outcomes, but have not yet mastered the art of devoting equal resources to relaxation.

Exercise 3.21: Testing understanding through coaching

Now repeat the above exercise by coaching someone else, e.g. one of your team, to achieve a goal. As many of you will have found, from tennis to project management, going through the process of coaching someone forces you to truly question and understand it.

Exercise 3.22: Applying outcome frame to projects

How does this apply to project goals? Many of the big IT 'failures' that you will have read about in the press would not pass this test. Although they are often expressed in outcome format, they are not well formed in that they fail several of these criteria. Typical examples are projects driven by political policy. Think of one of the reported failures currently in the press. Which of these criteria do you think it fails on?

3.13 TIME – MANAGING IT AND LIVING IN IT

'Nothing is worth more than this day'

Johann von Goethe

Have you ever noticed how some people always seem to be behind the clock, constantly rushing, often late, while others seem to cruise through life? As a PM, have you noticed that some people regularly get their progress reports in on time while others have to be chased every week? Some people give you a plan, while it is easier to draw teeth than get a plan out of some people, let alone get them to work to it.

On the other hand, which are the people that you would pick to write your communications plan, to go to speak to the unions about a change program, or handle a tricky HR issue? Maybe some of those self same people who don't plan?

Have you worked on international projects, or had people of different cultures in your team? Which cultures tend to be timely, and which can cause frustration at apparent lack of understanding or respect for deadlines?

3.13.1 Time management

The irony of many time management courses is that they are written by 'through-time' people for 'through-time' people. They make little sense to people who are predominantly 'in-time', yet they are the ones who really need time management tools. (And being mismatched, they are not in rapport so the communication is likely to be doomed anyway.) The essential skill for time management is to be able to plan through-time.

> 'How does a project get to be a year behind schedule? One day at a time'
> Anne Wilson Schaef

3.13.2 NLP Timelines

Timelines were briefly introduced in Section 2.16. The NLP meta-program for time helps us to determine which groups people fall into. (Like all meta-programs, however, note that they are context based, so you may behave differently in work situations than in leisure situations. If so, all the better, as you have a good basis for flexibility).

Figure 3.19 Different timelines

	Through-time (Typically American-European model of time)	**In-time (Traditionally Eastern culture, though adapting to working with the West)**
Indicators	• You tend to have dissociated memories. • You are dissociated from the 'now'. • You are able to keep your emotions separate from events. • You are aware of time passing. • You tend to plan ahead. • You are aware of deadlines and are good at keeping them. • You are very aware of the value of time. • You are goal-orientated. • You are conscious of turning up for appointments on time. • You find living in the now is difficult and avoid it.	• You feel your emotions very strongly. • You are associated in the 'now'. • You tend to have associated memories. • You are not aware of time passing. • You like to keep your options open. • You tend not to plan. • You avoid deadlines or are not good at keeping them. • You are good at multi-tasking. • You are good at living in the moment.
Good for	• achieving goals; • planning; • processes; • delivery; • appointments and meetings.	• building relationships; • dealing with difficult relationships; • enjoying yourself; • being creative.

Exercise 3.23: Determining your timeline

1. Close your eyes and imagine a line containing your past and your future.
2. Does the line pass through you or not?
3. Is your past behind you or not?

For through-time:

- Timeline lies outside of you body.
- Often the past is to your left and the future to the right.

In-time:

- Timeline passes through your body
- Often the future is in front of you and past behind.

Which type are you?

3.13.3 Changing your timeline

OK, so now you know what your normal timeline is. Rather than just give you an excuse for not planning, or not being good at one-on-one situations, the main purpose of NLP is to develop flexibility. Wouldn't it be good to choose which timeline you are operating on depending on the task? Well, you can change you timeline because you created it in the first place and can recreate it if you choose.

You can change the orientation of your timeline so that you can experience a different mindset without changing any of the individual memories and events that your timeline is made up of.

Figure 3.20 Choosing timelines

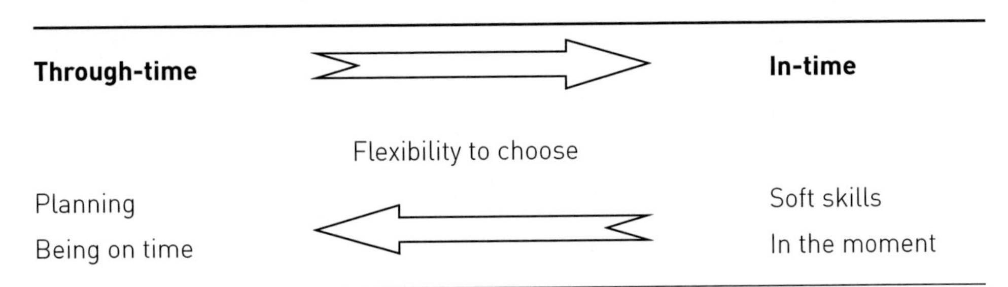

Exercise 3.24: Changing your timeline

If you are a goal-oriented person who generally operates through-time but you want to operate in-time for a delicate meeting then you can, with practice.

1. Close your eyes and imagine your timeline. For through-time this will generally be in front of you running left to right (or visa versa).
2. Now step on to the timeline.
3. Give yourself a minute to adjust as it can be disorientating, especially as you become more practiced at the switch.
4. How does that feel? You may feel more grounded, more in the moment.
5. Turn your head so that it faces your future. Imagine your future.
6. Now rotate your head so that your timeline is running from your future, through your body, to your past.
7. Take a moment to reorient.
8. Immerse yourself in your planned task and let time slip away. (I like to imagine a clock melting away like a Dali painting while I am doing this.)
9. Now open your eyes.

Conversely, if you are generally an in-time person but you have a deadline to meet, you may wish to choose to operate through-time for a period.

1. Close your eyes and imagine your timeline. For in-time this will generally be running through your body.
2. Now step to the side, off your timeline.
3. Give yourself a minute to adjust as it can be disorientating, especially as you become more practiced at the switch.
4. You may feel a little more objective, a little more able to take an overview.
5. Turn your head to look up and down your timeline, which will now be in front of you. You are now observing time and have control over it.
6. Imagine your task superimposed along this time line, with key activities laid out in the correct order.
7. Feel your internal clock running like your own metronome.
8. Now open your eyes and let your internal clock guide you through the day.

As you go through your day, think about the most appropriate way to be operating with regards to time according to what you are trying to achieve. Practise the technique and the changes will move from subtle to dramatic. Being in-time or through-time is a choice, not who you are.

3.13.4 Use of future pacing and as-if reframes

In several of the exercises in this book you will see the final stages being to 'future pace'. This is similar to one of the exercises on reframing, where we act 'as-if' something has already happened, test our reaction and look back. The advantages of going to a future state are that it dissociates the individual from difficult situations. It also allows people to move past obstacles that they cannot resolve when they are in front of them but can see a way through much more clearly when looking back to how they might have been resolved.

Exercise 3.25: Future pacing

- Imagine a problem/obstacle preventing project completion.
- Now, imagine you have successfully finished the project and are at the lessons learned/celebration meeting.
- Looking back:
    - o How did you solve it?
    - o Who helped you?
    - o What was the critical step?
    - o What was the one thing that you had to do to move forward?

Conversely, verb tenses can be used for putting a problem into the past, for example: 'That *has been* a problem, *wasn't* it?' (Note that the grammar is purposely mixed to confuse the conscious brain so that the instruction to put things in the past can speak directly to the subconscious. A slight change of emphasis also acts as instruction.)

3.13.5 Gaining rapport through matching timelines

Have you realised yet how much easier it would be to gain rapport and understanding with other parties if you could match their timeline? It is difficult to explain to someone who is in-time while standing through-time, and visa-versa. Some of the give-aways for which timeline people generally operate in are shown in Figure 3.19 above. You can find out a lot about how people think about time, together with their critical sub-modalities, by listening to their language, for example:

- It was in the dim and distant past.
- He has a bright future.
- I'm looking *forward* to a holiday.
- Put the affair *behind* you.
- Time is running out.
- Time is on my side.

Think of one of your key project stakeholders. Recall how they behave and what they say. Do you think that they operate in-time or through-time? How could you check? What might you do before your next meeting?

3.14 SEEING THE BIGGER PICTURE WHILE MANAGING THE DETAIL

> 'Nothing is particularly hard if you divide it into small jobs'
>
> Henry Ford

We often hear people talking about 'needing to see the big picture', but what are they actually talking about? Well, some people at work would naturally see a 'helicopter view' of a project, such as purpose, global budget, key stakeholders, rough duration and likelihood of success. Often, they will see this all together in a holistic picture with half a dozen key features. Others would ask to see a project plan, budget breakdown, risk log, etc. and want to look at the detail. We need both types of behaviour to deliver a project, though these could be in different team members.

3.14.1 Chunking

It doesn't matter where we start from in terms of preference for chunk size, as we can arrive at the same place. In NLP the process of chunking is used extensively to get to the right level of information; for example, chunking up to arrive at a motive in order to establish alternative strategies, or chunking down to arrive at sufficient detail for an action plan. Some approaches to project management lend themselves to the former, while method-based approaches tend to support the latter. Both have a place.

Figure 3.21 Chunking up and down

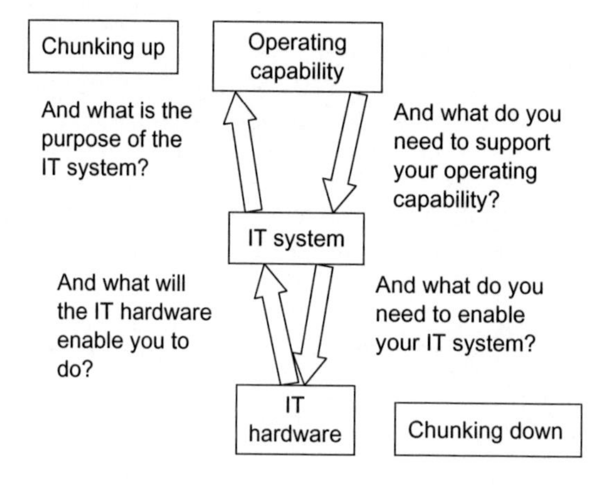

3.14.2 Work breakdown structure

To me, the big picture approach is good for portfolio management; that is, linking delivery up to the organisation's strategy and maintaining a balance of resources, as well as risk/reward profile. Unless we want to manage by the seat of our pants, however, we need a breakdown into component projects, phases, deliverables, work packages, milestones and activities in order to plan and control execution. In general, project management tools and techniques cater for the two aspects through the structure illustrated above, especially phasing of a project and use of work breakdown structure. Indeed, on reviewing the UK nuclear industry's £70 billion life-cycle baseline decommissioning program, the whole could be viewed as one entity, important to establish overall budgets and resources for approval, or drilled down through seven layers of work breakdown to reveal individual discipline-based work packages in any one of thousands of projects in order to benchmark them.

3.14.3 Behaviour and roles

Do you feel more comfortable in a supervisory role or a leadership role? Would you see managing a project in another discipline as a development opportunity or as a nightmare? What about working in a different industry altogether? Some of this, aside from how experienced and confident you are, is related to whether you take a big picture perspective, which is largely transferable, or focus on the technical detail. (Though the meta-program preference for 'sameness or difference' also comes into play.)

Exercise 3.26: Finding your preference

Before you read on, look out of a window for 30 seconds. Now quickly write down the first five things that you remember. Did you words show a clear preference?

Big picture	Detail
• Trees	• Tall tree with golden leaves.
• Wall	• High wall with ivy covering the majority of it.
• Clouds	• Pale blue sky with scattered clouds.
• Buildings	• Georgian double-fronted manor house.
• People	• A family with a young child.

3.14.4 Changing meta-programs

We have spoken about the need to be flexible as project managers, and nowhere is this more so than in relation to the meta-program for 'big picture/detail', because as project managers you will have to develop the ability to switch between the two options. Not only are some tasks more suited to one option than the other, but you will need to reflect the bias of your senior stakeholders when reporting to them and also balance this with the preference of your team.

Don't worry, though you probably have a strong preference, it can be changed at will. (Nearly all of us have a strong preference for using our right or left hand, but you can learn to brush your teeth with the other hand with practice, even though you would never be inclined to do so and it doesn't feel natural until you have made it routine.)

As with all meta-programs, they are context specific, that is, you may exercise one option while at work but the opposite at home. For example, you might be talking in the boardroom at work about shaping the overall portfolio, but when you get home you might be faced with the detailed planning and execution of keeping a family running, with time slots for picking kids up or baby feeding.

3.14.5 Communicating with big picture and detail

Do your key stakeholders have a preference for 'big picture' or 'detail'? You are likely to have a mixture of both. You would normally expect to get more 'big picture' people higher up the organisation, but this is not always the case, especially where people are promoted within a discipline, e.g. for IT, engineering or finance. Similarly, you would expect to get more 'detail' oriented people doing delivery, but I have been caught out by this when working in creative sectors such as media. If you do not communicate with them according to their preferences then you are going to lose rapport. Have you ever tried to give a 20 page progress report to the project sponsor, or five bullet points to an accountant?

Find out what your client's preference is and communicate with them in their preference, both with written and verbal communication. If you can't work out your client's preference then ask them 'How would you like me to present x?', 'How much detail would you like me to go into?' Remember, if you are communicating with a detailed person, make sure that you do a thorough spellcheck or your credibility will be severely questioned. (When getting this book reviewed I picked a mix of types. Some advised that I was missing a section while others would pick up on grammar and spelling – we need both.)

Exercise 3.27: Listening and using appropriate vocabulary

Big picture	Detailed
Summary	Precisely
Overview	Schedule
In a nutshell	First, second, next...
Generally	Plan

3.14.6 Options and procedures

A related meta-program is that for 'options or procedure'. Some people naturally focus on a range of options when presented with a challenge, while others start to plan out the detail of the most obvious option. The latter tend to be the 'doers', and if left unchecked, will head of into delivery without a proper options appraisal.

Exercise 3.28: Which meta-programs are most suited to the task in hand?

PM activity	Big picture or detail?	Options or procedure?
Outline business case		
Executive report		
Project approach		
Sourcing strategy		
Project review		
Resource plan		
Financial budget		
Schedule/plan		
Risk management		

3.15 BUILDING RAPPORT WITH STAKEHOLDERS

'Rapport is meeting someone on their map of the world'

NLP presupposition

The NLP fundamentals of rapport were introduced in Section 2.14, and here we will focus on its application to project management. Under emotional intelligence frameworks, social awareness and relationship management come under this topic. Successful people create rapport, and rapport creates trust. Many people think that it can't be learned, and you either have the ability or you haven't. All NLP courses, however, have this as one of the first skills that they teach, as rapport is one of the pillars of NLP. In fact, it is safe to say that without the ability to establish rapport, none of the other techniques of NLP will work. Before we expect to make any significant progress in any relationship we must establish understanding and trust.

3.15.1 Stakeholder management

Structures for projects can give the notion that a PM reports to a sponsor and manages a team, or set of teams, and that is where relationships start and end. You will be aware, however, that there is a whole host of people who have an interest in your project, including perhaps many outside your own organisation. Some have the ability to stop you achieving your objectives. Some may be initially for it, but you can be sure that for any change initiative there will be an array of people who would prefer things to remain as they are and so be resistant to you and your project.

Some PMs may assume that the project sponsor is managing all the other stakeholders. Sponsors certainly have accountability for it,[154] though much of the responsibility, including tracking, is usually left to the PM. Since stakeholder management has become one of the most important aspects of project management, and probably more important to the perception of project success than managing to time, cost or scope, it is best to draw upon any additional tools and techniques readily available to support you.

You probably do a good job in identifying your key stakeholders and keeping them abreast of your project. But maybe there are one or two where occasionally things don't quite gel for some reason.

3.15.2 It's not about being mates or a pushover

There are some common misconceptions about what it takes to build rapport. For clarity, it is not:

- Being a 'yes man'. Though it is easier to get people to like you if you agree with them, sycophants do not have a legitimate place in the workplace and you will soon find yourself in a corner where it is impossible to agree with everyone, as there will be many opposing views in a complex project environment.
- Being 'a pushover' – you still need to be assertive and hold what ground you need to, otherwise you risk losing respect.
- 'Passing the time of day'. Though it is important to take an interest in people and have an understanding of them as a whole, walking into an office to talk about football results every morning can be a big drain on time, and stakeholders might take a view that you are lazy or unfocussed.
- Finally, perhaps surprisingly to some people, rapport is not friendship. You probably would not want to spend your leisure hours with many of the people you interact with at work.

3.15.3 Prerequisites for rapport

To be able to create rapport at ease, or even at will, you need to be curious and take an interest in people. Often we can be so task focussed by deadlines that we forget about people, especially when we are in virtual teams spread around the country or even globally, and end up at the extreme of sending cold emails to strangers. Many of us like to people watch and observe others when we are in restaurants for example but seem to lose this ability when we are under time pressure at work. NLP believes that everything that is going on in the inside is expressed on the outside by language and behaviour, so everything that you may need to know is there to see if you take the time and make the effort to observe. In terms of the meta-programs, this is one of the occasions when you should attempt to be 'in-time': fully aware of the moment and in tune with your senses.

> 'Behind every behaviour is a positive intent'
>
> NLP presupposition

To be able to understand anyone we have to suspend judgement. Even if someone does something that we don't agree with, we should not judge the person. Until we can see things from their perspective and understand why they do things, we are unlikely to be able to anticipate their choices and affect their behaviour. (At the extreme, you can see people in traditional martial arts or cage fighting contests bowing and showing respect to their opponents before and after beating each other up. They are also experts in sensory acuity and rapport, as it is in the interests of their noses to be able to anticipate every move and behaviour of their opponent.) It is an instinctive skill that we all have within us that many of us just don't get around to using much or developing.

3.15.4 A word about matching and mirroring – stop copying me!

Matching and mirroring were described in Section 2.14, but NLP has had some bad press in the past and it mainly arose from application of this technique. When done properly it is a very persuasive technique, and this was not lost on salesmen in the early days. Rather than try to establish rapport, however, they used some physical matching and mirroring techniques to mimic it. This usually comes over as incongruent, as their motive and action are not aligned, and at best leads to the concept of 'buyer's remorse', where people regret the decision once they are away from the influence.

So let's go back to ethics, integrity and desired outcome. If you are trying to establish understanding and trust with someone in order to reach a mutually beneficial agreement, then all of this will work. For people whose own ethics and integrity would allow it, who want to try to use these techniques in order to trick someone, then they would be better looking elsewhere, as at best they will come over as 'creepy'.

Probably the NLP technique most badly performed is mirroring, and that is at least partly due to people reading a book, like this one, and thinking that they are competent to go out and bend the world to their will. If you are able to observe two people who are in love then this will be obvious through their body language. The ultimate example is the courting arrangement of two swans, which naturally match and mirror during their courtship display. In my view, matching of body language is an output measure, that is, an indication that two or more people are in rapport. It should only be attempted on the world at large when very competent and natural.

I was at a meeting with a large project-based organisation and their head of PM knew that I had NLP training. He spent the first 10 minutes adopting unnatural body positions, affecting facial characteristics, displaying negative body language, avoiding eye contact etc. to try to have some sport watching me attempt to mimic him. Fortunately, I only matched breathing and language, which bought us into line anyway, and he soon dropped the charade and realised that NLP was not so superficial.

So, my advice to you, particularly when starting out, is to be aware of body language but let it fall into line naturally rather than attempting to mimic it. If you match your breathing only you will find that you soon align in terms of energy, pace and pitch, which are prerequisite for rapport anyway. If you add into this matching of language you will quickly notice improvement in communications that lays the foundation for understanding and trust.

Of course, as we conduct a lot of our meetings over the phone, breathing and language remain good underpinning. For email correspondence, use of similar language, particularly recognising preferred modalities and reflecting any evident meta-programs improves the chances of common understanding.

3.15.5 Hierarchy of rapport

There is a well-established hierarchy of neurological levels for NLP, as discussed in Section 2.7 and illustrated in Figure 2.6. In terms of rapport, connection at higher levels leads to stronger connection.[155]

To put the reservations expressed above into context, rapport established through matching and mirroring is addressing the challenge from the bottom of the pyramid. To my view it is much more effective to start from the top to look for points of connection. The following could be considered from a project context:

Figure 3.22 Connecting neurological levels in the project context

Neurological level	Considerations for connection in the project context
Purpose	Joint venture projects and collaborations have been shown to be more likely to succeed if a clear super-ordinate goal has been established. If two parties are bought into a common purpose then it is more likely that they will work together constructively, even setting aside old rivalries. If the stakeholder can align to the purpose that you promote then it will be much easier to work together. You may have to 'chunk up' to identify this common purpose.
Identity	Who we are is very important to the human condition. From a project perspective this supports the need for a clear project identity and branding. When you speak to stakeholders be clear what hat you are wearing; that is, present yourself as 'the project' rather than as an individual. (Where you have an established personal brand or reputation, you may consider switching this around and connecting the project to the brand, just as some successful investment funds promote themselves through the fund manager where they have a strong track record.)

(Continued)

Figure 3.22 *(Continued)*

Neurological level	Considerations for connection in the project context
Beliefs and values	It used to be common to see corporate 'value statements' and this has spread to some projects, but avoid the cliché and the superficial. The values are what people do, not what is written down. If the project says that creativity is valued then don't stifle it with process and command and control. For projects such as public private partnerships (PPPs) I found early on that it is essential to bridge the gap in perception of different values between the public sector and the private sector. It is important to stress that all parties are trying to bring about a successful outcome.
Capabilities	People from similar professions or vocations have a natural affinity whenever the link can be established. Aside from the common linkage of the project, many people today have had a range of roles in their career and you may find commonality in history and experience.
Behaviours	It is easier to build rapport across similar behaviours. Where you identify that you normally have different behaviours then look at your preferred options for key meta-programs and consider those of the second party. (There is an exercise below.)
Environment	This can be taken to be working on the same project, in the same location, or under the same organisational structure. Whatever it is, emphasise it. 'We are all in the same boat.'

For all of these aspects, where you are looking for commonality it is obviously easier if you are working from a matching rather than a mismatching perspective.

On leading transformation on my first major public private partnership, we were paving the way in terms of governance arrangements. The public sector partner would usually insist on chairing project boards, but the expense of the projects was borne by the private sector partner. The potential for massive overruns in scope, cost and time had the potential to make the £250 million contract loss-making.

At the first formal program board, as we did introductions, most of the 20–30 people in the room advised that they were 'representing' such-and-such department. I introduced myself as being accountable for successful delivery of improvements for citizens. This struck a chord with the chairman, who had joined the council from the private sector and was also very focussed on delivery of benefits rather than assets. He nodded to me in recognition – we had established common purpose.

After the meeting he contacted me to arrange a more informal discussion. I put my cards on the table, telling him what my internal constraints were with regard to budget and expectations, and he told me what he needed and what his political masters wanted. We traded the stuff in the middle and set about to deliver as much as we could together with the resources that we had. The next thing we did was to communicate a competition and prize for a name for the program. Alongside joint working, we had started to establish a common identity.

Although the program was defined contractually in terms of deliverables, we agreed that we were actually trying to improve outcomes. The most prominent of these were those around customer service, as measured by the national auditing body. The program took on a slightly different direction, with less focus on the IT and more on changing behaviours, improving operating models and providing supporting training.

Private sector capabilities in delivery were acknowledged, and we in turn recognised the public sector knowledge and contact with its own customers. We seconded some of their people into the team and offered training to any who wanted it, creating a whole that was more than the sum of the parts.

During my time there we always behaved as a common team with a common purpose. Differences, potentially backed up by a contract and severe financial penalties, were reconciled in a way that meant that delivery was maintained and neither party was taken advantage of. All of this was underpinned by constant dialogue to get to learn more about each other, in terms of personalities as well as capabilities.

The partnership won major PPP of the year, not for having a brand new IT infrastructure, but for measurable improvements in customer-focussed services (that were enabled by the infrastructure). All of this was only possible, not by the latest technology, but from the earliest skill – the ability to connect.

3.15.6 Finding the connection

You may be familiar with the concept of six degrees of separation, which says that we are connected to everyone in the world by no more that six friends or contacts. Since this concept was first postulated in the nineteenth century, my own view is that this route may be even shorter today. Certainly, using professional networking sites such as LinkedIn, I can find my route to most famous people around the world in a maximum of three steps. So, next time you meet a 'stranger' you might like to practise by playing the game of discovering your connection. I like to set myself the target of finding three connections, though I include examples from all of the neurological levels. I use this technique as an ice breaker in workshops and have had people finding more than 10 connections with apparent strangers in less than 10 minutes.

Exercise 3.29: Finding the connection

If you use a stakeholder management grid then consider the dimension of 'connection' for each of your key stakeholders, or at least those where things may not be running as smoothly as you would like. This could be any aspect, for example: having studied at the same university, studied the same topic, worked for the same company, common friend, born in the same town, or even sharing the same hobby or football team. You probably don't have enough information for many of your stakeholders to construct this at the moment, but it should give you the prerequisite inquisitiveness to start to find out, which will build rapport in itself.

3.15.7 How do they see, or hear, the world?

Now we have an excellent starting point, but how do we start to understand their map of the world? Of course, we could ask them, and should. This is particularly important when we are dealing with customers and end users. Simple questions like 'How do you see things?', or even 'What is important to you in terms of outcome?' can be most enlightening. They can be even more so with the help of NLP to understand the underlying structure of what they are saying, as this will reveal their behaviours, i.e. meta-programs, and also their primary representational systems. Knowledge of preferred representational system will help to reflect in appropriate language, e.g. with a bias to visual or auditory words. Very subtle modifications to questioning can also reveal some of their values and beliefs in relation to the topic and context.

3.15.8 Rapport and meta-programs

Having similar ways of looking at the world and similar behaviours will help to establish rapport. But which meta-programs help to establish rapport in the first place?

Exercise 3.30: Meta-programs for rapport

For the following meta-programs, choose the option that you think is most appropriate for achieving rapport. For example, if you think that it is easier for outgoing, extrovert people to develop rapport with others then mark this option in the box. On the other hand, you may think that extroverted people only have shallow relationships, and being introverted helps to develop sufficient depth.

Best for building rapport?	
Self/Introvert Need to be alone to recharge their batteries. Few relationships with deep connections. Interested in a few topics but to great detail.	**Other/Extrovert** Relax in the company of others. Have a lot of surface relationships. Know about a lot of things, but not in detail.

(Continued)

Best for building rapport?

Match Notice points of similarity.	**Mismatch** Notice differences.
Associated Feelings and relationships are important.	**Dissociated** Detached from feelings. Work with information. Task oriented.
In time Live in the moment. Creative but poor with deadlines.	**Through time** Good at keeping track of time and managing deadlines.
Proactive Initiates action.	**Reactive** Analyses first then follows the lead from others.
Person Centred on feelings.	**Thing** Centred on tasks.

Do you remember what your orientation was with these meta-programs? Which ones would you like to develop flexibility with to help with this?

3.15.9 Tailoring reports

In terms of your stakeholder, knowledge of how they view the world can assist in how you behave and relay information. Again this can be interpreted from language and actions. In terms of reporting, key meta-programs to consider are their preferences for:

- General or specific – it could be assumed that the higher up the organisation an individual is then the more of a 'helicopter view' they may take, but this may not be the case.
- Options vs procedure – hopefully higher management are focussed on generating options, but in some professional backgrounds there is an organisational filter that pre-selects people with a disposition to procedure and method. Note that there has been a growing trend in project management since 2000 for procedure-based methods.
- Convincer pattern – what is their evidence base?

There are four basic ways that some people are convinced, as shown in the column on the left of Figure 3.23. You may think that you have convinced someone by telling them about it, whereas their preference could be to read a document. Once we have the preferred channel then we have to satisfy a frequency criterion. Some people will believe what they read/you tell them on face value, while others may take a lot of persuasion through repetition or over a period of time. At the extreme, some will always remain sceptical.

Figure 3.23 Dimensions and options for the convincer meta-program

What convinces someone?	**How often does something have to be demonstrated for another person to be convinced?**
They have to see something to believe it.	Automatic – they take things at face value.
They have to hear someone else say that they can do it, e.g. a reference.	They need two or three occasions before they make up their minds.
They have to read about it, e.g. a report or a CV.	They make up their minds over a period of time – no point repeating yourself or trying to rush them.
They have to experience doing something before believing it.	Consistently – they only consider you as good as your last performance (and almost expect to be let down).

Perhaps this sheds some light on why we sometimes struggle to convince some people. The safest option, especially when working with groups of people, and now being used in the educational system, is to provide all of these options where possible. For a project this would involve you:

1. sending out a report and providing all the details in an appendix;
2. getting an advocate or early adopter to talk about it;
3. giving them a tour/demo;
4. letting them try it;
5. maintaining the communications channels and not just doing it the once.

Of course this sits on top of the other aspects of effective communication that we have already dealt with, such as using both big picture and also detail, and with language appealing to different representational systems. And of course you have to keep doing it. This is one of the reasons that we bring in communications professionals to help us with change management programs. Otherwise we might just communicate according to our own meta-programs and in the language of our own representational system and lose most of the audience.

3.15.10 The language of rapport

Lessons learned workshops for projects invariably come up with a recommendation for 'better communication'. But this should not be taken as more, but rather better quality. So how do we make our communication better?

This is relatively straightforward for one-on-one situations. Here we just tailor our language to the preferred representational system (and meta-programs) of the recipient.

As covered in section 2.10, we all have a preference for a particular representational system based on the senses. Below are some examples of words and phrases that you might hear to indicate a person's preferred system, and which you might like to reflect back to them in your conversations.

Figure 3.24 The language of rapport

Visual	**Auditory**	**Kinaesthetic**
Appear	Clear as a bell	Those affected
Bird's eye view	Sounds right	Crash
Clear cut	Let's discuss it	Foundation
Focus	Harmonise	Get a grip on
Illustrate	In a manner of speaking	Impact
In the light of day	Outspoken	Lukewarm
With hindsight	Out of tune	Muddled
Graphic	Hear the results	Nail
Illusion	Hidden message	Pressure

Note that these are not casually used, but consistently, i.e. unless someone is deliberately attempting to vary vocabulary then they will tend to use the same type of words. (Good authors will attempt to use descriptive words from all representational systems in order to connect with a wider audience.)

If someone has a visual preference for example, and uses words like 'Let me *see* the evidence', you will not be doing yourself any favours by responding with phrases like 'Wait until you *hear* the results'.

Similarly, if people use language appropriate to a particular option for a meta-program, you will struggle to connect if you use language from the opposite option.

Figure 3.25 The language of meta-programs

You are likely to hear them say:

Proactive Lets do it! Go for it! JDI	**Reactive** Analyse, consider, think about The important thing is to... Set up a study group
Towards Outcomes, objectives, results Achieve, deliver Milestones, deliverables	**Away from** Overcome, solve Prevent, avoid Issues, risks
Internal reference We recommend We are/will	**External reference** What's your opinion? Has anyone else used this approach? Benchmark
Match Common, same, I remember a situation like this	**Mismatch** Doesn't fit Different
General Overview, executive summary, flavour	**Specific** Precisely, exactly, specification, data, specifics
Options Choice, options, possibilities, alternatives, variety, capability	**Procedures** Proven, tried and tested, logical, robust, process, method Firstly..., then
In time Lets do that now I'm sorry that I'm late, I just lost track of time	**Through time** Let's schedule that in I will see you at 1pm (Where is everyone?)
Sameness Same, similar Like this Replacement Reminds me of Usually, normally That's not the way *we* do it	**Difference** New ways of working, radical, transformation, change Make a difference Project

(Continued)

Figure 3.25 *(Continued)*

You are likely to hear them say:

Independent	**Cooperative**
Accountable	Let's, we, the team
Control	We will start right away
I will/have...	Teambuilding
When do you need it?	Collaborate
Person	**Thing**
People's names and their relationships	Where is the procedure for ...?
Who shall I ask/needs to know	What software are you using?
Talk about	Do

Figure 3.26 Rapport bridges the communication divide

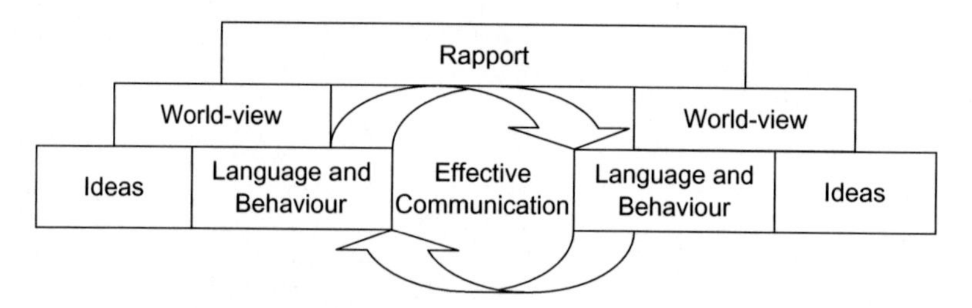

3.16 LISTENING SKILLS – HEARING WHAT'S NOT BEING SAID

> 'The meaning of the communication is the reaction to it'
>
> NLP presupposition

An alien observer may reasonably conclude that conversation is simply taking it in turns to talk, though I have witnessed 'discussions' with everyone talking at the same time. The most important part of conversation, however, is usually listening, not talking. Listening is more than hearing. Under stress, people's hearing improves but listening diminishes. We are mostly poor at listening, and have a number of natural obstacles to overcome in order to improve.

3.16.1 Listen with more than just your ears

> 'The most important thing in communication is to hear what isn't being said'
>
> Peter Drucker

Being able to pick up and decode what is being communicated outside of obvious words will give you an edge in everything from negotiation to leadership. We learned to communicate as animals long before we had language. Some studies have shown that the actual words used in conversation can account for less than 10 % of construed meaning,[156] with meaning being picked up from tonality and body language. Hence, the first part of an NLP practitioner course is usually spent on exercises to develop sensory acuity. The key starting point, whether we are listening or speaking, is to be 'present'/'in-time' rather than thinking where we need to be next or focusing on our own agenda, otherwise we will miss most of the meaning.

3.16.2 Meaning, words and distortions

In section 2.15 I introduced the meta-model, which describes the way the language we use distorts meaning and ways of challenging it using the 12 patterns of the meta-model. Which of those patterns regularly fall out of your mouth?

Exercise 3.31: Clarifying meaning using the meta-model

1. Refer to the Figure 2.16 (in Section 2.15) to remind yourself of the 12 patterns of the meta-model.
2. Think of someone that you don't quite relate to, or don't quite understand their behaviours.
3. Listen to the language they use and note examples against the 12 patterns of the meta-model.
4. What are the common patterns of distortion that they use?
5. What do the common patterns being used tell you about their view of the world?
6. Given that this view is their reality, are there any changes you could make to your language in order to meet them on their map of the world?
7. If you were to challenge their map of the world, what would be the key clarification to use?

3.16.3 What makes them tick – meta-programs and preferences

We have already mentioned some meta-programs to adopt when listening, such as being 'in time' and 'matching'. To get a good connection, it helps to match meta-programs through language. Listen to their language to work out:

- Are they towards goals or away from problems
- Big picture or detail
- Options or procedure, etc

Reflect these meta-programs through complementary words. If they talk about 'wanting to see the big picture' and you respond by offering to 'take them through the detail', then you may as well be talking different languages. It may sound obvious, but observe conversations and you will hear these miss-matches a lot, especially in groups such as Project Boards where you have a mix of grades and roles.

Similarly, listen for their preferred representational system. Are they visual or auditory? What words do they use? Reflect them, and change them according to the person you are speaking to in a group. This exercise will also enable you to move out of your own head and internal dialogue into the head of the person you are trying to communicate with. Being able to adopt '2nd position' is what really separates out good communicators from those who just talk.

3.16.4 Modelling of good listeners – some basic do's and don'ts

Practise talking and listening to people where the opportunity arises. (I leaned this from my father, who seemed to make friends with everyone he came into contact with, from the checkout girl to the chairman). Here are some common things to bear in mind:

- Be present (that is, 'in time').
- Give them your attention – this will also help you to move into a situation of rapport.
- Suspend your personal view on the issue while listening and just try to understand theirs.
- Listen from a position of respect for the person.
- Listen without judgement – do not impose your own 'map of the world', values or beliefs.
- Focus on what you have in common rather than the (often trivial) differences. in opinions. (This one is especially important for people like myself who are at the 'miss-matcher' end of that meta-program.)
- Know when someone's style is just thinking out loud.
- Playback and summarise, but don't paraphrase – use their language.

And a few things to avoid:

- Don't 'help' others to say what (we think) they want.
- Don't 'mind read' peoples intentions from their actions – keep everything evidence based. Or ask them.
- Don't jump in and problem solve – despite what we may think it can be quite insulting.
- Don't tell people that you know how they feel.

Identify someone who is a good listener and observe them with a view to modelling them.

3.17 REFRAMING DIFFICULT SITUATIONS AND DELIVERING BAD NEWS WELL

> 'The meaning of any experience in life depends on the context that we put around it'
> Anthony Robbins[157]

There is no such thing as reality, only the meaning that you give to it, which is dependent upon your past experiences, attitudes, values, beliefs etc. When the frame changes then the meaning changes with it. How you think about a situation determines your behaviour, which in turn, affects your outcome. You can use reframing to help yourself in difficult situations and you can also use it to help take the emotion out of situations for other people by offering an alternative perspective.

In a nutshell, reframing is looking at situations in 'out-of-the-box' ways to help yourself or others feel better about situations in order to gain positive results.

Frames were introduced in Section 2.9 and here we will look at their application to project management.

3.17.1 Bad news

> 'There is nothing either good or bad, but thinking makes it so'
> William Shakespeare

Although effective PMs adopt the mottos 'no surprises', and 'under-promise, over-deliver', given the range of stakeholders, suppliers, risks and issues that we have to manage in a project it is inevitable that there will be things that do not go to plan. It is very tempting to get into a 'witch hunt', but this 'blame frame' is not constructive, especially when we still need to solve the issue and go on to deliver the project. We should adopt an 'outcome frame' which will help us to resolve the problem.

Look at the following two lists. Think about a recent issue you've had at work and tick either the left or right hand column depending on which reflects how you were thinking about the issue (if you did both kinds of thinking, which did you spend the *majority* of your time in?)

Figure 3.27 Blame frame versus outcome frame

Blame frame	Outcome frame
What's wrong?	What do we need?
Why do you have this problem?	How shall we resolve this challenge?
How late is it?	How will we know when we have achieved it?
What is holding you back?	What resources would help us to move this forward?

(Continued)

Figure 3.27 *(Continued)*

Blame frame	**Outcome frame**
Who's fault is it?	Who has experienced similar challenges?
How could this happen!	What can we learn from this?
What does this problem stop you from doing?	What resources do you have that could help you to move forward?
Why haven't you solved it yet?	What are you going to begin doing now to get what you want?
This is going to reflect badly on us.	When we look back on this, what actions will stand out in helping us to have solved the challenge?

Think about how the left hand column makes you feel and how the right hand column makes you feel.

3.17.2 Reframing of context

According to NLP, all behaviours are useful in some context. It's just that sometimes we develop behaviours in one context but continue to use them in a context where other behaviours would be more useful. Jokes are an excellent example of context reframe, where the twist at the end 'reframes' the original meaning and makes the thing funny.

'How many project managers does it take to change a light bulb?
It depends on what you want to change it into'

Politicians are also excellent role models for reframing. During the 1984 presidential campaign in the USA there was considerable concern about Ronald Reagan's age. Speaking during the presidential debate with Walter Mondale, Reagan said, 'I will not make age an issue of this campaign. I am not going to exploit, for political purposes, my opponent's youth and inexperience.' Reagan's age was not an issue for the remainder of the campaign!

While leading a change management project in local government, I was warned to avoid a couple of 'troublemakers' who were asking awkward questions during a briefing by their director. When I put on my best innocent face and asked why, I was told that they were cynics. I offered a reframe: I said that I often found that cynics were people with passion about a situation that were brave enough to voice an opinion that was not popular, and some had experience of previous failures that might be able to help avoid making the same mistakes again. If you can win over the cynics, I said, they can become your biggest zealots in a change program.

While not being convinced of this transformation from sinners to saints, the reframe gave me the scope to get a meeting with several 'ringleaders' to hear their concerns, while at the same time asking for help and advice. Feeling listened to alone disarms much hostility, and asking for help more so. Cynics, for this campaign at least, quietened down, which helped my credibility with the director. One, a prominent union official, joined the change team and helped to forge better working relations with the range of union representatives on site. Inevitably, some changes involved detriment to individuals, including redundancy, but these were resolved through fair process in constructive dialogue, rather than adversarially through lengthy tribunal process.

Whenever battle lines start to get drawn, there is always opportunity to reframe where the skirmish will take place and who the protagonists are.

Figure 3.28 Examples of context reframing

Frame (Problem?)	**Context reframe (When/how would this behaviour be useful?)**
Too stubborn	Resilient Can be relied upon to get the job done
Can't work late tonight	Honest Prioritises Values work/life balance
Won't delegate	Sees things through Takes care of the details Takes ownership

3.17.3 The 'as if' frame

The 'as if' frame is particularly good for resolving conflicts. It allows you to come up with ideas that you might not have already thought of, giving you the flexibility to think outside of the box, which will provide more of a chance of gaining a positive outcome. Remember, 'choice is better than no choice'. To help resolve problems, try one or more of the 'as if' frames on yourself or with another party. (You can think of it as a grown up version of 'let's pretend'.)

Figure 3.29 Use of 'as if' frames to overcome barriers

As if frame	Steps
Future switch Useful for stepping back from the issue and giving some perspective to enable creative thinking.	1. Imagine yourself some time in the future when this project is finished. 2. Look back to now. 3. Ask yourself how you solved this issue.
Person switch Useful for de-personalising the issue and looking for resources that you might need. (Also a good technique for 'self coaching'.)	1. Imagine that you are someone else whom you respect (famous or a personal colleague, friend or family member). 2. Ask what you would do about the issue if you were that person.
Information switch Good for identifying missing resources.	1. Imagine that you have all the information you need in order to solve the issue. 2. What information do you need to know now to get you to where you want to be? 3. Where might you find it?

3.18 BRIDGING THE DIVIDE – NEGOTIATION, PERSUASION AND MANAGING DIFFICULT PEOPLE

> 'When two people agree 100% of the time then one of them is 100% redundant'
>
> Former boss

There is a huge body of knowledge on negotiation and arbitration,[158] but here we will be focussing on what NLP can bring to bear, though this covers most of the fundamentals along the way. As NLP recognises that people each have their own views and filters on the world, it also has a range of techniques for discovering them and finding accommodations.

It is very likely that you will get conflict in projects as from the outset you are trying to constrain the desire for more scope within limited resources, and also trying to accommodate an array of stakeholders, often with conflicting views. Negotiation is at the core of PM. As we saw in Section 1.2.1, two of the models for project management are those of a negotiation and as a decision-making process. So, before dealing with the NLP aspects, it is worth revisiting some of the tools and techniques available in project management for minimising conflict in the first case.

3.18.1 Minimising conflict using project management

As we saw in Section 1.7, there is a wide array of tools and techniques to support effective project management. Having these agreed and explicit helps to avoid conflict down the line, as most project management organisational structures are transient, and actors have probably worked with an array of different methods and processes.

Agreeing the governance structure up-front with clear reporting and escalation routes is essential to avoid conflict escalating to damaging levels. Similarly, agreeing clear roles and responsibilities and having these explicit in a tool such as a RACI (a table of those Responsible, Accountable, to be Consulted, and Informed for key deliverables) minimises doubt and confusion.

Sections below will describe active processes for stakeholder management, but effective PMs will already have a comprehensive stakeholder management plan, listing all known key stakeholders, assumptions about what they need and want, and how they will be engaged and by whom. This informs the communication plan. Often, conflict arises just because people were not consulted and informed at the right time, and this is mostly avoidable with good project management. Of course, clear documentation made available to stakeholders is an effective form of communication in itself, but the form has to be tuned to the audience – in NLP terms, you have to go to their world rather than expecting them to come to yours. Presenting casual project participants from the business with huge Gantt charts, risk registers and other tools of the trade is not likely to impress them, let alone get your message over.

Reporting should follow the principle of 'no surprises'. Don't bury the bad news inside a 20 page report or in the detail of an earned value chart. Give regular reports, ideally face to face, in plain language. If you don't, then you are likely to find yourself deluged by various project reviews and health checks as key stakeholders lose confidence.

Within the project life cycle, dispute is more likely towards the end, but this is when we have least influence over outcome. The early stages of a project decide whether it will be successful, not the mad rush and heroic endeavours at the end. Appraisal of options is where we have most chance of choosing the most benefit with the least resistance. In our urge to start doing stuff, however, we sometimes skip this stage and rush into defining a solution rather than exploring the problem. Similarly, gathering of requirements is often poorly done, leading to dispute at the end. I find this phase the hardest work, as the customer and end users are difficult to engage when things are still abstract, so you really need to be assertive.

Risk and issue management is clearly fundamental to conflict management. On one major government IT project a gateway reviewer commented that the strategy for risk management appeared to be to let them mature into issues and then fire fight those. Risk management was described as risk administration, i.e. a process of bureaucracy. It is obviously easier to avoid or mitigate risks than deal with them all as issues, though the latter may be more in keeping with the preferred 'heroic' mode of some PMs. To this I would add assumptions – you had to make them, but you also need to make them explicit and visible and monitor that they are still valid through the life cycle of the project.

Many projects involve partners, engaged through contracts and service level agreements (SLAs). It is often said that good contracts stay in drawers. Rather than mean that they are useless, this equates to 'good fences make good neighbours', i.e. when everyone knows where they stand there is less risk of dispute. Contracts also define escalation and dispute procedures, though the techniques described below, in combination with basic project management as above, should keep you the right side of fully fledged arbitration.

3.18.2 Perceptions, values and beliefs

People have different filters, see things quite differently and have different maps of the world. They have different values and beliefs, and no matter what you believe, this is their reality, so there's no point arguing with their perception, especially since it's got equal chance of being seen as 'right' to an observer as your perception. The trick is to try to understand their map of the world, values and beliefs and speak from it.

3.18.3 Meta-programs

We have seen that NLP describes some people with a meta-program for 'big picture' and others for 'detail'. Neither is right or wrong, but they are more useful in different contexts. In the context of gaining agreement, a 'big picture' approach is much more likely to lead to agreement than a detailed approach.

While working in R&D projects, I was asked to arbitrate in a dispute over which project took control over which laboratory. In short, one project that had failed to plan properly wished to claim priority and ownership of a laboratory that had been refurbished by a better planned but lower priority project. Since these were nuclear facilities, the lead time to get a laboratory decommissioned and refurbished to purpose was long, as well being costly, so the stakes were high. 'Big guns' had been brought in to argue their corner. It looked like one of those funny shaped arguments with two sides and no end.

As insults were already flying, the first thing to do was to try to take the emotion out of the situation. The technique of putting representative bullets on a flipchart and saying, 'This is the problem that *we* are trying to solve', while pointing at the board had the effect of starting to move everyone towards solving a common problem. (As these were R&D staff, problem solving was one of their motivating meta-programs). As everyone was from a research background, however, the predominant meta-program was detail. They were all familiar with work breakdown structure so we were able to chunk up to a common problem of shortage of facilities. With the problem-solving brains of a dozen people with PhDs now engaged in generating options, we were very quickly able to generate a flipchart full of options. (About half the room would have been options orientated, with the rest being mainly process driven. Those process-oriented people were then able to take the lead in putting the options through 'the machine', listing criteria, ranking and rating, and coming up with recommendations.)

The preferred solution was one of the options created in the process, which was to do a three-way move, bringing in another lab which required no decommissioning and relatively modest refurbishment. Those with a detailed/specific orientation then happily went away and planned out all the component work to make it operational.

Rather than having a blood bath and simmering resentment and personal vendettas for years, by chunking up to a bigger picture we were able to align a very creative joint team to imagine options and provide a process for accommodation. Although everyone had to give a little, everyone could see that it was best for the organisation and the process had been fair. As a group we all claimed credit for helping to sort out the department's facilities problems, further cementing us together to make things deliverable.

Which do you think is easiest to gain agreement from, when you are operating from 'sameness' or 'difference'? Are people motivated by 'away from', which can be fear, or 'towards', which could be greed? How would you change your approach?

3.18.4 Winning the battle but losing the war?

> 'Never argue with an idiot. Bystanders have problems working out who is who'
>
> Former boss's advice on being promoted into his job

As Dale Carnegie said, 'You can't win an argument'; both sides lose over time as resentment builds up and relationships suffer. Of course you don't have to negotiate or resolve conflicts. You can always go into denial and avoid the issue, give in, compromise or even attempt to push out your chest and dominate. All of these options have their problems, however, even if we can minimise resultant stress on the PM. Compromise should be a last resort as it can leave ongoing resentment. As everyone says, you need to look for 'win-win', but this cannot be gained by force or capitulation.

When we are dealing across cultures we must also remember that issues such as 'face' can be very important. You are rarely forgiven for causing someone unnecessary embarrassment by airing mistakes or poor judgment.

3.18.5 Dealing with emotions/anger

> 'You cannot shake hands with a clenched fist'
>
> Indira Ghandi

Conflict has two basic types: substantive and emotional. Mostly we are dealing with residual emotional conflict long after the original cause of the conflict has ceased to be significant. We need to deal with strong emotions before attempting to problem solve using logical tools.

In NLP, one of the underlying principles is to separate out the behaviour from the person and not to take issue with the individual (though it is human to do so). It is also very easy for the other party to become the anchor for the issue. Hence, try not to be in the direct line of sight of people experiencing negative emotions. Instead, try to anchor the issue to an inanimate object such as a whiteboard or a piece of paper on the desk and refer to 'How are we going to resolve *this* issue', with reference to the neutral object.

Should you remain calm in the face of anger and hostility, maybe adopting the demeanour of a Buddhist monk? If you have ever been annoyed enough to have a rant at the 'customer services' of your mobile phone operator or similar utility, how did it make you feel to be met with a calm and level tone? Maybe it works for you, but it makes me angrier. In NLP terms they are mismatching me in terms of energy, pace, probably language, and apparently on values and beliefs. If someone is angry with you then avoid being angry back, but respect their emotion and attempt to match their energy and pace, which will give you much more chance of getting them to tune in to what you are saying. Initially of course, just let them get it out of their system and check understanding. What makes me most angry is when I feel that my concerns are not being listened to. Once you have listened to them, and they have signalled that they feel that they have been heard, agree to go away and investigate their concerns and make an appointment to come back to discuss 'the issue'. When they come back you may not be able to give them what they need but most of the emotion should have gone out of the situation and you will have a better chance of finding a logical accommodation.

3.18.6 Meta-mirror and meta-positions

> 'In the house of ignorance there is no mirror in which to view your soul'
>
> Kahlil Gibran

The meta-mirror technique, developed by Robert Dilts,[159] is based on the assertion that in our subconscious minds we see in others that which we don't like in ourselves. (Perhaps this is why we hear the accusation of hypocrite so often.) Hence, as per one of the presuppositions in NLP, we have all the resources within ourselves to deal with the situation. Personally, I didn't relate to this concept during training until I had a facilitated session to deal with a recurring confrontation and figuratively found myself looking back in the mirror. (NLP has a number of techniques for resolving parts of ourselves that are in conflict. They require facilitation and are outside the scope of this book but you can find pointers in the appendix on 'taking things further'.)

When one of the founders of NLP, John Grinder, modelled people who were good at negotiations, he found that their core skill was being able to experience situations from many different perspectives. It is said that Mahatma Gandhi would sit in the chairs set aside for delegates before important meetings and try to see the world from their perspective, rotating around the seats time and again until he had a good mental model of the overall human system.

3.18.7 Using meta-positions to explore difficult situations

This exercise highlights what's really going on in the situation and helps you to feel differently about the person and situation. It is sometimes referred to as perceptual positions, and was the technique that sold me on NLP 15 years ago when it helped me to resolve repeated conflict with an old boss. I find it best to anchor the positions with chairs set at the appropriate points.

Figure 3.30 Perceptual positions

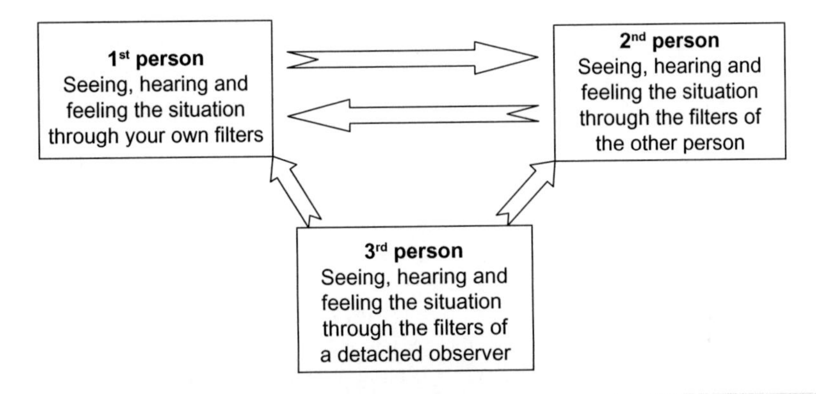

Exercise 3.32: Exploring conflict through meta-positions

1. Think of a situation where you are struggling to build a good relationship or find mutual understanding.
2. Sit in 1st position and imagine that you are looking across at the other person with whom you are having difficulty (in 2nd position).
   a. What are you thinking/experiencing/feeling when you see X?
   b. What would you like to say to X?
3. Break state by standing off 1st position and shaking it off.
4. Sit in 2nd position and imagine that you are looking back across to yourself as you were in 1st position.
   c. What are you thinking/experiencing/feeling when you see Y?
   d. What would you like to say to Y? Make sure you respond in the first person; "I ...".
5. Break state by standing off 2nd position and shaking it off.
6. Sit in 3rd position so that you have a detached and impartial overview. Looking at yourself in 1st position, how do you respond to the 'you' there?
   *e.*What would you like to say to yourself?
   f. What would you like to say to X?
   g. Having listened to both sides, what insights do you have that would help to move the situation forward?

7. Break state by standing off 3rd position and shaking it off
8. Go back and revisit 2nd position. Ask, *'How is this different now?', 'What's changed?'*
9. Finish by going back to 1st position. Ask, *'How is this different now?', 'What's changed?', 'What's happened for you since the beginning?'*

3.18.8 Needs and wants through language

'You get what you need in life, not what you want'

Anthony Robbins

Would your colleagues, friends and family describe you as being flexible?

In classical negotiation terms you need to work out what your minimum requirements are before your walk away/go to war decision. Often people have difficulty distinguishing between what they want and what they need. In one classic negotiation exercise we usually end up with two parties coming to blows over a pumpkin that they both 'need', whereas in fact one wanted the pumpkin skin to make a Halloween mask and one wanted the meat to make a pie – a classic potential win-win where they could have shared the cost and labour. A fundamental of NLP is the meta-model (Section 2.15) that helps us to make our language precise by minimising distortions, generalisations, deletions and equivalences, e.g. pumpkin skin = pumpkin.

Figure 3.31 Using the meta-model in negotiation

Type	Example	Response
Comparative deletion	'This is the best deal that you will get'	Compared to what?
Simple deletion	'I'm disappointed'	Disappointed about what?
Unspecified verbs	'You explain things badly'	How specifically do I explain things badly?
Cause and effect	'What you say makes me angry'	How specifically does what I say cause you to be angry?
Complex equivalence	'You didn't deliver on time, you are a failure'	How does an unavoidable change to the plan make me a failure?
Mind reading	'You think that I don't know what I am doing'	How do you know what I think?

3.18.9 Framing the problem

Frames are very important in NLP. What is referred to as the agreement frame is where we look at scoping the issue in terms of the areas of agreement that sit around it. For example, we agree that: we want to finish the project within cost, we can't use any more time and we don't have any more resources. Now we can explore our common problem with considerations such as 'Which are the parts of scope that can be deferred to another phase?'

3.18.10 Chunking to agreement

Project structures like public private partnerships can be described as 'same bed, different dreams'. The secret to making them a success is to find a 'superordinate' goal that both parties can sign up to. In soft systems methodology (SSM) this would be called finding an 'accommodation'.[160] Successful joint ventures are said to depend on establishing a superordinate goal that allows both organisations to address a common purpose.

We may disagree on whether we need an ICT system at all, let alone which system, but could chunk up to agree that we need 'a system'. Defining the system and process could then lead to a separate question of 'Which is the best option for achieving our agreed requirement?' I have been caught up in arguments over which finance systems to procure, when chunking up would have revealed that the superordinate goal was to improve financial governance, which would actually have been better addressed through clear accountability and training on the existing system, and for a lot less money and disruption.

Figure 3.32 Chunking to common purpose

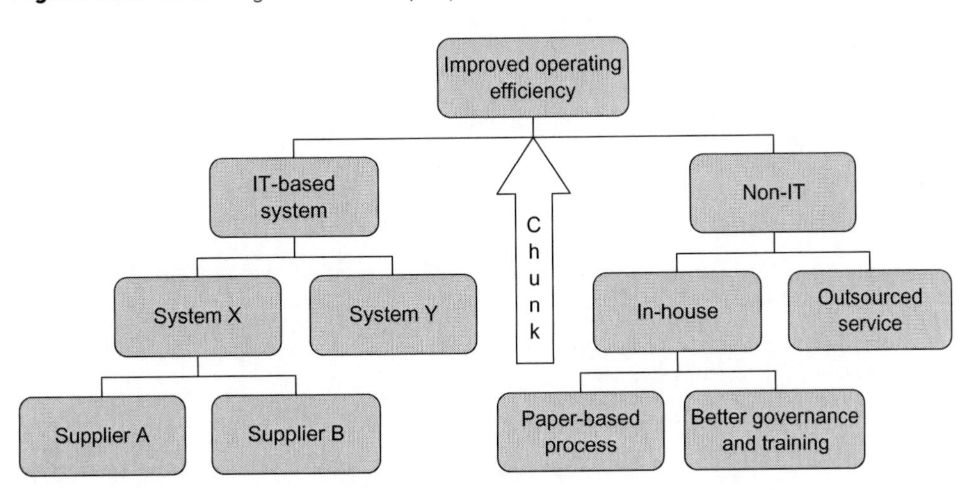

3.18.11 Modelling

If you are not experienced in negotiation, or not yet confident in it, then you should consider 'modelling' someone who is. Do you know someone who is good at resolving conflict or negotiation that you could try to model? What do you think their meta-programs might be? (Modelling is covered in Section 3.21.)

3.18.12 Summary and end-to-end process

As we have heard in this section, NLP has a lot to contribute towards finding agreement and resolving conflict. Just to recap on fitting some of these into an overall process:

1. To minimise risk of conflict, have project management processes and tools in place and sorted up-front, especially stakeholder management.
2. Use the techniques that you have started to learn to gain rapport – without this there will be no trust.
3. Anchor resourceful states (such as confidence, enthusiasm, commitment, curiosity and motivation) in order to manage your own psychological and emotional state before going into the negotiation/persuasion/conflict resolution.
4. Prepare your 'outcome frame' so that you know what your desired outcome is in the situation you are facing.
5. Separate out your needs from your wants, and be specific in your language.
6. Outline the overview first and then go into the detail afterwards so that you appeal to people with 'big picture'; and 'detailed' preferences in order to help them to understand you.
7. Get good at listening and reading other people's non-verbal communication. Start to recognise when someone really believes what they are saying or whether they are lying, being honest or testing you.
8. Use all of your linguistic power to influence the discussions.
9. Are they motivated by 'towards' (greed) or 'away-from' (fear)? Do you need to 'dangle the carrot' or 'wave the stick'? If you are dealing with a group of people, choose language which appeals to both preferences.
10. Use your questioning skills to uncover any deletions, distortions and generalisations, as this will help ensure that you are both on the same page and that there are no misunderstandings.
11. Reframe situations if there are any obstacles or objections so that the person can look at the situation from a different point of view.
12. Chunk up to a point of agreement before dropping back down to deal with areas of difference one at a time, easiest first.
13. Use metaphors to get your point across on an unconscious level if you meet conscious resistance.

3.19 MOTIVATING THE PROJECT TEAM

> 'You've got a goal, I've got a goal. Now all we need is a football team'
>
> Groucho Marks

It is the role of any leader to create a climate for success, and there is a great deal written about team building. This section does not intend to be comprehensive on team building, but to show how some NLP techniques can be applied to team building. Saying that, NLP does have a lot to offer in terms of motivating high performing teams. When the allied forces were mustering for the push into Kuwait and Iraq during the first Gulf war in 1990, the commander of allied forces called on NLP guru Anthony Robbins to deliver a motivational speech to the Special Forces who would be the first to go into hostile territory. (Compare this to the commander of the allied forces in the second Gulf war, reported as disheartening troops with a John Wayne speech about how 'some of us aren't going to be going home…'.)

3.19.1 Role of the PM in motivating the team

> 'Your most precious possession is not your financial assets. Your most precious possession is the people you have working there, and what they carry around in their heads, and their ability to work together'
>
> Robert Reich (American economist)

PMs often lack direct authority, as the resources on the project may belong to functional groups in a matrix organisation or be contracted in. PMs themselves may be contracted in. In any event, the project itself will be temporary and the team disbanded at some point. Nonetheless, projects are a team effort and the PM usually sets the mood of the project.

As a PM, for the team you will:

- Set the culture and tone for the project, whether by intention or not. If you come in late or deliver late then the team will norm to this behaviour, not what you say. Live the behaviours that you expect.
- Lead on communication. If you let the team stay in the dark then don't be surprised if you are kept in the dark and have a lot of nice surprises. You are a conduit, not a black hole.
- Agree expectations and enforce the rules. If you don't have any expectations then there won't be any. If you don't agree and enforce rules with the team then there aren't any.
- Choose the team. Your starting line-up may not have been in your control, but you may wish to switch your goal keeper from playing centre forward and make a couple of tactical substitutions down the line.
- Build the team. The individuals and the whole should be better performers at the end of the project than at the start, not worn down by the grind.
- Get the team to believe in you. Or not. Be true to your word.
- Be flexible enough to know when to lead, manage, supervise or coach.

3.19.2 Teams – a collection of individuals

> 'There is no such thing as society – only a collection of individuals'
> Margaret Thatcher

I have worked on a lot of projects where the plan said we needed x resources and we got x, usually minus a bit. But the old school question of 'How many men do you need to dig a hole?' rarely applies to projects. Not only do we need a range of different skills, but we should also have a range of personality types to avoid common modes of failure, or 'group think'. De Bono described different types of team roles, and Belbin and others have been used, but at the end of the day we need a mix. Cassandra/Black Hat figures are not usually popular, but every project needs one, though perhaps looking at risk rather than leading the project. If we put our team together correctly, or at least change the roles of the players we get to suit their aptitude, then the whole should be greater than the sum of the parts.

We cannot treat any team as a collection of clones. We all have different maps of the world, different values and beliefs, and different filters for language and behaviour. We need to consciously match our language and motivators to the individuals rather than blandly use those that apply to ourselves.

3.19.3 Working style – we all want to be in teams, right?

From most job ads it would appear that we all have to be team players. In a working environment, however, only about twenty per cent prefer to work as a cooperative team and have shared responsibility, according to the studies by Rodger Bailey.[161] A similar proportion want to have clear accountability and work independently. The majority prefer proximity – clear responsibility but have others involved. Hence, most people prefer well-defined responsibilities to be productive and stay motivated, and if accountability is not clear then most people will become disengaged.

How would individuals in your 'team' score on this meta-program?

> When I worked with a human resources department to recruit top level scientists and engineers into an R&D department they were preoccupied with talk of team players and questions to filter this orientation. (Most of the people in HR were of a cooperative style.) I explained to them that most of the candidates had research PhDs in maths and nuclear physics, and these were the types of activities that attracted independent workers. The projects that they worked on required a multidisciplinary team of experts, but the amount of interaction between individuals didn't need to be huge. I joked that for some of the people we could write a 'hard sum' on piece of paper and slide it under the door and they would just slide the answer back when they had finished and be very effective at it, probably even forgetting to eat or sleep until it was complete. This is an extreme, but we should not get too carried away with 'being a team player', as most people are not.

We did bring in specialists to engineer the new R&D facility around the concept of people dynamics and interaction to maximise casual cross-fertilisation of ideas, and I appointed a 'social secretary' to help with team building and morale, especially as most people were single and relocated to the job, which was in the middle of nowhere in case we got careless with the plutonium. Attempts at usual project team building exercises, like being blindfolded on a raft on a lake, were not so successful.

3.19.4 Working organisation – facts or feelings?

In projects there is a lot of focus on getting things done. One camp seems to be focussed on doing this through task and process, while another advocates an approach of relationship management. This reflects the meta-program for working organisation. A majority naturally focus on task or object, while less than twenty per cent naturally pay attention to feelings and thoughts of themselves and others. About a third sit somewhere on the continuum between. If you are trying to motivate a people-oriented person then don't over-emphasise the task aspects, but rather the interactions. For task-oriented people, just give them the goal and let them go, but not before you have got them to acknowledge the other people that they should speak to about it and keep informed as otherwise they may 'forget', as it will not be their focus. For task-oriented people, RACI charts are a very useful process tool for them to follow, clearly articulating for each activity who is responsible for actually doing it, who is accountable for the results, who needs to be consulted, and who should be informed. For people-oriented people, they are likely to have a preference for stakeholder management plans and communication plans (though they might not actually like the process of creating them!)

As a manager, try to understand the differences and use the right tool/person for the right job, as the saying goes: 'when you have a hammer in your hand, even a screw looks like a nail'.

3.19.5 Identity, beliefs and values for the team

As a long-established project reviewer, I have seen a lot of projects outside the ones that I have been personally involved with over the last 25 years, and creation of a strong project team greatly increases the prospect of success. To make our job as PMs easier, it is best to create a project team identity. This is often started through creation of a unique project name, though some still use accountancy reference numbers. For those projects with dedicated communications professionals, they should support internal communications by helping to create the team identity. A project kick-off meeting helps to engender identity, and many large projects have 'away days' to start to norm behaviours. Co-location of the core team is invaluable in creating identity, especially when resources report to different functional departments, or even different organisations.

Although there will be some natural norming of behaviour where there is co-location, it is best to explicitly agree some expectations with the team. Some projects have produced cards with 'team values' and 'team behaviours' on them.

Figure 3.33 Team charter for values of beliefs in high performing projects

Team values	Team behaviours
• We are a high performance team. • We achieve our goals. • We deliver value to the business. • We are true to our word. • Under promise, over deliver. • etc.	• We will turn up on time for team meetings. • We will submit reports on time with no chasing. • We will meet our commitments, or ask for help if we meet challenges. • We will notify our fellow team members of changes via the project plan and change log. • etc.

What are the values and behaviours of the team that you would like to be part of? Add them to the list. Rather than draft or impose these, the PM or nominee should facilitate the co-creation of these so that the team has maximum ownership. Although there will be peer pressure support if these are explicit, the PM is accountable for enforcing the agreed values and behaviours. If individuals are allowed to bad mouth other team members, or submit late or poor work, then only what gets enforced are the actual values and beliefs.

3.19.6 What are the rules?

A very important meta-program in management is working rule structure, which has two dimensions:

Figure 3.34 Working rule structure

	Rules for self	Rules for others
My/My	My rules for me	My rules for you
My/Your	My rules for me	Your rules for you
No/My	No rules for me	My rules for you
My/Don't care	My rules for me	Don't care about you

My rules for me and my rules for you is predominant in the workplace. Basically, people with this inclination do not appreciate that others have different maps of the world and different beliefs or values. They are always giving people advice/instructions, as they think that they know 'the' rules. (If you get a combination of this with meta-programs for detail, process and self then you are in big trouble – I worked for one of these and nearly imploded.) Do you think that they would take to NLP?

My rules for me and your rules for you can appear like someone not in control as a manager, but they actually appreciate that people are different and instead try to lead rather than marshal. They will tell you what they want but let you do it your own way. This combination is great for arbitration and negotiation as they can see all sides to a situation. A natural NLPer?

No rules for me but my rules for you are definitely not the people who 'walk the talk' or lead by example. The great dictators, past and present, would fall into this category. Some people call them hypocrites, but they know better. In combination with My/My, it seems most people at work want to tell you what to do and how to do it.

Own rules for self but no rules for others is a combination that really makes people angry. It appears as if they do what they want and don't care about the consequences for others. Fortunately they are a small minority in the workplace. (Though I think that they used to live in the flat above me.)

What do you think your current preference is? Do you think that your team would agree? Ask them. In surveys, most managers say they demonstrate a coaching style but staff respond that most managers are autocrats. But remember, with the help of NLP, we can change what we choose to, and change it back again when it suits us. We just need the acuity to know what strategy is best for the context/situation, what our 'normal' behaviour is and how to change it.

3.19.7 Why people don't do what they're supposed to

You have probably found out by now that people will not do what you say just because you are the PM. The days of formal hierarchies and 'command and control' are largely gone. Many PMs in any case work across structures, often without formal authority, so must learn to work by influence rather than status anyway. But no one comes to work to screw up, so why don't people do what they are supposed to? In his bestseller on the subject, Fournies gives the following reasons:[162]

- They don't care because they don't understand the need.
- It is not their priority.
- They don't know what they are supposed to do.
- They don't know how to do it.
- They think your way will not work.
- They think their way is better.
- There is no reward or recognition for doing it.
- They think they ARE doing it.

- There are positive consequences for not doing it.
- There are negative consequences for them from doing it.
- They anticipate a negative consequence.
- There are no negative consequences for poor performance.
- There are obstacles beyond their control.
- Their personal limits prevent them from performing.
- It is not possible.
- They have personal problems.

My interpretation of the common themes from these reasons are:

- lack of planning;
- lack of ownership;
- poor communication;
- lack of capability.

3.19.8 Planning for success

Few projects now exist without a formal project plan. For me, the main issue with plans is lack of ownership by the team when they are produced in isolation by the PM or a designated planner. If an unrealistic plan is foisted on me, or perhaps even a good one that I have had no part in, then I am not likely to be motivated to meet it. To my mind, the plan is effectively the contract between the team, and as such should be drawn up together through a process of co-creation. This is readily accomplished using workshop tools such as mind maps, especially the software versions that can export directly to MS Project and other tools. Estimation should always be a group exercise unless the organisation is mature enough to have a database of estimate versus forecast for similar activities. Many plans are hopelessly optimistic – projects don't necessary take too long, but insufficient time may have been given in the plan. This is particularly prevalent in public sector projects where parameters for the project are often top down rather than based on planning and estimation. The best plans use three-point estimation, encompassing best likely time/cost, i.e. the one that usually goes into the plan – engage your optimists for this, and the worst time/cost – you need your pessimists in the room too. From these ten per cent and ninety per cent probability points, we stand a much better chance of estimating our fifty per cent probability plan, i.e. one where we have as much chance of coming in early as late. (Software tools for this approach will generate probability curves and contingency, but more importantly, give prominence to the activities with most uncertainty that should be at the front of the PM's risk management plan.)

> 'Failing to plan is planning to fail'
>
> Alan Lakein

Once you have ownership of a common plan then be sure to use it as a communication tool and keep it updated against progress. After all, it was only the best guess of the team at the time – maybe you should have taken more notice of Cassandra?[163]

3.19.9 Clear communications

> 'Tell me and I will hear. Show me and I will see. Involve me and I will understand'
> Chinese proverb

Most projects now, especially change management projects, have communications plans and often dedicated resources to deliver them. This plan should be expanded from the Stakeholder Management Plan. These communications plans, however, are usually outward facing, that is, concentrate on stakeholders other than the project team. It is worth having a separate internal project communication plan. The communications plans should utilise those NLP tools described to address people with different meta-programs and preferred reference systems through a mix of channels and language.

3.19.10 Matching modal operators

People have a strong bias to the modal operators that they use. If we want them to properly compute what we say to them, then we *should* match their choices when practical.

Figure 3.35 Matching modal operators

	Positive	**Negative**
Possibility	Can, will, able to	Cannot, etc.
Necessity	Must, should, have to, ought	Must not, etc.

For example, if someone says that they *cannot* do something, then responding that they *should* mismatches their filters and is not likely to be heard. If people say that they *can't*, then tell them that they *can*, or are *able*.

3.19.11 Presuppositions

'*When* you start to use the skills in this book ...' presupposes that you will use the skills in this book. Similarly, 'when we complete this activity/project on time' presupposes that things will be done on time. Presuppositions usually slip under the radar and go unchallenged, which is why they are very common in sales training. Always presuppose success in your language.

Figure 3.36 Use of presuppositions to lead us to success

Typical language	Use of presuppositions
If we finish this project on time.	When we finish this project on time.
If the suppliers deliver on time.	When we find a way to get the suppliers to deliver on time.
Assuming we get budget approval.	After budgetary approval.
Requirements are a mess.	After requirements have been clarified.

3.19.12 Matching the meta-programs

When you ask for an update from a team member do you get a 20 page in-depth step-by-step description of what's happened or do you get a one-page summary? The first person is 'detailed', while the second person is 'big picture'. If you need more detail from the 'big picture' person, refrain from being angry at the one-page summary, simply be clearer in your instructions of what you expect. 'I need a detailed account for last week covering x and y.' Conversely, be more specific to the 'detailed' person if you only wanted a one-page summary. Use of templates helps, though one problem is that most of them are written by 'detail' people (with a 'process' orientation).

Figure 3.37 The motivational language of meta-programs

Meta-program	Option and appropriate language	
Motivational direction filter	**Towards** Talk about goals, objectives, achievements and benefits.	**Away from** Talk about the problems we are trying to solve, barriers that we are trying to overcome, and the risks that we need to manage.
Chunk size	**Big picture** Give an overview before you go into any detail. Use phrases like 'helicopter view', 'in a nutshell'.	**Detail** Follow up an overview with some detail, and refer to where more detail can be found. Use words like exactly and precisely.
Action filter	**Proactive** Ask them what they think needs to happen.	**Reactive** Tell them what needs to happen.

(Continued)

Figure 3.37 *(Continued)*

Meta-program	Option and appropriate language	
Reason filter	**Options** Talk about scope and the need to be flexible and open minded.	**Procedure** Talk about the phases and processes for the project.
Relationship filter	**Sameness** Bring out the similarities of this project to others.	**Difference** Emphasise some of the things that are new to this project.
Self/other	**Self** Talk of opportunities for development and progression.	**Other** Talk about the team and benefits of the project for the organisation.
Work organisation	**Person** Talk about the personalities and the interactions. Use peoples' names.	**Thing** Talk about the systems and processes that will be used. Talk about technology. Plans and activities.

What motivates you?

3.19.13 Metaphor – the key to the unconscious mind

Metaphor is like storytelling. Use of metaphor is about relaying a story to others in order to communicate with them on an unconscious level. Use all the modalities of the senses and get them to really imagine themselves in the picture that you're painting, hear what's happening and feel, smell and taste everything around that story. Whether the metaphor is a simple ('he's as cold as ice') or a more elaborate tale, as a PM, you can use metaphors to motivate others, to make sense of others' experiences and to overcome opposition, resistance and conflict. The great leaders all used them to effect, and you will find plenty of them in the holy books for good reason – the stories relay meaning and opinion that goes unchallenged. Maybe you remember parables like 'the good Samaritan' and 'Aesop's monkey'. Have you heard the one about the PM who communicated through the power of metaphor?

3.19.14 Hypnosis and the power of command

We do not cover hypnosis in this book, but its role in motivation is second to none. How else can you motivate someone to jump on a table and behave like a chicken, other than putting them in a 'reality' show? Basically, the human mind is very susceptible to direct command, especially when the conscious mind is distracted. If you want someone to do something, then tell them directly in a clear strong voice, rather than having a rambling conversation and hoping that they work out from it what your expectations are.

If you want to be more subtle about it, for example when you want to get seniors to do things for you, or the odd prima donna, then you may wish to try embedded command. This is where the command is disguised inside a harmless sentence but given a subliminal emphasis. For example, 'If you *SEND me that report on Monday…'*, then it will usually appear on your desk. Subtlety is required, so on this occasion CAPITALS does not mean shouting, only a slight emphasis in pitch or volume, or even a nod of the head.

3.20 GIVING AND RECEIVING FEEDBACK

> 'Feedback is the breakfast of champions'
>
> Ken Blanchard

We can regard feedback as of two types: motivational or developmental. We covered motivational feedback for ourselves and others under separate sections. Hence we will concentrate on developmental feedback in this section.

Continuous improvement through lessons learned reviews at the end of projects, and continuous professional development (CPD) for project managers, are cornerstones of the profession. In my experience, however, feedback is rarely done well, if at all.

3.20.1 Believing in yourself

Our brain is wired for feedback from the physical world. The classic example is a baby learning to walk. How many times does it fall over before mastering the technique? As many as it takes. And no one ever says on seeing it fall over for the tenth time, 'That baby will never learn to walk', or 'That baby is a terrible walker.' But that's what we seem to do in real life. As a consequence, people start to believe that, not only do they fail at things, but that they themselves are a failure. 'You can't write decent reports', or 'You are terrible at planning', become self fulfilling prophecies. When people start to believe that they can't do something, clearly given away in language by use of such words as 'can't', then it is difficult to motivate them to even attempt such tasks in the future.

3.20.2 'Failure' and resilience

> 'That which does not kill us makes us stronger'
>
> Friedrich Nietzsche

In America, some refer to having a business failure behind you as 'the million dollar MBA'. That, of course, depends on two things: if we are resilient enough to bounce back, and how the feedback was delivered and received.

One of the characteristics of high performing project managers, and CEOs for that matter, is resilience. One of the NLP meta-programs is internal or external referencing. Personally, I am high on internal referencing, which means that I seek feedback mainly as information, but have an internal view of myself and my own capabilities. Those that are mainly externally referenced, however, can be damaged easily by crude feedback.

Another relevant meta-program is 'towards/away from' for motivation. I am naturally an 'away from' person. This means that I want to know what can be improved, rather than what I do well. Fortunately, I have a *belief* in my own abilities, which means that I can take negative feedback without too much risk of damage. But be wary, too much 'could do better', without balance, can gradually erode self confidence and change beliefs. Sometimes it is those that appear most confident that can be hurt, as they may be wearing a mask to protect themselves.

3.20.3 Giving sandwich feedback

Why do the words, 'Can I give you some feedback?' often send alarm bells ringing? In practice it may mean, 'Can I give you my opinion/criticise you/embarrass you/castigate you/belittle you/do a hatchet job on you …'

A favourite technique for feedback in NLP is referred to as the 'meat sandwich'. The middle layer, the 'meat' of the behaviour that we are trying to improve, is sandwiched between layers of specific and general praise to reduce resistance and make the suggestion more palatable. Give it a try.

Figure 3.38 Sandwich feedback model

Step	Example
1. What they are doing well specifically – removes barriers	I like that you got the progress reports out on time again this week. I know it takes a lot of effort to get all contributions in.
2. What they can do even better next time – the behaviour that you want to improve	I think it would be even better if we put a simple dashboard on the front to summarise the overall project status next time.
3. What they did well overall	I am impressed with you overall contribution to the project – keep it up!

In terms of delivery:

- Timing – don't wait until end of year reviews. Give people feedback at least at the end of each piece of work.

- Get into rapport – if there is 'distance' between you then your message is not likely to be heard.
- Use their language where you are aware of it.
- Use fact, not opinion. You may be a mind reader, but most of us are not, and as we all have different maps of the world, we should not guess at the motivation of others.
- Language – Use 'do', not 'do not'. Express things in the positive as the subconscious brain filters negative precursors.
- Tone – avoid aggression, sarcasm, trying to show someone up, etc. It will not have the desired effect but will rebound on you at some later time.

3.20.4 Receiving feedback

Here are some tips on how to receive feedback. Firstly, if it is a straight compliment then accept it graciously and say a simple 'thank you'. Many of us are poor at accepting compliments. If it is likely to require some change of behaviour, however, then read on.

Exercise 3.33: Receiving feedback

- Reframe the situation – someone is going to help me to be even better!
- Set your goals – I am going to turn a critic into a supporter by meeting their needs.
- Manage your state – I am going to stay calm and open minded.
- Present yourself – imagine that your best friend is going to give you some good advice that will help you to meet your longer term needs.
- Dissociate behaviour from identity – no one is meaning to criticise you, only possibly your behaviour in this context.
- Accept things at face value – don't argue. Perspective is the only reality, and they have a different world-view to you. Respect it, and remember that a definition of rapport is meeting someone on their map of the world.
- Let them finish – don't try to cut them off.
- Paraphrase to check understanding. This does not give you licence to challenge, interpret, exaggerate or distort.
- Offer reasons if applicable. If they point out that you are often late, you can point out that you assumed you were working flexi-time, or that it is your week to drop the kids off etc. Reasons are not excuses though. Check what is an acceptable compromise if necessary.
- Thank them. Give them a genuine thank you for helping you to improve. It will help to diffuse even the bleakest situation, as they don't want to cut you down, only to see some improvement. Acceptance of a need to change is most of the way there in any change management project.

- Agree actions. If you can, agree actions going forward. It may be more appropriate to the situation, however, if you agree to consider what they have said and come back with a proposal. For any proposed changes, use the goal setting section of this book and clear success criteria so that you will know when you are done.
- Check information after the event if necessary. If what they say doesn't ring quite true, then check with others, but avoid going into denial as it will destroy the relationship.

3.20.5 Seeking feedback

'There is no such thing as failure, only feedback'

NLP presupposition

Now that you appreciate that feedback helps you to improve and is not to be feared, think of how you may get even more and even better feedback.

I was once fortunate to be in an organisation that ran 360 degree appraisals for senior staff. (With 360 degree appraisal you get structured feedback against set questions from clients, superiors, peers and subordinates). I was given the advice by a close friend in HR to send it to people that I thought I may have issues with, rather than those that I knew would give me a good report, as it was a good tool for bringing problems into the open and resolving them through fact and process, rather than letting them fester. It was a turning point in my career, as I found that one superior had fundamental issues with my behaviour, and this was based upon a simple misunderstanding of motive.

Exercise 3.34: Seeking feedback

If you don't have the luxury of 360 feedback in your organisation, then do your own.

1. Draw up a list of your personal key stakeholders, e.g. client, project sponsor, team leaders, head of finance, key resources, head of project management office, etc. (You can keep a generic list of the roles and then just change the names as you change projects).
2. Now write down what you think about them. Do you think that you have a good relationship with them? Do they understand what you do? Do you understand what they do? Do you think they appreciate what you do, and why you do it?
3. Now write down things that have gone well with them.
4. And things you think may have not gone so well.
5. Are you sure this would be their perspective?
6. Now make appointments to see some of them informally.

7. Say something like, 'I am putting together my personal development plan and would value some constructive feedback from you on things I have done well and should do more of and things I should work on for next time'. The latter part gives people a chance to say in constructive way things they may not be happy with.
8. Refresh yourself on how to receive feedback.
9. Attend the meetings.
10. Any surprises?
11. Now, draw up a development plan for yourself containing things people think you do well and things to work on.
12. For things to work on, look at the sections in this chapter on coaching and modelling.
13. Congratulations – you are already on your way to being an even better project manager.

Figure 3.39 Stakeholder map for 360 feedback

Position	Name	Went well	Not so well	Feedback
Sponsor				
Line manager				
Lead for finance				
Head of PMO				
Senior user				
Lead contractor				
Lead analyst				
HR manager				
Head of procurement				
etc.				

3.21 MODELLING EXCELLENCE

'Modelling is the pathway to excellence'

Anthony Robbins

Do you know any really good PMs, or ones that do some aspect of the job better than you, e.g. run a workshop? You are in luck, as the primary approach of NLP has been to model effective behaviours. I gave a brief introduction to modelling in section 2.18, and will now introduce the practical steps of modelling. Please note, however, that effective modelling requires a number of competences in itself, some of which have been introduced to this point, but it is not usually taught until Master Practitioner level. Of more than two dozen NLP books on my shelf, half only mention modelling in passing and the rest contain only a cursory outline for modelling of simple strategies. Proper coverage, aside from facilitated practice, needs a book all to itself. The pioneering work for modelling in business was by Robert Dilts,[164] based in large part around modelling of leadership skills at Fiat. My own modelling project, on entrepreneurs in the project management sector, took over a year to complete and achieve my desired outcomes. But PMs are clever people, so we will make a start.

3.21.1 Why modelling is important

As professionals, we are required to demonstrate ongoing professional development. In project management, after a few months of book learning, effectiveness comes down to being able to model the skills we see in others. It is your ability to learn that is important, not a trainer's ability to push information between your ears. Once you understand the thinking patterns and behaviours used by people who excel, you can emulate that competence.

In today's competitive environment, organisations have to build competence or be overtaken in the marketplace by those that do. The best rely on structured mechanisms to replicate the behaviours and results of their top performers. Whereas in the past people tended to consider 'knowledge is power', and organisations protected 'intellectual property', today in consulting and contracting, the most valued organisations and individuals are those that are willing and able to effect 'knowledge and skills transfer'. The real test of modelling is being able to transfer a skill to a third party.

3.21.2 Simple process to complex behaviour

Many areas of excellence that we experience are complex composites of many beliefs, values, behaviours and skills. Just as the APM's competence framework lists 'human resource management' as a key soft skill, this can obviously be broken down into further levels of detail until we eventually arrive at something that is finite enough to be able to model in a relatively short process. For example, 'presenting' could be broken down into a number of components, such as: presenting yourself, engaging your audience, use of language, projecting your voice, dealing with questions, use of tools such as Powerpoint, etc. The more finite the process is then the better your chance of achieving the same outcome.

Where you are trying to master a larger topic, some success can be achieved by spending a lot of time with people who are experts and mimicking what you see and hear. (Some of your preference for approach will depend on your own meta-programs, e.g. for process, big picture, etc.) For martial arts, this is equivalent to just mimicking the Master, which was the common form of instruction when it originated. For PMs, I certainly recommend spending time with your peers and getting involved in best practice groups. Aside from picking up knowledge, some of the behaviours will 'rub off'. (The appendix on 'taking things further' will point you in the right direction for communities of practice and best practice groups.)

3.21.3 Modelling simple strategies

Think of a simple skill that you would like to learn; for example, remembering names. My first experience of modelling was in the early 1990s. I wasn't comfortable using the telephone, but had the fortune to witness a colleague in the PMO who appeared confident and achieved good results. I will use this example for illustration in the process below. Please note that, although the process is shown linear and can be read through in a minute, it usually requires repeat cycles for you to be able to replicate the skill. Yet more time and practice is required to move it from being consciously competent to a subconscious and internalised skill. The true test of whether you have accurately modelled a skill is whether you can transfer it to a third party. Remember that it is your job to discover what it is the person is doing to be successful because they will not have conscious awareness of it.

Exercise 3.35: Modelling process for a simple strategy

1. Identify a gap or improvement that you would like to address through modelling.
2. 'Chunk down' the skill until you have something small and concise enough to complete in a reasonable time frame.
3. Identify suitable resources who seem to have this skill. One will do, but more helps in later stages to identify core and non-essential components.
4. Ask permission to model the skill. Most people will be flattered. Usually they do not realise they have this skill, as it is 'natural' to them and they often assume that everyone can do it.
5. Spend time observing people with this skill to get a kind of holistic overview of things they seem to have in common. During this time you will also be doing some subconscious modelling through the natural process of induction, similar to how you learned most of your skills early in life.
6. Establish rapport. You are well placed to make this easy as you have genuinely praised their skills and you should be listening intently to them. Later, you will also be mimicking both their body language and verbal communication, which naturally leads to rapport.
7. As important as how people do things is why they do them. Values and beliefs underpin success. Where we have recognised a skill gap we probably have a belief that we are not good at it, which needs to be addressed. The negative language can be easily corrected, e.g., 'Now that I have an excellent model I will soon be even better at (communicating by telephone).' In this instance, my model had a clear belief that information should be shared to avoid confusion and mistakes, so would routinely phone people up just to ask them if they had heard about so-and-so and generally how things were going. People often don't know why they do things, so some gentle questions along the lines of, 'And why is that important?' help them to explore what is buried between their ears.

8. Ask what their desired outcome is, and how they will know when they are achieving it. How will they know when they are not moving towards their desired outcome?
9. What starts the sequence? What are they doing? What are they seeing/hearing/feeling/saying to themselves?
10. Observe people's physiology when you get them to act out the task. In this example I observed that my model always stood up to make important phone calls. He said he liked to imagine walking up to them when he said 'hello'.
11. The most important revelation to me was that he managed to completely ignore the telephone, which had become a negative anchor for me. Instead, he recalled a picture of the person he was going to call, heard their voice and then, in his head, he was effectively having a face to face conversation. Usually, people who have a skill are not aware of how they do it, but these features can be elicited by a combination of focused questions, such as, 'And what are you thinking about now?' and 'Why is that important?'
12. If you have developed sensory acuity, observing the model's eyes when they are mentally replaying the activity will reveal any incongruence in what they say is happening. In this example, the model said that they imagined the person's voice, but their eyes revealed that they were recalling visual memories first, and subsequent questioning revealed that they first accessed the face to help to retrieve the voice, which would be normal for someone with a visual preference.
13. Ask what they will do if they are not achieving their desired outcome. How do they recover the process?
14. Once you are happy that you have elicited a good enough model to make an improvement, then try it out. Ideally, get your model to watch you, as seeing a 'mirror' will remind them of any steps or thought processes they have missed out. This learned strategy for the telephone proved a very effective starting point for me, especially in overcoming the barrier of making more calls in the first place and relying less on email.
15. The real test for a model though is to be able to transfer it to someone else. If you can't then there is probably a step missing.
16. As with any skill that we start to see an improvement on, I was motivated to improve further as I got the hang of it. You can refine the model by testing for bits that can be taken out without affecting the result. Modelling of other 'callers' also revealed that it was not necessary to stand, only to be comfortable, avoid looking down and relax the diaphragm in order to project your voice for clarity.
17. Is the strategy effective in all situations in which you want to use it in? The strategy was not effective when calling strangers, and had to be adapted. I gleaned this from a 'cold caller' in sales, who told me they imagined they were phoning up someone they knew who was in some way related to the purpose of the call, i.e. different purpose, different 'dummy'.

18. Models can be improved over time as you discover new resources. Matching of pace and energy, matching of language and preferences, etc., all built on to this skill over subsequent years.

(I later realised that my mother hated the telephone and would avoid answering it, so I was unpicking an induced behaviour.)

If you study NLP and modelling further you will see notation for modelling relating to this, particularly to the eye accessing cues. It is, however, easy to misread these cues unless you have had practical training and have 'calibrated' for your model; that is, tested how far and fast their eye movements are for a range of questions related to the senses.

'Children have more need of models than of critics'

Joseph Joubert

3.22 SUMMARY OF PART 3

In this chapter we have seen that there are a lot of NLP tools and techniques that can help to develop awareness of ourselves and those around us, and also to control ourselves and influence social engagement. All of this helps us to be even more effective and to deliver projects successfully.

We started off by considering ethics within the wider framework of professional communities and aligned the need to be ethical in our approach to NLP. We built on the work of Covey and other management gurus who promoted the need to 'sharpen our saw' and maintain a thirst for continuous development. We were introduced to a process for changing limiting beliefs. From Plato onwards, we were advised that our most fundamental requirement is for self awareness, and we explored the use of language and behaviour profiling of our sixty-plus meta-programs to understand ourselves and where we needed to develop flexibility.

After doing some exercises to know ourselves better, we moved on to exercises to help to manage our emotional state. In NLP we believe that we can choose our state, and prefer to be in resourceful ones, especially as we are often presenting ourselves in some way. We learned the 'circle of excellence' technique to manifest additional positive resources when we needed them. We were introduced to further meta-programs related to handling stress, and in particular where, when and how to move between associated and dissociated behaviour.

Assertiveness is an important skill for PMs, and we discussed how to occupy the high ground between the troughs of submissive and aggressive behaviour. More importantly, we explored the different leadership models, and the TOTE model was introduced to help develop flexible behaviour.

The NLP pillar of being outcome focussed was described and mapped over to goal setting in projects, and simple tools for prioritisation were practiced.

Timelines are a big theme in NLP, and tools for developing flexibility in being people focussed or task focussed were introduced. Better ways to match the natural inclinations of different stakeholders using language patterns were discussed.

Sometimes in projects we need to be able to see the big picture, while at other times we need to manage the detail. Sometimes we need to explore options, while for some activities we need to manage the process. NLP techniques to choose preferences were practiced, as was matching of language to different stakeholders with different preferences.

We covered a lot of different techniques to help us to build rapport with a wide variety of stakeholders, all underpinned by an attitude of genuine curiosity. An appreciation that everyone has different maps of the world and sees things in a different way to ourselves is required to establish the need for a structured approach. Different levels of rapport were introduced, from the superficial to those at an identity level, alongside examples of how to achieve them. Illustrations were given on matching of representational systems, predicates and the language of preferred meta-programs. Implications for progress reports and presentations were illustrated.

The meta-model of the deep structure of meaning of language was a cornerstone in the development of NLP and its usefulness in helping us, in the words of Peter Drucker, 'to hear what isn't being said', was exemplified through several exercises. Models for good and contrasting poor listeners were presented.

The use of reframe to change our interpretation of events, particularly in difficult situations, was described. Examples of how to do this and where it had been successful were given. As well as reframing of context, use of 'as if' and 'future pacing' were introduced to help to overcome difficulties and blockages.

Use of 'meta-positions', exploring first, second and third person perspectives, was described as a tool to help us deal with difficult situations and people. Various techniques for helping to reach agreement were discussed, including 'chunking' to common purpose. An end to end process for reaching agreement was laid out.

One of our biggest challenges as PMs is to harness the potential of the project team. The fact that the team is a collection of individuals with different world-views, values and behaviours was discussed. Different working rule structures, and their impact on the team, were described. Ways to create a project identity and norm behaviours were illustrated, e.g. through a 'team charter'. Common reasons for people not doing what they are asked were discussed, before addressing some of the root causes of these. Use of presupposition, metaphor and subtle command were illustrated.

All of this may be worthless unless we get feedback on what works and what needs further practice, so we dealt with giving and receiving feedback. The 'sandwich feedback' model was described, and an end to end process for seeking and receiving feedback was laid out.

We concluded with an introduction to the modelling of excellence – the starting point for the development of NLP. An end to end process for the modelling of a simple strategy was given, with an example of its use.

I am convinced that this approach and these and similar tools will improve your performance in the world of project management. I am also assured by family and friends that they help in our private lives too.

Appendix 1 gives pointers on how to take things further, other aspects of life that can be supported by NLP, and where to find additional resources.

Appendix 2 provides a virtual 'Week in the life of an effective PM' who has learned the lessons in this book. We will not learn these skills and behaviours by simply reading about them, however, but now that you are engaged and persuaded you are on the road to self improvement by practising their use, ideally with support in some form.

Appendix 3 provides an illustration of a counsellor-facilitated session for changing beliefs that limited professional development.

APPENDICES

APPENDIX 1
TAKING THINGS FURTHER

NLP seems to be one of those things that you either hate or you love it. I guess by now you will realise that it depends on your map of the world! Assuming that this book has stimulated your interest and you want to take things further, then I will give you some pointers here.

Of course, my first port of call must be the **supporting website** for this book: www.nlp4pm.com. It contains:

- Supplementary material
- Templates for use with exercises
- Reference material
- Links to other NLP sites
- Links to PM sites, those of the professional bodies, and PM communities of practice
- Details of upcoming free talks across the UK and abroad
- Details and dates for related training and workshops, including a practical one week course on NLP for PM that will embed all of this knowledge
- Details and dates for other courses leading up to formal qualifications as practitioner and master practitioner
- A blog
- A community of practice including space for your feedback and questions

The first NLP book that I read was *Frogs to Princes* by the founders of NLP Richard Bandler and John Grinder.[165] This is basically a transcript of one of their early training sessions back in 1975. It contains lots of dialogue, including a live phobia cure, so you can still **learn from the mouths of the founders of NLP**. You can follow this all the way to over 1500 pages on the subject in the encyclopaedia of NLP.[166]

Modelling is at the core of NLP but requires some practical tuition to take it further. Robert Dilt's books describe some of the modelling work that he did in top organisations, including leadership with Fiat.[167] For my dissertation on modelling, I modelled entrepreneurs in PM, i.e. those that had successfully started significant PM businesses and achieved a strong reputation. What made them different and how could I get it? (I also did a lecture based on this dissertation to Master's students studying the psychology of business.) An introduction to modelling successful behaviours is included in the associated course on NLP4PM.

NLP has been widely adopted as a tool for **motivation and personal development** and popularised by gurus such as Anthony Robbins.[168] Get along to one of his long weekend road-shows and discover what NLP can do for you.[169] Though you will be alongside several thousand others in a large venue, I guarantee that you will have an illuminating experience. You will also have the opportunity to do 'the fire walk' on hot coals to demonstrate the principle of beliefs (and also trance).

Although we only made passing reference to **hypnosis and self-hypnosis**, it can be very effective in resolving deep rooted problems.[170] Some of my associates have succeeded in modelling the patterns of Milton Erickson and have had great success.[171] Self hypnosis can be effective for state management and relaxation and I intend to make downloads available via the website.

Timeline was introduced in this book in relation to managing projects, but timeline therapy, as developed by Tad James,[172] is one of my favourite tools for re-interpreting past events. Do you want to know why you are angry with X or don't get on with Y? Maybe it is because your sub-conscious mind has associated them with a gestalt of other experiences lost in the mist of time (as I discovered on one occasion). Timeline regression and timeline therapy are introduced in many NLP training courses. (Timeline therapy also forms a part of a short add-on course for health that can be taken in combination with study of five days or more).

Top **sports** stars have long ago discovered NLP to achieve peak performance and control their conscious mind. The concept of 'the inner game' has been developed from its origins in tennis coaching all the way through to business.[173]

I made several references to NLP and **health** issues in the text and there are some good NLP books on the subject.[174,175] Aside from issues around stress, NLP is common in treatments of phobias, compulsions and addictions.[176] I have personally dealt with a number of clients with inner conflict issues. Colleagues, who are also fully qualified clinical psychologists, deal with issues at the extreme end, right up to 'car crash' celebrities. Be cautious who you deal with in this area as it tends to attract fringe elements with beliefs that fall right off my map of the world. If you need advice then call me and I will refer you.

And finally, **counselling, coaching and mentoring** can also be arranged through the supporting website www.nlp4pm.com via the 'contact us' page.

Have a good journey!

Peter Parkes

APPENDIX 2
A VIRTUAL WEEK IN THE LIFE OF AN EFFECTIVE PROJECT MANAGER

So, now that we are trained in NLP, when and where do we put it into practice in the management of projects? Every place and every time. Let's look at a virtual diary of an effective project manager who is starting to put all of this into practice over the course of a working week...

Monday Morning

On my way into work this morning I was thinking about the challenges facing me this week as the project nears the end of a crucial phase. Fortunately, I had some good 'me time' over the weekend with family and friends and felt happy and well rested. I carried the positive mood with me on to the client's site and was met in turn with a warm response.

As usual, we started off the working week with a meeting of the different parties working on the project. Rather than just invite my immediate team, I now try to include a wide variety of parties to get as many perspectives as I can on what needs to be done, and agreement on good ways of going about it. Some of the users have commented to me that they now appreciate all the work that goes into getting the project delivered and have gone out of their way to be more helpful. (It seems our old page on the intranet wasn't getting to most of them, though some appear to visit it regularly.) People used to turn up late for meetings, or skip them at the last minute, but since we drew up a team charter together everyone seems to play by the rules. (Of course there was one individual who tested our rules, but a private conversation to enforce our agreement seems to have resolved that smoothly.) Since Paul had expressed an interest in developing his leadership skills, I asked him prior to the meeting if he would facilitate the meeting. (I find that getting someone else to facilitate gives me the opportunity to listen and observe more, and pick up on some of the things that are not being said.) But first I did my usual overview of the breadth of the project and what was going well. We kept a separate note of anything that sounded like a risk or an issue to enter into the logs for review later. I concluded the meeting by summarising what was going well, what challenges we faced together, and what we had each agreed to do. I thanked everyone for their efforts. (One of the team had been very quiet in the meeting, so I had a brief word afterwards, but it turned out to be a personal matter – they thanked me for noticing anyway.)

I had arranged a meeting with a senior user that some of the staff had complained to me about. I feel that it is important to show the staff that I am there to support them and back them up. I used to invite people over to my office to save me time, but now I have got into the habit of going over to their workplace – this gives me a mental anchor of 'visiting their map of the world'. I have a lot to get through this week and felt quite rushed, but I wanted to give him my full attention, so I imagined stepping on to an imaginary timeline as I crossed the threshold of his door so that I could be more 'in time' – I find that it is much easier to concentrate on the other person in this state. Rather than getting straight down to my issues, I like to ask stakeholders what's happening in their world. (It turns out that big efficiency targets have been announced in Operations and they are taking staff cuts – probably why my people have been complaining that staff have not been released for workshops. I am sure that there is an accommodation to be found, perhaps if I pay for overtime to cover the time for training from the project budget. I will speak to the Sponsor about it.) I didn't use to like the guy that much, but we discovered at a team ice-breaker that we studied the same subject at university and we seem to have connected a lot better since then. (I am always amazed at where chemists turn up.) He uses a lot of 'doing' words, so I find it is easier if I talk to him in similar language rather than stick to my own visual expressions. It seems to strike a chord, and we both agreed to 'get on with it'. (I mentally stepped back off my timeline as I left his office as I had some other appointments to get to.)

Tuesday

We got together today for a workshop to update the risks and issues logs. First we reviewed the log of our assumptions, constraints, and dependencies. Had our world changed? Not as far as we knew, but I will check them with the project Sponsor when I meet him later in the week, as I am not aware of all that is happening across the business. I try to be upbeat in most meetings, but for the first half of these meetings I try to become a 'miss-matcher' and find reasons why things may not work. I usually like to be 'big picture' – a bit like the conductor of an orchestra, but for this session I wanted to be 'in the pits' with the players, so I adopted detailed behaviour so that I could understand peoples' concerns more easily. Having sounded out a range of pessimistic and optimistic scenarios, we agreed on a fairly realistic picture of the health of the project. I will run this by the Sponsor on my regular weekly meeting to hear if this matches his perception. One of the actions has not been updated – I will go around to see the action owner, as we had agreed for our team charter that we would all update our actions by Friday every week. Not many of them used to get updated at first, but now that they know that it is expected they conform most of the time. It saves all the chasing we used to have to do.

I have to go over to a supplier's offices today. They have not sent anyone to the team meeting or risk workshop for two weeks. I used to send an email and copy in their boss, but I realised that this behaviour never seemed to work. I could see that they were stressed and I commented that they looked tired. They confirmed that they had all been working late and weekends to recover another project. It turns out that they had not captured all of the client's change requests and now had to do a lot of re-work. I understood why my project was down his list of priorities. I agreed to cut him some slack on the provision that he would chair our monthly review of change requests – I wanted everyone to realise that we were not doing it for the sake of bureaucracy. I find that a lot of the staff like to hear theory and lessons first hand rather than go on a lot of training in methods, so I try to get people to pass on their experiences as much as I can.

I used to think that lunch was for wimps, but on my way back to the client's site I stopped off for lunch in the park. I have a relaxation tape that I play on my iPod and after twenty minutes I feel really relaxed, which restores perspective on my day.

I met with the new client who had a reputation for being antagonistic. His secretary kept me waiting and when he called me in he was assertive to the point of aggression. To that point I had been quite calm, which at least helped me to listen more and pick up the fact that he was 'hearing' a lot of 'noises' that he didn't like the 'sound' of. Although I did not match his aggression, I matched my tone to his and moved my breathing up to the middle of my chest where aurally oriented people tend to breath from, giving my breathing a similar pace to his. I didn't bother to ask him if he had read the progress report. I chose my words carefully, as I figured that they were important to him. I started out by reminding him that we all wanted a successful outcome from this partnership. I told him what had happened, what went well, what the challenges were, and asked him for his advice on helping to resolve them. He spoke at some length, giving me his opinions on the world while I dutifully nodded and made mental notes. I asked him what would make him sound happy about the project. He responded that it would be when his staff told him that things were ticking over properly. When he had finished giving me an ear bashing, he thanked me for coming to see him. I thanked him and made a mental note to update the communications plan to do a regular walk around the staff offices. (From experience I was confident that he would be much less aggressive next time, now that he was being listened to.)

Wednesday

We have a planning meeting today for the next project. I am good at the tools and used to knock these up myself and post them out to the team, but found it difficult to get people to update them. Now I like to get representatives from each of the groups in the room when I pull them together. It takes a bit of skill to stop everyone going straight into the detail – I use a 'chunking technique' to bring those people up to a high level and then travel back down the work-breakdown structure together. It really helps to get the dependencies aligned and have everyone understand the impact of any delays that they introduced. We used to encounter an optimism bias too, in that people would say when things could be done, but when challenged these were always best case scenarios assuming that the project was highest priority and fully resourced. Either that or else they put so much fat into the estimate that they were under no pressure themselves. We use a three point estimating method for activities now: an earliest realistic completion date, a last acceptable date, and an average or likely date given real world pressures. This seems to get the optimists and the pessimists on the same page and produce realistic plans that people can sign up to. Funny, but having had a hand in creating the top-down plan, people seem easier to persuade into updating their progress as they seem to want to see how things turn out themselves.

I take one of the guys out for lunch to discuss his personal development plan. He wants to be promoted and knows that the best way to do this is to keep improving his competence and experience. (He also wants to become a chartered practitioner and knows that this is now competence-based and experienced-based.) We work back from his goals to get a realistic timeline for his personal achievements – a bit like planning his own personal project. I give him feedback on specifics that he has been working on, emphasising the positives and pointing to what would make him even more effective. I also suggest someone for him to observe and try to model them for one area where he is having difficulty.

Thursday

I have a meeting with the finance department today. I have been asked to update the business plan, but I am not sure why they need all these tables and numbers. If we are on time then we are to budget, and if we are late then it costs money, simple as that in my map of the world. Rather than tell them about my world, however, I confess that all the spreadsheets and the finance system leave me a bit bewildered and I do not give them the priority that I maybe should. They say that at least my projects are running to cost, so I must be doing something right. I tell them that I am very careful to get a realistic plan and robust estimates, and then just track those. They say that if I show them how I put my estimates together then they will translate them to their format. Apparently they need them in this standard format so that they can consolidate figures across all projects to report up to the CFO, who uses them to make sure that we have sufficient cash-flow in the company to pay our salaries. They even offer to show me how to check the progress of orders using the on-line financial system, so that I know if they are delayed or not. I may start to let one of them come to the project team meetings – if they promise to leave Excel behind.

Now that I have all my financial information sorted I can finish drafting the progress report. I like to use highlights and exceptions, but some people just can't seem to get enough detail, so I update standard tables as appendices. One of the senior users likes me to use 'smiley/sad' faces – it keeps her happy and lets everyone know at a glance how we are doing. I will run my draft past the Sponsor before I send it out, as she will do an upward briefing to other directors and it is good to sing from the same hymn sheet, as we have some stakeholders who can be difficult if they are not actively managed. Some of the staff don't seem to read email so I always give the highlights at key meetings the following week to make sure everyone is on message.

Friday

I have lunch with my boss to discuss my performance. I am lucky in that she is responsible for developing the project management capability across the company. I tell her what things I am happy with and where I think that I could improve. I tell her that I am not comfortable with Finance and we discuss options. I suggest that I could get someone in to help me, or go on a training course. She proposes instead that I meet with one of her other project managers who comes from a finance background and get him to mentor me in this aspect. She asks that I offer to facilitate some risk workshops for him in return, as his risk log never quite matches reality. She suggests that I move my desk to the finance department while I am focussing on finance, to get a better understanding of their world. She also reports back that the new client said that he liked what I had to say.

At lunchtime I go for a run. I never used to make the time and often felt too tired, but now I find that I actually have more energy and even sleep better. A virtuous circle really.

After lunch I meet with the project sponsor. I mentioned that we had reviewed the assumptions log and asked if there were any changes that we might need to accommodate. He replied not, but that we were in changing times, so we should review them regularly. I emailed the draft progress report over last night to give him time to read it, but I will go through it anyway. He wants me to make more of the issues that we are facing, as some people think that we are over-resourced and he is worried about being another project failure. We agree to add a pictorial 'probability impact grid' to provide an overview of the number and magnitude of risks, but to colour code them to show that they are generally under control with this level of resource. I mention the meeting with the client and ask for some casual support in convincing them and other stakeholders that we are doing this *for* them, and not *to* them. (He tells me that they play in the same jazz band, and that he is a nice chap when you get to know him.) I also mention the conversation with Operations about people not turning up to workshops, and ask if we can pay overtime to mitigate the issue. He tells me to speak to Finance about it to see if we have scope, but says that finance have warned him that my Business Case may be late. I report that I have met with them to ask for help and that my boss has also appointed a mentor to help me with it. He says he feels well informed and reasonably assured. We exchange pleasantries about our plans for the weekend, I go back to my office, make the agreed changes and send out the report. He used to want to check it again after changes, but now seems to trust me.

I review my week: what I have accomplished, what challenges I have faced, and what I have learned. I make a list of things to do for the next week and then go home to my family for some serious R&R. And there are those that say the life of a project manager is an unrewarding and stressful one – only if we let it be.

APPENDIX 3
CHANGING BELIEFS THAT LIMITED PROFESSIONAL DEVELOPMENT

We have heard that some beliefs can limit our achievement and become self fulfilling prophecies. We can use Belief Change techniques as illustrated in Section 3.4 to help with these. We can also use direct intervention with the help of a counsellor/facilitator. I will walk you through a story to illustrate, with annotation for NLP components.

I had a friend who knew of my counselling work and was finally driven to visit me to ask for help, which is surprisingly difficult in most cultures. He had been working on a Master's for many years, and was now rapidly approaching his time limit for submission before he was automatically failed. (Note that this is not the same as those accustomed to leaving everything until the last moment to get sufficient 'away from' motivation to put the effort in.)

Client: I have never passed any exams before'. (Universal Distortions 'never' and 'any')

Counsellor: 'Never, any?' (Addressing Universal Distortions)

Client: 'Well, apart from …' (challenge accepted)

Counsellor: 'So, you can successfully pass exams, as already evidenced. (Supplying evidence for belief change.) Moving on, again, why are you here?'

Client: 'I have to finish my dissertation.'

Counsellor: 'Have to, or want to? Who doesn't want you to? (Looking for 'Part' causing conflict, usually associated with significant figure during up-bringing.)

Client: 'How do you know about that?' (Surprise and assumption that I am mind reading, whereas I am just following process.)

Counsellor: 'You just told me about it (viz in response). Do you really think that *they want you to succeed*?' (Use of redundant negative to express positive, viz 'they want you to succeed' – the subconscious does not hear negatives.)

Client: 'They (named) never had the chance of a proper education.' (Displaying subconscious empathy with part modelled on carer – very common.)

Counsellor: 'Does anyone else in your family have qualifications?'

Client: 'Oh yes, my brother has loads' (Wall of old belief about not deserving qualifications in mis-placed empathy for carer starting to tumble down.)

Counsellor: 'So, people in your family pass exams like this as a matter of routine. (Second induction at Belief change.) And I bet *your family were really proud'.* (Re-enforcer.)

Client: 'Oh, yes' (possible confirmation of belief change).

Counsellor: 'And when you *complete this dissertation and pass* (use of command tonality alongside future pacing), everyone will be really proud of you' (installing motivators.)

Client: 'Oh yes' (Confirmation via '3 yeses' technique beloved of sales people.)

Counsellor: 'So remind me. Give me ten reasons why ***you want to complete this dissertation now'*** (Overt use of embedded command as resistance has now disappeared.)

Client: Reels of list with sparkle in the eye. (Physical evidence of belief change.)

Counsellor: 'And didn't you finish renovating your house recently? It looks really nice now that *it's finished.* (Close of process.) Can you imagine how happy you will be when *your dissertation will be finished.* (Command and applying anchor to positive experience.) *Think how happy you will be at your graduation. How happy your family will be. And you will* ***look back at today*** *and remember that* ***now*** *is the time that everything* ***changed***. (Use of future pacing to establish belief change on timeline.)

This is obviously a contracted example, as subjects tend to try to distract the facilitator and wander around in circles, meaning that sessions like this can take an hour and may need to be repeated.

Having read the chapter on NLP and sections on Ethics and well formed outcomes, you will not be alarmed at the use of techniques to change people's beliefs and behaviours, but in short:

- We can only effect change when we have been given permission
- The Desired Outcome must be congruent with the well-being of the subject and those affected by the actions.

NOTES

1. www.majorprojects.org

2. (2010) *A History of the Association for Project Management,* APM Publishing.

3. Robert Dilts and Judith DeLozier, 'Encyclopedia of Systemic NLP and NLP New Coding', www.nlpuniversitypress.com

4. Stevens, M. J. (Ed.) (2002) *Project Management Pathways: Better Projects Are Better Business*', APM Publishing.

5. Turner, J. R. (1993) *The Handbook of Project-Based Management: Improving the Processes for Achieving Strategic Objectives*, McGraw-Hill.

6. (2008) *A Guide to the Project Management Body of Knowledge (PMBOK Guide)* 4th Edition, PMI.

7. Office of Government Commerce (OGC) (2009) *Managing Successful Projects with PRINCE2 2009 Edition Manual*, The Stationery Office.

8. Office of Government Commerce (OGC) (2007) *Managing Successful Programs*, The Stationery Office (TSO).

9. (2010) *A History of the Association for Project Management*, APM Publishing.

10. Winter, M. and Szczepanek, T. (2010) *Images of Projects*, Gower.

11. (2010) *History of the Association for Project Management*, APM Publishing.

12. Stevens, M. J. (Ed.) (2002) *Project Management Pathways: Better Projects Are Better Business*, APM Publishing.

13. Winter, M., Smith, C., Cooke-Davies, T. and Cicmil, S. (2006) 'Rethinking Project Management', *International Journal of Project Management*, 24 (8), 650–662.

14. Turner, J. R. (1993) *The Handbook of Project-Based Management: Improving the Processes for Achieving Strategic Objectives*, McGraw-Hill.

15. (2006) *APM Body of Knowledge*, Revision 5, APM Publishing.

16. (2009) *Sponsoring Change: A Guide to the Governance Aspects of Project Sponsorship*, APM Publishing.

17. (2006) *Directing Change: A Guide to Governance of Project Management*, APM Publishing.

18. Obeng, Eddie (1995) *All Change! The Project Leader's Secret Handbook*, Financial Times/Pearson Publishing.

19. Pellerin, C. J. (2009) *How NASA Builds Teams: Mission Critical Soft Skills for Scientists, Engineers, and Project Teams*, Wiley.

20. Project Evaluation and Review Technique (PERT) was developed by the US Navy Special Projects Office in 1957 to support the Polaris nuclear submarine project (Wikipedia).

21. Parkes, P. (1998) *Best Practice for Project Management of R&D*, Master's dissertation, Lancaster.

22. Phillips, R. (1998) 'BAE project "a shambles": Aerospace giant accused of wasting taxpayers' money on ill-managed research work', *The Independent*, Sunday, 3.

23. www.ogc.gov.uk/documents/rpa_guide.pdf

24. The OGC transferred to the Cabinet Office in 2010 as the Efficiency Review Group (ERG).

25. Parkes, P. (1998) 'Strategic Technical Alliances and Outsourcing', *International R&D Management Conference*, Avilla, Spain.

26. (2009) *Sponsoring Change: A Guide to the Governance Aspects of Project Sponsorship*, APM Publishing.

27. Turner, J. R. (1993) *The Handbook of Project-Based Management: Improving the Processes for Achieving Strategic Objectives*, McGraw-Hill.

28. Mehrabian, A. and Wiener, M. (1967) 'Decoding of Inconsistent Communications', *Journal of Personality and Social Psychology*, 6 (1), 109–114.

29. Cabinet Office (2005) 'Transformational Government: Enabled by Technology', HM Government White Paper.

30. Office of Government Commerce (OGC) (2007) *Managing Successful Programs*, The Stationery Office (TSO).

31. Hammer, M. (1996) *Beyond Re-engineering: How Process Centred Organization is Changing our Work and Our Lives*, Harper Business.

32. Parkes, P. (1998) *Best Practice for Project Management of R&D*, Master's dissertation, Lancaster.

33. Parkes, P. (1997) 'Marrying R&D to the Business', *International R&D Management Conference*, Manchester.

34. Cooper, R. G. (1986) *Winning at New Products*, Addison-Wesley.

35. www.ogc.gov.uk/what_is_ogc_gateway_review.asp

36. Office of Government Commerce (OGC) (2009) *Managing Successful Projects with PRINCE2 2009 Edition Manual*, The Stationery Office.

37. Clegg, R. (1996) 'Developing a Culture for Innovation', Master's dissertation, Lancaster University Management School.

38. Dr Sue Ion led BNFL's R&D directorate and was made a Dame in the New Year's Honours list 2010.

39. (2010) *Project Magazine*, APM Publishing/Headlines, October, Issue 232.

40. Jenner, S. (2010) *Transforming Government and Public Services: Realising Benefits Through Project Portfolio Management*, Gower.

41. (2005) *Directing Change: A Guide to Governance of Project Management*, APM Publishing.

42. APM Governance SIG (2009) *Sponsoring Change: A Guide to the Governance Aspects of Project Sponsorship*, APM Publishing.

43. www.standishgroup.com

44. www.nao.org.uk

45. www.ogc.gov.uk/documents/cp0015.pdf

46. Cobb, M. (1995) (Treasury Board of Canada Secretariat), presentation at CHAOS University, reported on www.standishgroup.com/chaos/intro1.php.

47. 'Creating Value in Project Management Using PRINCE2', A study by Queensland University of Technology 2010.

48. Phillips, R. (1998) 'BAE project 'a shambles': Aerospace giant accused of wasting taxpayers' money on ill-managed research work', *The Independent*, 3 May.

49. Stevens, M. J. (Ed.). (2002) *Project Management Pathways: Better Projects Are Better Business*', APM Publishing.

50. (2007) *Models to Improve the Management of Projects*, APM Publishing.

51. http://www.ogc.gov.uk/documents/p3m3.pdf

52. (2002) Typical Terminologies by Industry (for Life Cycle Stages), *Project Management Pathways*, APM Publishing.

53. Turner, J. R. (1997) 'Cultural Profile for Project Management', *The Handbook of Project-Based Management*, McGraw-Hill, 504.

54. APM Governance SIG (2009) *Sponsoring Change: A Guide to the Governance Aspects of Project Sponsorship*, APM Publishing.

55. Flyvbjerg, B., Holm, M. S. and Buhl, S. (2002) 'Underestimating Costs in Public Works Projects: Error or Lie?' *Journal of the American Planning Association*, 68 (3), 279–295.

56. Chapman, J. (2006) *Project and Program Accounting: A Practical Guide for Professional Service Organisations and IT*, Project Manager Today.

57. Flyvbjerg, B., Holm, M. S. and Buhl, S. (2002) 'Underestimating Costs in Public Works Projects: Error or Lie?' *Journal of the American Planning Association*, 68 (3), 279–295.

58. Parkes, P. 'Risk Management', www.peoplealchemy.com

59. Pullan, P. and Murray-Webster, R. (2010) *A Short Guide to Facilitating Risk Management: Engaging People to Identify, Own and Manage Risk*, Gower.

60. The Specific Interest Group (SIG) for Risk Management holds an annual conference on soft skills, see www.apm.org.uk/riskmanagement.

61. Parkes, P. 'Consulting and Contracting', www.peoplealchemy.com

62. Jenner, S. (2010) *Transforming Government and Public Services: Realising Benefits Through Project Portfolio Management*, Gower.

63. Parkes, P. (2008) 'Lost in Translation', *Project Magazine*.

64. Parkes, P. 'Performance Management and Scorecards', www.peoplealchemy.com

65. Wake, S. (2004) *Earned Value Analysis (EVA): A Real Guide to Cost and Schedule Control*, Steve Wake Projects Ltd.

66. Fournies, F. F. (1999) *Why Employees Don't Do What They Are Supposed To Do*, McGraw-Hill.

67. GAPPS – Global Alliance for Project Performance Standards – www.globalpmstandards.org

68. Whiddett. S. and Hollyforde, S. (2003) *A Practical Guide to Competences*, Chartered Institute of Personnel and Development (CIPD).

69. Boyatzis, R. (1982) *The Competent Manager: A Model for Effective Performance*, Wiley.

70. Miller, J. 'Competence Frameworks', www.alchemyformanagers.co.uk

71. (2008) *APM Competence Framework*, APM Publishing.

72. Turner, J. R. (1993) 'Traits of Effective Project Managers', *The Handbook of Project-Based Management: Improving the Processes for Achieving Strategic Objectives*, McGraw-Hill, Section 18.5.

73. Portny, S. E. (2001) *Project Management for Dummies*, Wiley.

74. Covey, S. R. (1989) *The 7 Habits of Highly Effective People: Powerful Lessons in Personal Change*, Simon & Schuster.

75. Office of Government Commerce (OGC) (2009) *Managing Successful Projects with PRINCE2* 2009, Edition Manual, The Stationery Office.

76. Gadeken, O. (2000) 'What the Defence Systems Management College Has Learned From Ten Years of Project Leadership Research', Proceedings of PMI Research Conference, 274.

77. Goleman, D. (1996) *Emotional Intelligence: Why It Can Matter More than IQ*, Bloomsbury.

78. Carter, P. (2009) *Test Your EQ*, Kogan Page.

79. Mersino, A. (2007) *Emotional Intelligence for Project Managers: The People Skills You Need to Achieve Outstanding Results*, American Management Association.

80. Turner, J. R. (2006) 'Leadership: The Project Context', *Project Manager Today*, November, 29.

81. Lee-Kelley, L. and Long, K. L. (2003) 'Turner's Five Functions of Project-Based Management and Situational Leadership in IT Services Projects', *International Journal of Project Management* 21 (8), 583–591.

82. Dr Charles Wilbe @ www.projectdoctors.co.uk

83. Hughes, B. (Ed.) (2004) *Project Management for IT-Related Projects* (Textbook for ISEB Certificate in IS Project Management), BCS Publications.

84. Kruger, J. and Dunning, J. (1999) 'Unskilled and Unaware of It: How Difficulties in Recognising One's Own Incompetence Leads to Inflated Assessments', *Journal of Personal and Social Psychology*, 77 (6), 121.

85. www.apm.org.uk/apmprojectprofessional.asp

86. SFIA – Skills Framework for the Information Age @ www.sfia.org.uk

87. Grinder, J. and Bandler, R. (1975) *The Structure of Magic I: A Book About Language and Therapy*, Science and Behaviour Books.

88. Korzybski, A. (1994) *Science and Sanity*, Institute of General Semantics, (first published 1933).

89. Pribham, K., Miller, G. and Gallanter, E. (1960) *Plans and the Structure of Behaviour*, Prentice Hall.

90. Miller, G. (1956) 'The Magic Number Seven, Plus or Minus Two', *Psychological Review*, 63, 81–97.

91. Berne, E. (1961) *Transactional Analysis in Psychotherapy*, Souvenir Press.

92. Perls, F. (1969) *Gestalt Therapy Verbatim*, Real People Press.

93. Satir, V., Bandler, R., and John Grinder, J. (1976) *Changing with Families*, Science and Behaviour Books.

94. Grinder, J. and Bandler, R. (1975) *The Structure of Magic I: A Book About Language and Therapy*, Science and Behaviour Books.

95. Grinder, J. and Bandler, R. (1975) *Patterns of the Hypnotic Techniques of Milton H. Erickson*, 1 & 2, Meta Publications.

96. O'Connor, J. (2001) *NLP Workbook*, Element.

97. Robbins, A. (1987) *Unlimited Power,* Harper Collins.

98. Bandler, R. and Grinder, J. (1975) *Patterns of the Hypnotic Techniques of Milton H. Ericson*, Meta Publications.

99. Owen, N. (2004) *More Magic of Metaphor: Stories for Leaders, Influencers and Motivators*, Crown House.

100. Shapiro, D. (1996) *Your Body Speaks Your Mind: Understanding How Your Emotions and Thoughts Affect You Physically*, Piatkus.

101. Dilts, R. (1983) *Applications of NLP*, Meta Publications.

102. Charvet, S. R. (1995) *Words that Change Minds: Mastering the Language of Influence*, Kendall Hunt.

103. Bandler, R. and Grinder, J. (1981) *Reframing*, Real People Press.

104. Dilts, R. (1998) *Modelling with NLP*, Meta Publications.

105. Mehrabian, A. and Wiener, M. (1967) 'Decoding of Inconsistent Communications', *Journal of Personality and Social Psychology*, 6 (1), 109–114.

106. Robbins, A. (1992) *Awaken the Giant Within,* Simon & Schuster.

107. Brown, D. (2006) *Tricks of the Mind*, Channel 4 Books.

108. Bandler, R. and MacDonald, W. (1988) *An Insider's Guide to Sub-Modalities*, Meta Publications.

109. McDermott, I. and Jago, W. (2001) *Brief NLP Therapy* (Brief Therapies series), Sage.

110. James, T. (1989) *Timeline Therapy and the Basis of Personality*, Meta Publications.

111. McDermott, I. and Jago, W. (2001) *Brief NLP Therapy* (Brief Therapies series), Sage.

112. Satir, V., Bandler, R., and John Grinder, J. (1976) *Changing with Families*, Science and Behaviour Books.

113. Grinder, J. and Bandler, R. (1975) *The Structure of Magic I: A Book About Language and Therapy*, Science and Behaviour Books.

114. Bandler, R. and Grinder, J. (1975) *Patterns of the Hypnotic Techniques of Milton H. Ericson*, Meta Publications.

115. Perls, F. (1969) *Gestalt Therapy Verbatim*, Real People Press.

116. James, T. (1989) *Timeline Therapy and the Basis of Personality*, Meta Publications.

117. Woosnam, I., Alder, H. and Morris, K. (1997) *Masterstroke: Use the Power of Your Mind to Improve Your Golf with NLP*, Piatkus Books.

118. Grinder, J. and Bandler, R. (1975) *The Structure of Magic I: A Book About Language and Therapy*, Science and Behaviour Books.

119. Bandler, R. and Grinder, J. (1975) *Patterns of the Hypnotic Techniques of Milton H. Ericson*, Meta Publications.

120. People Alchemy for Managers @ www.peoplealchemy.co.uk

121. Carnegie, D. (1936) *How to Win Friends and Influence People,* Simon & Schuster.

122. Covey, S. R. (1989) *The 7 Habits of Highly Effective People*, Simon & Schuster.

123. Carter, P. (2009) *Test Your EQ*, Kogan Page.

124. Godbold, A. (2009) 'Ethics in Project Management', *Presentation to the APM Annual Conference*, London, October.

125. Laborde, G. Z. (1984) *Influencing with Integrity: Management Skills for Communication and Negotiation*, Crown House.

126. O'Connor, J. and Prior, R. (1995) *Successful Selling with NLP*, Thorsons.

127. Covey, S. R. (1989) *The 7 Habits of Highly Effective People*, Simon & Schuster.

128. *APM Competence Framework* (5th Edition), APM Publishing, 2008.

129. Carnegie, D. (1936) *How to Win Friends and Influence People,* Simon & Schuster.

130. Robbins, A. (1987) *Unlimited Power,* Harper Collins.

131. Dilts, R. (1990) *Changing Belief Systems with Neuro-Linguistic Programming,* Meta Publications.

132. Ornish, D. and Bodian, S. (2006) *Meditation for Dummies,* Wiley.

133. Handy, C. (2000) *21 Ideas for Managers*, Jossey-Bass.

134. Briggs Myers, I. (1980) *Gifts Differing: Understanding Personality Type*, Davies-Black Publishing.

135. de Bono, E. (1990) *Six Thinking Hats: An Essential Approach to Business Management*, Penguin.

136. Belbin, R. (1991) *Management Teams: Why They Succeed or Fail*, Butterworth.

137. Honey, P. and Mumford, M. (1982) *Manual of Learning Styles*, Peter Honey Publications.

138. Gallwey, W. T. (1986) *The Inner Game of Tennis*, Pan.

139. Essex, A. (2004) *Compassionate Coaching*, Rider.

140. Hammer, M. (1996) *Beyond Re-engineering*, Harper Business.

141. Pedler, M. (2008) *Action Learning for Managers*, Gower.

142. Wenger, E. (1999) *Communities of Practice: Learning, Meaning, and Identity* (Learning in Doing: Social, Cognitive and Computational Perspectives), Cambridge University Press.

143. Adams, D. (1995) *The Hitchhiker's Guide to the Galaxy: A Trilogy in Five Parts*, William Heinemann.

144. McKenna, P. (2009) *Control Stress*, Bantam Press.

145. Robbins, A. (1992) *Awaken the Giant Within*, Simon & Schuster.

146. Grose, R. (2010) 'Sell Yourself', *IT Now*, May, 2.

147. Mehrabian, A. and Wiener, M. (1967) 'Decoding of Inconsistent Communications', *Journal of Personality and Social Psychology,* 6 (1), 109–114.

148. Gillen, T. (1998) *Assertiveness*, Chartered Institute of Personnel Development.

149. Bolton, R. (1979) *People Skills,* Touchstone.

150. Compiled from leader articles in *The Sunday Times*, January–March 2008.

151. Turner, J. R. (2006) 'Leadership: The Project Context', *Project Manager Today,* November, 29.

152. Branson, R. (2006) *Screw It, Let's Do It,* Virgin.

153. Office of Government Commerce (OGC) (2007) *Managing Successful Programs*, The Stationery Office.

154. APM Governance SIG (2009) *Sponsoring Change: A Guide to the Governance Aspects of Project Sponsorship*, APM Publishing.

155. Dilts, R. (1990) *Changing Belief Systems with NLP*, Meta Publications.

156. Mehrabian, A. and Wiener, M. (1967) 'Decoding of Inconsistent Communications', *Journal of Personality and Social Psychology,* 6 (1), 109–114.

157. Robbins, A. (1987) *Unlimited Power*, Harper Collins.

158. The Chartered Institute of Arbitrators @ www.ciarb.org.

159. Dilts, R. (1990) *Changing Belief Systems with NLP*, Meta Publications.

160. Checkland, P. and Poulter, J. (2006) *Learning for Action: A Short Definitive Account of Soft Systems Methodology*, Wiley.

161. Bailey, R. Unpublished work, cited in Charvet, S. R. (1995) *Words That Change Minds: Mastering the Language of Influence*, Kendall Hunt.

162. Fournies, F. F. (1999) *Why Employees Don't Do What They Are Supposed To Do*, McGraw-Hill.

163. In Greek mythology, Cassandra was gifted with being able to foretell the future, but Apollo subsequently gave her the curse that no one would believe her.

164. Dilts, R. (1998) *Modelling with NLP*, Meta Publications.

165. R. Bandler and J. Grinder (1975) *Frogs into Princes*, Real People Press.

166. R. Dilts and J. DeLozier (2000) *Encyclopedia of systemic NLP and NLP New Coding*, NLP University Press (www.nlpuniversitypress.com)

167. R. Dilts (1998) *Modelling with NLP*, Meta Publications.

168. A. Robbins (1992) *Awaken the Giant Within*, Simon & Schuster.

169. www.tonyrobbins.com

170. S. Lynn and M. Yapco (2003) *Trancework: An Introduction to the Practice of Clinical Hypnosis*, Brunner-Routledge.

171. Grinder, J. and Bandler, R. (1975) *Patterns of the Hypnotic Techniques of Milton H. Ericson*, Meta Publications.

172. James, T. and W. Woodsmall (1988) *Time-line Therapy*, Meta Publications.

173. Galwey, T. (1974) *The Inner Game of Tennis*, Pan.

174. McDermott, I. and J. O'Connor (1996) *NLP and Health*, Thorsons.

175. Thomson, T., K. Khan and R. Bandler (2008) *Magic in Practice: Introducing Medical NLP – The Art and Science of Language in Healing and Health*, Hammersmith Press.

176. Paul McKenna (2007) *Quit Smoking Today*, Bantam.

GLOSSARY OF NLP TERMS

NLP has developed its own shorthand and specific meanings for some common terms. The following are some practical definitions of terms as used in this book. (Full definitions and explanations can be found in the 'encyclopedia of NLP' @ www.nlpuniversitypress.com).

Anchoring The process of associating an external trigger with an internal response, e.g. a resourceful state.

'As-if' frame Pretending that some event has happened or situation holds, for example, acting 'as if' I am a presenter, or 'as if' we have already overcome the issue.

Associated In tune with feelings of an event, along with the sights, sounds, tastes and smells of an event. The event could be in the here and now, recalled, or constructed.

Back-track frame Review or summarize using the other party's key words.

Beliefs The generalizations that we make about the world and hold to be true.

Calibration Adjusting our reference point to the individual, e.g. when noticing non-verbal signals such as eye movements, breathing, posture, etc.

Chunking Stepping up or down a logical level. Chunking up involves more generalization, whereas chunking down requires more specific detail.

Complex equivalence One of the meta-model violations. Two unrelated statements that are considered to mean the same thing, e.g. 'She is not looking at me, so she is not listening to what I say'.

Congruence The words of a message convey the same meaning as non-verbal aspects such as posture and tone of voice.

Content reframing Taking a statement or situation and giving it another meaning.

Context reframing Changing the context of a statement to give it another meaning. (As often used in jokes.)

Cross-over mirroring Matching a person's body language with a related movement, e.g. crossing your legs when they cross their arms.

Deletion One of the meta-model violations. Missing out part of an experience in speech or thought.

Dissociated Seeing or hearing an event as if an onlooker with detached feelings rather than as a participant.

Distortion One of the meta-model violations. The process by which something is inaccurately represented in internal experience.

Ecology The ethics of the overall system, including the second and third parties.

Elicitation To consciously evoke a state or gather information through observation or questioning, e.g. about a person's strategy for doing something.

Eye accessing cues Movements of the eyes in certain directions which indicate visual, auditory or kinaesthetic thinking.

Future pace Mentally rehearsing an outcome to ensure that the desired behaviour will occur. Acting 'as if' something has happened.

Generalization One of the meta-model violations. Speaking/acting as if one example is universally true.

Incongruence Where the mind and body are not acting as one, or where language is not aligned to body language.

Internal representations Patterns of information stored and recalled in your mind in the form of pictures, sounds, feelings, smells, and tastes.

Kinaesthetic Tactile sensations and internal feelings.

Lead system The representational system that you use to initially access information, e.g. sight, sound or smell.

Matching Adopting parts of another person's behaviour, such as particular gestures, facial expressions, forms of speech, tone of voice etc., for the purpose of increasing rapport.

Meta Existing at a higher logical level to something else. (Derived from Greek, meaning above.)

Meta-model A model that identifies language patterns that obscure meaning in a communication through the processes of distortion, deletion and generalization. From this, a set of specific questions to clarify and challenge imprecise language in order to re-construct meaning.

Metaphor An indirect comparison. Likening one thing to another, e.g. in a fable.

Meta-programs Habitual and systematic filters that we put on our experience, e.g. optimist/pessimist.

Milton model A model of the hypnotic language patterns of the therapist Milton Erickson. Artfully vague language patterns designed to confuse the conscious mind and allow access to the unconscious mind. (The inverse of the Meta-model.)

Mirroring Precisely matching aspects of another person's behaviour, especially in order to accelerate rapport.

Miss-matching Adopting different patterns of behaviour to another person, especially to purposefully break rapport in order to interrupt or terminate a meeting or conversation.

Modal operator of necessity A linguistic term for rules, e.g. should, ought, must etc.

Model A practical description of how something works. (The purpose of a model is to be useful in some application, not necessarily accurate.)

Modelling The process of determining the sequence of ideas and behaviour that enable someone to accomplish a task. The basis of accelerated learning.

Perceptual filters Unique ideas, experiences, beliefs and language that shape an individual's model of the world.

Predicates Verbs, adverbs and adjectives that can be categorized into one or more representational modalities.

Pre-suppositions Statements that have to be taken for granted for a communication to make sense.

Primary (preferred) representational system The sensory system that an individual uses most to think consciously and organize experience.

Rapport A heightened state of trust.

Re-framing Changing the frame of reference around a statement to give it another meaning.

Representational system How we code information in our minds in one or more of the five sensory systems (visual, auditory, kinaesthetic, olfactory or gustatory).

Sensory acuity The (trained) ability to discern detail of situations, communications and body language.

Strategy Sequence of thought and behaviour to obtain a particular outcome.

Sub-modality A level of detail of our representational systems of sight, sound, feeling, taste and smell, e.g. brightness and colour for sight. (Our memories are coded using sub-modalities and their meaning can be changed by changing the sub-modalities.)

Surface structure The grammatical structure of language.

Trance An altered state with an inward focus of attention.

Up-time A state of heightened awareness where the attention and senses are committed outwards.

INDEX

Enabling the
information society